W9-BNZ-295

Literacy Before Schooling

Emilia Ferreiro *and* **Ana Teberosky**

Translated by
Karen Goodman Castro

Preface by
Yetta Goodman

Heinemann Educational Books
Exeter, New Hampshire and London

Heinemann Educational Books
4 Front Street, Exeter, New Hampshire 03833
22 Bedford Square, London WCIB 3HH

EDINBURGH MELBOURNE AUCKLAND
HONG KONG SINGAPORE KUALA LUMPUR NEW DELHI
IBADAN NAIROBI JOHANNESBURG
KINGSTON PORT OF SPAIN

Library of Congress Cataloging in Publication Data

Ferreiro, Emilia.
  Literacy before schooling.

  Translation of: Los sistemas de escritura en el
desarrollo del niño.
  Bibliography: p.
  1. Language arts (Preschool) 2. Language arts
(Elementary) 3. Language arts—Latin America.
I. Teberosky, Ana. II. Title.
LB1140.5.L3F4713 1982   372.6   82-15839
ISBN 0-435-08202-7 (U.S.)
ISBN 0-435-80474-X (U.K.)

Printed in the United States of America

Contents

FOREWORD

Learning to read and write is not just a matter of distinguishing letter shapes, drawing those shapes, following a text with the eyes, and so on. These and similar skills are quite secondary when it comes to understanding the nature and function of writing. Some gifted psychologists and teachers have always been convinced that learning to read and write could not be reduced to a set of perceptual-motor skills, or to willingness or motivation, but must grow from a deeper layer of conceptual development.

Until recently, however, this conviction remained intuitive, and few efforts were made to study the conceptualization that affords the beginning reader entry into the cultural world of written language, despite every effort to teach him good perceptual-motor habits and letter-recognition skills. Emilia Ferreiro and Ana Teberosky explored this conceptualization by studying the acquisition of literacy in a new way; they succeeded in translating the correct though vague ideas of their precursors into hypotheses that can be tested experimentally and opened up a previously unknown world of child thought.

The authors belong to the school of the great epistemologist and psychologist Jean Piaget. They introduced the essence of his theory and scientific method into an area that Piaget had not studied. According to Piaget, knowledge in any field is acquired through the subject's interaction with the object of that knowledge. The child's understanding of the writing system used in his or her culture is no exception. The authors show that children have ideas, and indeed, hypotheses and theories, which they continually test against the many examples of written text they encounter in their environment and against the information they receive from others.

The Piagetian method of exploring children's thinking through dialogue allows the experimenter to create testable hypotheses about the reasoning behind the child's words and gestures and turns out to be—in this field as in many others—a most fruitful approach. It permits basic ideas held by many children to be distinguished from the passing reactions of a child who is impelled to say or do something, never mind what, just to respond to a question. The method also allows researchers, who apply it as ably as the authors of this book have done, to see how a concept that may have taken humanity a great deal of time to establish is recreated by the child.

While a fresh theoretical and experimental approach to the study of literacy opens new horizons, it cannot provide ready-made solutions to pedagogical problems. But after reading this book, psychologists and educators will be able to pursue their own research and consider new ways of teaching, without the risk of blind alleys or vague notions that do not lend themselves to experimentation or pedagogical application.

Although intended primarily for educators and psychologists, this book deserves a much wider audience: linguists, historians, parents, poets—all those interested in the world of child thought and in the written word should be fascinated.

To write a foreword for such a book is a pleasure indeed, and if, as one of its first readers, I may formulate a wish, it is that the authors will bring out their next volume without delay.

Hermine Sinclair
University of Geneva

PREFACE

Teaching reading and writing is viewed as one of the major responsibilities of the educational system. Too many children fail as they are being introduced to literacy. The objective of this book is to propose a new approach to this problem. We intend to demonstrate that learning reading, understood as the child's explorations of the nature, function, and value of written language as a cultural object, begins long before the school imagines and takes unsuspected paths. In addition to methods, manuals, and instructional materials there are knowing subjects actively seeking understanding, posing problems, and trying to solve them following their own methodology. Children are active seekers of knowledge and not simply willing or unwilling to acquire a particular skill. This has been forgotten in the area of written language by psychologists too concerned with finding specific aptitudes, particular abilities, or always poorly defined levels of maturity.

The reflections and the theses presented in this book are the results of an experimental project we undertook in Buenos Aires from 1974 to 1976. The project carried out in 1974 was part of our university work as staff members of the University of Buenos Aires. We followed it up later with no official backing or financial support. We are indebted to the educators who authorized our work in elementary schools and preschools. Without their collaboration this study would not have been possible. We extend our profound thanks to them although we cannot state their names. We also thank all the children we interviewed who, without knowing it, caused us to reflect tremendously and to modify our hypotheses more than once.

Our initial work team remained intact during the three years in spite of all vicissitudes. New collaborators were added during the last year of our work. All the members of the initial team should be coauthors of this book, an impossibility due to current geographic dispersion. They are: Susana Fernandez, Ana Maria Kaufman, Alicia Lenzi, and Liliana Tolchinsky. All of us—each one from her current place of work—continue to be involved in this area, attempting to unveil the mysteries of the preschool story of written language.

Emilia Ferreiro
Ana Teberosky

PREFACE TO THE ENGLISH EDITION

Tanya, a five-year-old child with large black eyes, is sitting next to her brother on a TWA jet waiting for take-off. She is animated and excited about her first flight. As the fasten-your-seat-belt sign lights up, her little brother pops his two fingers into his mouth. Tanya pokes him and says, "Take your fingers out of your mouth, Rubin, we're ready to go."

"Why," replies Rubin continuing to suck his fingers as hard as before. "Don't you see," she says, pointing to the no smoking sign above their seat. "It says no bad habits."

What does such a vignette tell us about Tanya's knowledge of written language? Some might respond by saying that's a very bright child—so precocious; others might say, isn't that cute. However, we now know, thanks to the authors of this book, that similar examples of preschoolers throughout the world have great significance for understanding how children in a literate society come to know written language.

Emilia Ferreiro and Ana Teberosky are enriching a growing, although small, body of research exploring literacy development in young children prior to school instruction. As psychologists and researchers based in Piagetian tradition, the authors have ingeniously devised reading and writing tasks within the framework of Piagetian theory to explore how children come to know literacy.

They raise significant questions. How do children come to know written language? How do children determine what is readable? How do they learn to compose written language? How do they become aware of the forms written language takes? Which hypotheses about written language are original constructions developed by children and which can be attributed to cultural transmission on the part of adults? How do children differentiate or incorporate drawing, illustrations, numbers, cursive writing, and print in relation to the whole writing system? These problems may seem much too complex for linguists, psychologists, or teachers to solve. Yet in this volume, Emilia Ferreiro and Ana Teberosky discover how children as young as four, from middle class and lower class environments, solve these problems as they become literate. The authors start by posing specific questions and allow their results to pose new ones. Their tasks, questioning techniques, and conclusions are based on Piaget's theories that children hypothesize about the nature of reality.

This particular work provides many important insights. In the introduction the authors raise sociocultural issues about literacy which must be considered, especially in countries where large numbers of children fail, drop out, or are pushed out of school before completing the primary years. Although the authors focus on Argentina, the insights apply to many countries.

Each chapter explores literacy development and suggests how children ages four to six progress through various hypotheses about written language until they develop notions similar to those of literate adults. In chapter 2, they explore how children respond to graphic information such as letters, numbers, and punctuation marks and when such characters become readable to the subjects. In chapter 3, they explore how children respond to and interpret the relationship between drawing and writing. Chapter 4 explores both how children establish correspondence between the oral response to the text and graphic aspects of the text and how printed words become apparent to children. Chapter 5 explores how children decide if someone is reading by oral and silent behaviors as well as how they determine differences in texts based on newspaper, story, and conversational modes. Chapter 6 explores how children produce written language and when they become aware that it has meaning. The importance of the child's own name is a main focus in this chapter. Chapter 7 explores how children respond to dialect differences and shows their concerns about correct pronunciation. Finally, in chapter 8, Ferreiro and Teberosky present their conclusions by summarizing their data and defining reading and writing, including implications for instruction.

The basic population used in this research is a group of Argentinean children from disparate socioeconomic groups. Whenever it becomes appropriate, the researchers refer to data from other studies.

Although the original work was published in Spanish in 1979, Ferreiro and Teberosky and their colleagues have been updating, extending, and modifying their experiments, tasks, and interactions with subjects. Emilia Ferreiro has confirmed the major developmental trends presented in this work with a French-speaking population in Geneva. In addition she has completed a longitudinal study with children ages three to six in Mexico City and is now engaged in research on the same topic with illiterate adults. Ana Teberosky has been working in Spain with bilingual kindergarten children exploring what happens when children are allowed to construct their knowledge about the writing system. In addition to this, the authors' coworkers are now conducting research in Israel and Venezuela.

Not only can we look forward to new insights and conclusions coming from the Ferreiro-Teberosky team, but they welcome adaptations of their work, critical analysis, and communication with other researchers. It is with their permission that I urge the reader who attempts similar research or applies the ideas to curricular areas to do so with a dynamic flexible view of experimentalism.

The original Spanish was retained for many examples of the child-researcher interaction because the careful presentation and analysis of the interactions clearly show how to conduct an interview with a clinical approach and how to make a qualitative analysis of a child's development. The basic procedures and philosophical attitudes of the Piagetian clinical approach must be kept in mind as the child is always encouraged to take the lead.

Most important, however, are the many audiences to whom this work speaks.

For psychologists, insights on how to extend Piaget's clinical approach to literacy development are provided. It documents how to set up tasks related to literacy experiences showing children's concepts about print and avoiding the all-too-common pitfalls of simplistic correlations between standardized test scores and Piagetian stages of development. As in Piagetian explorations, the authors believe that errors reflect the mechanisms of the construction of knowledge. Ferreiro and Teberosky carefully provide and describe the theoretical framework from which their research ideas come.

For researchers, a rich array of experiments, which need replication and extension, are provided. Replication in English-speaking countries will extend dynamically the knowledge of literacy development. The results presented here provide baseline data that can be used in comparing Spanish- and English-speaking children, adding to the knowledge of universals and differences in written language development in young children.

For teacher educators, knowledge useful in in-service and pre-service programs is presented so teachers can critically examine issues and questions about the state of the art in literacy development. In these days of rigid instructional programs and back-to-basic movements such examination is greatly needed.

For classroom teachers, specific examples are provided of how questions are asked to gain greater insights into children's understandings of written language. The authors also suggest ways of looking at children's responses to understand the strength of their intellectual functioning, thus helping build language arts and reading curricula to facilitate children's development. They point out that to understand what is easy for a child, the teacher must ask "easy for whom, easy from whose point of view and from whose definition of easy?"

For Spanish bilingual educators and researchers, issues are raised about traditional reading and writing instruction in Spanish. Simplistic notions about syllabication and letter-sound correspondence are explored. In addition, questions are raised about the differences between psychogenetic development and culturally transmitted aspects of literacy development.

For all of us concerned with humanistic education who want an exciting view of the dynamic nature of human learning, the authors describe the problem-solving strategies of the young child and suggest levels of progression as children change their hypotheses and move closer to adult conventions about the written language system.

I am proud to have played my own small role in bringing this volume to English-reading audiences. I somehow feel part of the creative efforts of this translation since I convinced my daughter Karen Goodman Castro to translate this work, encouraged Heinemann to publish it, and even occasionally participated with the translator as she labored over a particular word or phrase, making sure it was meaningful in English and close to the authors' meaning. The authors were giving of their own time to help keep ideas and concepts from straying too far from the original. However, translations do involve interpretation and the authors cannot be held responsible for any ideas lost or changed in the process.

Emilia Ferreiro and Ana Teberosky have written a text that excited me, stimulated my own thinking, extended my own views of literacy and human development. I am convinced it provides extraordinary knowledge about written language development which must be reflected in teaching at all levels.

The authors believe that, "To understand children we must hear *their* words, follow *their* explanations, understand *their* frustrations, and listen to *their* logic." Not only do the authors reveal their respect for the child but for research, language, and knowledge. The excitement of discovering how young children dynamically construct a written language system is waiting for the reader in the pages that follow.

Yetta Goodman

I INTRODUCTION

This book will attempt to explain the developmental processes of children learning to read and write. By process we mean the path children take to comprehend the characteristics, value, and function of written language, from the time it becomes an object of their attention (and as such, of their knowledge). This topic is highly debated in the field of education. We do not intend to propose a new method of learning or a new classification of learning disorder. Our objective is to interpret the process, from the point of view of the learner, on the basis of data obtained during two years of experimental work with children between four and six years of age. This is not meant as a thorough analysis of the educational situation in Latin America, but the effects of methodological and social factors are taken into account throughout the development of this book.

The Educational Situation in Latin America

Reading and writing occupy an important place in the concerns of educators. Despite the various methods used for teaching reading, a great number of children do not learn. Along with elementary arithmetic, reading and writing are the objectives of basic instruction, and their learning is a condition of success or failure in school. School officials have given this problem some attention; failures in this area lead numbers of students to drop out of school and thus impede the achievement of minimal objectives of instruction in a large portion of the population. School officials and teachers have attempted to reveal the causes of these failures. School failure in initial learning is an easily verifiable occurrence. It also confirms the persistence of the causes that provoke it. In spite of educators' and public officials' good intentions, the problem persists. One may ask, then, whether the causes of the failures stem from the educational system as a whole rather than from the schoolroom.

Some figures pertinent to the educational system in Latin America will help plot out our problem. Official statistics (UNESCO, 1974) show us that: (a) Of the total population between seven and twelve years of age in 1970, 20 percent were outside the educational system. (b) Of the total population entering school, only 53 percent reaches fourth grade, the minimal level necessary for literacy (as defined by UNESCO). In other words, half the population abandons its education permanently halfway through the elementary grades. (c) Two-thirds of all repeaters occur in the primary grades and around 60 percent of the students who complete elementary school have repeated one or more grades.

What do these figures mean? For one thing, they prove the existence of a problem of such magnitude that it cannot go unnoticed by national and international organizations. In 1976, official UNESCO statistics estimated that there were eight hundred million illiterate adults in the world. In 1977, UNESCO made an important decision, transmitted by *Le Monde* of Paris in its September 7, 1977, edition:

International Literacy Day will be honored September 8th in the UNESCO headquarters in Paris. It will be the first such ceremony in which none of the prizes for action taken to combat illiteracy will be awarded (the Mohammed Reza Pahlavi and Nadejad Kroupaskaia prizes). The jury has decided this due to the increase in the number of illiterates in the world, estimated in 1976 at 800,000,000 illiterate adults. The jury holds that literacy should be integrated into plans for national development of affected nations. In a public message regarding this international day, the director general of UNESCO, Amadou Mather M'Bow, exhorts nations to bestow upon literacy programs part of the funds designated for armaments, emphasizing that the "total cost of one single bomber with its equipment is equal to the salary of 250,000 instructors a year!"

This action is doubly important: first, in emphasizing the increase in the number of illiterates in the world it recognizes the failure (or at least the mass failure) of the multitude of literacy campaigns developed in recent years; second, and primarily, it is the first time that a director general of UNESCO makes a direct comparison between the cost of a warplane and the cost of a team of literacy workers, showing that the persistence of illiteracy is not a financial problem.

We cannot forget that literacy has two faces: one relative to adults, and the other relative to children. If literary programs for adults are directed toward correcting a deficiency, for children it is a matter of prevention, of designing programs that will keep them from becoming illiterates. Both tasks are the responsibility of nations that, as members of the United Nations, have accepted the Universal Declaration of the Rights of Man (1948). Article 26 of this declaration speaks of the right to education: "All people have the right to education. Education shall be free, at least in the elementary and fundamental stages. Elementary education shall be compulsory."

There is no doubt, then, that achieving just, egalitarian, and effective educational systems is an important priority for the international community and its constituent nations. However, this Rights-of-Man article dedicated to universal education is still a long way from being put into practice. This problem—the lack of basic education for the entire population—is officially alluded to as one of the endemic weaknesses of the educational system, generated by the numbers of students who repeat grades and eventually drop out of school. According to official explanations, absenteeism, repetition of grades, and, finally, dropping out are the factors preventing appropriate levels of education in the majority of the Latin American population. But what causes individuals to become repeaters, then dropouts, and thus ultimately undereducated all of their lives? Could it be an inability to learn that determines their failure? Is it, perhaps, a matter of individuals who drop out voluntarily with the possibility of someday reintegrating themselves into the educational system? When we analyze the statistics, however, none of these factors is found to be distributed proportionally across the population. To the contrary, they accumulate in certain sectors that for ethnic, social, economic, or geographic reasons are disfavored. The greatest percentages of school failures are concentrated among indigenous, rural, and marginalized urban populations.

To understand this issue we must analyze the factors cited as causes of failure. One such factor is school absenteeism. In truth, many children are absent from school for long periods of time. But why is this so? In some rural areas, climatic conditions or distance prevent regular attendance at school. Sometimes the necessity of assisting the family in productive tasks requires absence or dropping out. This is the actual situation, and without improving the living conditions of the population it will be very difficult to solve this problem. It is a matter of social condition, not of individual responsibility.

Repetition of grades is also cited as one of the major problems of elementary education (a phenomenon that, as we have seen, is concentrated in the primary grades). What does such repetition mean? When children fail in learning, they are offered a second chance. Is this a solution? To repeat an experience of failure in identical conditions? Does this not, perhaps, oblige children to repeat their failure? How many times can individuals repeat errors? We suppose as many times as is necessary to make them give up trying.

The central issue of this educational problem is dropping out. This term carries an implicit meaning that assumes a voluntary action by individuals—in this case, children—in abandoning a group or system to which they belong. In the case of the educational system, one must ask whether it is the system which abandons the dropouts if it lacks both strategies for keeping them and interest in reintegrating them. One must also question whether dropping out is an individual attitude, as the term suggests, or if there is a coincidence of individuals who share socioeconomic circumstances that make it difficult for them to remain within the rules of the established system.

In other words, this is more a matter of social dimension than a consequence of individual will. Because of this we believe that instead of endemic weaknesses, we must speak of the social selection of the educational system; instead of dropping out we must call it hidden expulsion. We are not simply changing terminology; we are establishing another interpretive framework in view of the social and economic inequality underlying the unequal distribution of educational opportunities.

When we speak of social selection, we are not referring to the conscious intentions of teachers as particular individuals but to the social role of the educational system. From the point of view of teachers or, more correctly, of the pedagogy that sustains educational action, there have been attempted solutions to this problem.

Traditional Methods of Reading Instruction

Traditionally, from a pedagogical perspective, the problem of learning to read and write has been posed as a question of methods.[1] Educators have been oriented toward finding the best or most effective method, creating controversy over two fundamental types: synthetic, which starts with elements smaller than the word; and analytic, which starts with the word or larger units. There is an extensive literature in defense of each method, referring as much to methodological execution as to underlying psychological processes.

The synthetic method has emphasized the correspondence between oral and written language, between sound and graphics. Another key aspect of this method involves establishing this correspondence by building on minimal elements, a process of going from part to whole. The minimal elements of written language are letters. For many years pronunciation of letters has been taught, establishing the rules for sounding out the written form of the corresponding language. The most traditional alphabetic methods endorse this posture.

Later, under the influence of linguistics, the phonetic method, which starts from oral language, developed. The minimal sound unit of spoken language is the phoneme. The process consists of beginning with the phoneme and associating it with its graphic

[1] Translator's Note: This discussion is related to methods of reading instruction used in Latin America. Although they are similar to and sometimes built on views or theories developed in English-speaking countries, they reflect linguistic and pedagogical differences which exist in Latin America.

representation. It is essential that learners be capable of isolating and recognizing the distinct phonemes of their language to be able, later, to relate them to graphic signs. In the following we refer to the phonetic method, since the alphabetic method has fallen into disuse.

Since this method emphasizes auditory analysis in isolating the sounds and establishing phoneme-grapheme (sound-letter) correspondence, two preliminary issues are posed: (*a*) that the pronunciation be correct to avoid confusion of phonemes; and (*b*) that graphemes of similar form be presented separately to avoid confusion of graphemes. Another important principle of this method is teaching one phoneme-grapheme pair at a time, without going on to the next until the association has been well established. The first phase of this learning involves the mechanics of reading (deciphering the text), which later gives way to intelligent reading (comprehending the text), culminating in expressive reading when intonation is added.

Whatever the differences between the defenders of the synthetic method, there is complete agreement on this point: initially, the learning of reading and writing is a question of mechanics, a matter of acquiring the techniques of text deciphering. Because writing is viewed as the graphic transcription of oral language, as its image (a more or less faithful image depending on the particular case), reading is equivalent to decoding written language into sound. Obviously this method will be more or less effective depending on the degree to which the writing system is in keeping with alphabetic principles; that is, how perfect the sound-letter correspondence is. Since there is no writing system in which speech and orthography are in total agreement, beginning with cases of regular orthography, words in which the graphics coincide with the pronunciation, is recommended. Primers or beginning readers based on this method are an attempt to combine all these principles: to avoid auditory and/or visual confusion; to present one phoneme and its corresponding grapheme at a time; and, finally, to work with cases of regular orthography. Meaningless syllables are used regularly, carrying the inevitable consequence of disassociating sound from meaning and reading from oral language.

These principles are not posed solely as methodological postures, but they respond to precise psychological concepts. In emphasizing auditory and visual discrimination and phoneme-grapheme correspondence, the process of learning reading is conceived of simply as an association between sound responses and graphic stimuli. This model, which is the one most in accordance with associationist theory, reproduces for the learning of written language the model proposed to interpret oral language acquisition. It also has received justifications from linguists. In particular, Bloomfield (1942) affirms: "the chief source of difficulty in getting the content of reading is the imperfect mastery of the mechanics of reading." He adds: "the first step, which may be divorced from all subsequent ones, is the recognition of letters. We say that the child recognizes a letter when he can, upon request, make some specific response to it." Psychology, linguistics, and pedagogy appear to have coincided in considering initial reading as pure mechanics.

Is this a satisfactory explanation of the learning process? Failure to differentiate the conception of the nature of the object to be learned—the alphabetic code—from hypotheses about the learning process leads to a confusion between teaching methods and learning processes. Moreover, it creates a dichotomy in the learning process: when one does not know, initially, one must go through a mechanistic phase; when one does know, one arrives at comprehending (stages clearly represented by the classic sequence of "mechanistic reading, comprehensive reading"). This is, in synthesis, the model of the synthetic method. If we have been extensive in discussing it, we have done so because it is one of the methods most in use today. Also, because as its theoretical postures defer to the crudest mechanics, its practical applications tend to exceed far beyond, sometimes to the point of appearing to be based literally on the old and dismal refrain, *la letra con sangre entra*. (Literally, "the letter enters with blood," a pedagogical application of the English adage, "spare the rod and spoil the child.")

For the defenders of the analytic method, on the other hand, reading is a global and ideo-visual act. Decroly reacts against the principles of the synthetic method—accusing them of being mechanistic—and postulates that "holistic vision precedes analysis in the child mind." What comes first, according to the analytic method, is the global recognition of words or phrases; analysis of the components is a subsequent task. The auditory difficulty of what is to be learned does not matter, since reading is fundamentally a visual task. In addition, instruction must begin with meaningful units. (From this comes the term ideo-visual.)

There are many discrepancies between the two methods, but they pertain mainly to the type of perceptual strategy used: auditory for some, visual for others. The so-called methodological controversy (Braslavsky, 1973) is a question of which perceptual strategies are in play in the act of reading, but both methods are based on different conceptions of the psychological functioning of the individual and on different learning theories. Because of this the problem cannot be resolved by proposing mixed methods which would benefit from the good points of each.

The emphasis placed on perceptual abilities ignores two fundamental considerations: (*a*) the linguistic competence of the child;

and (*b*) the cognitive competence of the child. By presenting these two considerations as focal, we intend to show how we must change our vision of the child who stands on the threshold of literacy.

Contemporary Psycholinguistics and the Learning of Reading and Writing

In 1962, extremely important changes arose in our understanding of oral language development in children. There was a virtual revolution in this field which had been dominated by behaviorist models. Until this period, most of the studies on child language were predominantly concerned with the lexicon, the amount and variety of words used by the child. These words were classified according to adult language categories (verbs, nouns, adjectives, and so on), and the studies examined how the proportions between these distinct categories of words varied and what relationship existed between increment in vocabulary, age, sex, school achievement, and so on.

No collection of words, no matter how vast, in itself constitutes a language; without precise rules for combining those elements to produce acceptable phrases, there is no language. The critical point at which the associationist models fail is in accounting for the development of syntactic rules. It has been demonstrated that neither imitation nor selective reinforcement—the two key elements of associationist learning—can account for the acquisition of syntactic rules.

Although it is beyond the scope of this introduction to provide a detailed analysis of the advances of contemporary psycholinguistics and the reasons leading to them, it is necessary to present a brief overview indicating some crucial points. The traditional associationist model of language acquisition is simple: children have a tendency toward imitation (a tendency different associationist positions justify in various manners). The social medium that surrounds children has a tendency to selectively reinforce vocal emissions corresponding to sounds or complex sound patterns (words) of the language of the social medium. In elementary terms: when a child produces a sound similar to a sound in the parents' speech, the latter manifest joy, make gestures of approval, and show signs of affection. In this way the environment selects, from the vast repertoire of initial sounds that leave the child's mouth, only those corresponding to the sounds of the adults' speech (the collection of phonemes of the language in question). These sounds must acquire meaning to be converted effectively into words. In this model, the problem is resolved like this: the adults present an object and accompany this presentation with a vocal emission (they pronounce a word which is the name of the object); by reiterated associations between the sonorous emission and the presence of the object, the former ends up converting into a sign for the latter and so becomes "word."

Our current vision of the process is radically different: instead of children who passively await external reinforcement of a response produced at random, we see children who actively attempt to understand the nature of the language spoken around them, and, in trying to understand it, formulate hypotheses, search for regularities, and test their predictions. Consequently they form their own grammar, which is not simply a deformed copy of the adult model but an original creation. Instead of receiving bit by bit a language entirely fabricated by others, children reconstruct language for themselves, selectively using information provided by the environment.

One example will suffice to demonstrate the difference in viewpoint. All Spanish-speaking children around the age of three to four years say *yo lo poní* (I putted it) instead of *yo lo puse* (I put it). Traditionally, this involves an error, because the children do not yet know how to deal with irregular verbs. When we analyze the nature of this error, however, the explanation cannot simply conclude that the child made a mistake, because children always make the same mistakes: they treat irregular verbs as if they were regular (saying *yo hací* [I maked], *yo andé* [I walkted], *está rompido* [it's broked]). After all, since *comer* (to eat) becomes *comí* (I ate) and *hablar* (to talk) becomes *hablé* (I talked), *poner* should become *poní*, and *andar* should become *andé*. (English equivalent: If look becomes looked and bake becomes baked, then why doesn't take become taked?)

When children always make the same mistakes, that is, when we face a systematic error, to simply call it error only covers up our ignorance. Children do not regularize irregular verbs through imitation, since adults do not speak this way (the only child does it too). Irregular verbs are not regularized through selective reinforcement. They are regularized because children look for regularity and coherence in language that would make it a more logical system than it is.

In summary, what was labeled previously as error from lack of knowledge appears to us now as proof of the surprising degree of knowledge young children have about language: to regularize irregular verbs, they must have distinguished between the verbal root and its inflection and discovered the normal (regular) paradigm of verb conjugation. (This can be considered a universal phenomenon since it has been confirmed for all languages for which there is reliable data.)

Evidence such as this (normal occurrences in child language development) suggests that language learning does not proceed through the acquisition of isolated elements which gradually join together, but rather through the formation of systems where the value of the parts continually redefines itself in function with the changes in the whole system. In addition, this evidence also demonstrates the existence of what we could call "constructive errors", that is, responses differing from correct responses but, far from impeding emergence of the latter, permitting subsequent development. The regularization of irregular verbs between two and five years is not a pathological occurrence, it is not an indication of future disorders, but it is totally the opposite.

The initial emphasis of contemporary psycholinguistics on syntax occurred not only because it was an almost totally unexplored area but, fundamentally, because the new psycholinguistics developed due to the powerful impact of the linguistic theory of Noam Chomsky (1974, 1976). The generative grammar proposed by Chomsky gives a central and privileged place to syntax, and psychologists took this model as a point of departure, attempting to test its psychological reality. Today the situation is much more complex. Although we are still far from having formulated an interpretive system which provides an integrated explanation of the multiple complex aspects of language development, a series of irreversible advances have come forth: (*a*) The shortcomings of the behaviorist model have become apparent in a domain which previously constituted one of its most solid bulwarks. (*b*) A series of new facts has been revealed and a series of original lines of research has been opened. (*c*) The conception of learning sustained by contemporary psycholinguistics coincides (although unintentionally) with the conception of learning sustained for some time by Jean Piaget.

What does all this have to do with the learning of reading and writing? A great deal, and for various reasons. In the first place, since writing is a particular way of transcribing language, everything changes if we suppose that individuals learning to read and write already possess a notable knowledge of their mother tongue, or if we suppose that they do not. (This will be seen more clearly when we discuss what reading is and in what way readers continually make use of their linguistic knowledge. See "Reading Is Not Deciphering; Writing Is Not Copying" in chapter 8.)

In the second place, it is easy to demonstrate that many habitual practices in the teaching of written language are attributable to what was known (before 1960) about oral language development. The classical progression, which consists of starting with the vowels, going on to form the first words by duplicating syllables (mama, papa), and, when it comes to sentences, beginning with simple declarative ones, reproduces quite well the sequence of oral language development as seen from the outside in (seen from observable behaviors and not from the process that engenders these behaviors). Implicitly, it has been judged necessary to pass through these same stages when learning a written language, as if relearning spoken language.

The concept of written language learning as a relearning of oral language is even more apparent when we think of notions so important to traditional instruction as those of speaking correctly and having good articulation. In fact, many difficulties in writing have been attributed to speech. (In chapter 7 we discuss the inevitable ideological consequences of this position.) Traditionally, it has been thought that to write correctly one must also know how to pronounce words correctly. But what criteria determines the correct manner of pronunciation? In the case of a linguistic community as vast as the Spanish-speaking community, who has the right to establish which pronunciation is correct? Is it possible to legislate in this matter as if linguistics were a normative science rather than a factual one?

Traditional instruction has required children to relearn the sounds of spoken language assuming that if they do not distinguish them adequately, they will not be able to write in an alphabetic system. This premise is based on two assumptions, both false: that six-year-old children do not know how to distinguish the phonemes of their spoken language, and that alphabetic writing is a phonetic transcription of oral language. If children in the course of oral language learning were not capable of discriminating between phonemes, at the age of six they would not be able to orally distinguish pairs of words such as *palo/malo* (an equivalent English pair: pan/man), something they obviously know how to do. The second assumption is also false, in view of the fact that no written language constitutes a phonetic transcription of oral language.

We do not dismiss the importance of breaking up speech into its minimal elements (phonemes), but we handle it in a different way: it is not a matter of teaching children to make a distinction but of making them conscious of a distinction they already know. Stated in other terms, it is not a matter of transmitting knowledge that children would not have otherwise but of making them aware of knowledge that they already possess. What we are saying here with respect to phonemic contrasts is also valid for all other aspects of language.

Children who enter school have a notable knowledge of their mother tongue, a linguistic "knowing" that they utilize unconsciously in their daily communications acts. Since Chomsky, the distinction between "competence" and "performance" has been widely accepted in psycholinguistics. This distinction guards against the tendency—markedly behaviorist—to equate an individual's real knowing about a particular domain with his or her actual performance in a particular situation. The fact that individuals are incapable of mentally calculating a complicated mathematical problem does not indicate ignorance in math. (Normally, to perform such operations we need special mnemonic aids, the simplest being paper and pencil, a necessity related to the limitations of our short-term memory but not to our real capacity for performing these operations.) In the same way, the fact that individuals cannot repeat unfamiliar words like "Nebuchadnezzar" or "Constantinople" (found on well-known tests of reading readiness) does not mean that they are incapable of comprehending and producing the phonemic distinctions of their language. (This distinction between competence and performance is also at the base of the Piagetian theory of intelligence.)

Schools may have had difficulty recognizing children's linguistic knowing before psycholinguistics made it evident, but how can we continue to ignore these facts now? How can we continue acting as if children know nothing about their own language? How can we continue requiring children to ignore everything they know about their language in order to teach them to transcribe it into graphic code?

We are not the first to point out the need to completely revise our ideas about written language learning on the basis of the discoveries of contemporary psycholinguistics. In 1971, a conference was held in the United States on the relationship between oral language and the learning of reading, constituting the first global attempt in this sense (Kavanaugh and Mattingly, 1972). Since then, authors like Kenneth Goodman, Frank Smith, Charles Read, and Carol Chomsky have produced important work in this area. We are probably the first to do so for the Spanish language and also the first to relate this perspective to cognitive development as seen in Piaget's theory of intelligence.

The Pertinence of Piaget's Theory to Understanding the Developmental Processes of Reading and Writing

In the literature on learning written language, one finds, basically, two types of treatises: those dedicated to promoting some methodology as being the solution to all problems, and those dedicated to establishing the list of capacities or aptitudes necessary for this kind of learning. Within the latter group we include the educational literature that attempts to establish the conditions necessary for initiating this learning, conditions commonly referred to as "reading readiness." Our work does not fall within either of these two groups.

The psychological literature dedicated to establishing the list of aptitudes or skills necessary for learning to read and write continually mentions the same variables: left-right directionality, visual and auditory discrimination, visual-motor coordination, and good articulation, to name a few. A rather curious view arises from articles that synthesize such research (Mialaret, 1975): all these factors correlate positively with successful written language learning. In plainer terms, if children have good directionality, if their emotional equilibrium is adequate, if they have good visual and auditory discrimination, if their I.Q. is normal, and if their articulation is adequate, then it is probable that they will learn to read and write without difficulty. In short, if everything is okay, then the learning of reading and writing will also be okay.

The least that can be said is that this reasoning is unsatisfactory. For one thing, one must not confuse positive correlation with a causal relationship. The fact that all of these variables correlate positively with school achievement in reading and writing does not mean that they are the cause of the observed achievement. For another thing, one cannot help wondering what in this drawn-out list of factors is specifically linked to reading and writing. Written language learning is a complex problem, but must one refer to a long list of aptitudes to become aware of this complexity?

We have searched unsuccessfully in this literature for references to children themselves, thinking children who seek knowledge, children we have discovered through Piagetian theory. The children we know through this theory are learners who actively try to understand the world around them, to answer questions the world poses. They are not learners who wait for someone to transmit knowledge to them in an act of benevolence. To the contrary, they learn primarily through their own actions on external objects, and they construct their own categories of thought while organizing their world.

We believe that these thinking children play an active role in learning written language. It is absurd to imagine that four- or five-year-old children growing up in an urban environment that displays print everywhere (on toys, on billboards and road signs, on their clothes, on TV) do not develop any ideas about this cultural object until they find themselves sitting before a teacher at the age of six. This is difficult to imagine knowing what we know about children of this age, children who wonder about the phenomena they observe, who ask the most difficult-to-answer questions, who construct theories about the origin of humans and the universe.

The controversy over instructional methods is unresolvable unless we come to know the learning processes of the child, processes that a particular method may favor, stimulate, or block. But the distinction between teaching methods, on one hand, and the learning processes of the child, on the other, requires a theoretical justification. Within a behaviorist framework, they appear to be one and the same, since a basic behaviorist principle is that stimuli control responses and that learning itself is no more than the substitution of one response for another. In a Piagetian framework, however, the distinction between the two is clear—and necessary—since a basic principle of this theory is that stimuli do not act directly but are transformed by the individual's assimilation systems (or assimilation schemes). In this act of transformation, the individual gives an interpretation to the stimulus (to the object, in general terms), and only by virtue of this interpretation does the behavior of the individual become comprehensible.

In Piaget's theory, then, a particular stimulus (or object) is not the same unless the available assimilation schemes are also the same. This means putting the learner at the center of the learning process, rather than giving the central place to what supposedly directs this learning (the method or the person who carries it out). Thus it is necessary to establish a clear distinction between the steps a method proposes and what actually occurs in the learner's head. We make this distinction because the confusion between teaching method and learning process leads to a conclusion we find unacceptable—that success in learning is attributed to the method and not to the learner. A recent historical example reveals the fallacy of this argument. For decades people have learned mathematical calculations in school using pencil and paper and memorizing arithmetic facts, but this does not prove that this is how one develops a notion of numerical quantity and learns to operationalize. Today we know from the work of Piaget and his collaborators that the processes leading to elementary mathematical notions do not advance through memorization or through repetitive mechanical activities (Piaget and Szeminska, 1952). Although people for generations have been able to formulate correct numerical notions, it has not been because of these methods but in spite of them. This is so because children do not wait to receive instructions from adults to begin classifying and ordering the objects of their daily world.

This example of elementary arithmetic leads to another very important point. Until recently, if not to this day, first grade has been conceived of as an "instrumental" year in which children must acquire the instruments that will enable them to acquire other knowledge. These instruments (elementary arithmetic, reading, and writing) are not viewed as knowledge in themselves but, more precisely, as instruments for obtaining other knowledge.

Today we know (again from Piaget's work) that this position is unsustainable regarding elementary math. In the process of acquiring elementary numerical notions children construct logical thought; they acquire a type of knowledge that has great powers of generalization. Piaget's work on the development of elementary numerical notions destroys in its very foundations the conception of first grade math as the acquisition of a nonreasoned mechanistic procedure.

Our question is: doesn't the same thing occur with reading and writing? To what point can one sustain the idea that children must go through *ma—me—mi—mo—mu* rituals (English equivalent: cat—fat—mat—rat—sat) to learn to read? What is the justification for beginning with mechanical calculations of phoneme-grapheme correspondences to proceed later, and only later, to comprehending written texts? Is there justification for the concept of initial reading and writing as a blind initiation (that is, with the absence of intelligent thought) to the transcription of phonemes to graphemes?

Many teachers find themselves trapped in contradictory pedagogical practice when it comes to the two areas that determine the scholastic destiny of the first grade child (elementary math and reading/writing). They are Piagetians (or try to be) at math time and associationists (sometimes without meaning to be) at reading time. This contradiction is unacceptable, not only for reasons of pedagogical consistency but also because it is based on two conflicting conceptions of children themselves—creative, active, and intelligent during math time and passive, receptive, and ignorant during reading.

We have often heard the following objection: how can one speak of a Piagetian theory of reading and writing when Piaget himself has not written anything on the subject? In truth, Piaget has developed neither research studies nor a systematic reflection on this topic, and one can barely find tangential references to these problems in his diverse texts. The issue here is the conception one has of Piaget's theory. Either it is conceived of as a theory limited to the processes of acquiring logical mathematical and physical knowledge, or it is seen as a general theory of the processes of acquiring knowledge. The latter, of course, is our interpretation. Piaget's theory is not a specific theory about a specific domain. It is a much broader theoretical framework which lets us understand any process of acquiring knowledge. (In the same way, Freudian theory is not a specific theory of neurosis or subconscious processes, but a general theory of affective functioning.)

Viewing Piaget's theory in this way does not mean accepting it as dogma, but as a scientific theory. One of the ways of testing its general validity is by applying it to domains not yet explored from this perspective. Of course efforts to generate new hypotheses and expose new observable data through this theoretical framework must be differentiated from half-baked attempts to use Piaget to support any position (like the hasty assertions that the global methods are most in accordance with Piagetian theory).

Piaget's theory allows us to introduce written language as an object of knowledge and the learner as a thinking individual. It also allows us to introduce the notion of assimilation. But there is more still.

The concept of learning (understood as the process of obtaining knowledge) inherent to genetic psychology rests on the basic assumption that there are learning processes that do not depend on methods (processes that could be said to pass through methods). A method may help or hinder, facilitate or complicate, but not create learning. Obtaining knowledge is a result of the learner's own activity. (It is useful to note here—although we cannot develop it fully—that only genetic epistemology postulates action as the origin of all knowledge, including logical-mathematical knowledge.) An intellectually active learner does not necessarily carry out observable activities. An active learner compares, excludes, orders, categorizes, reformulates, confirms, forms hypotheses, and reorganizes through internalized action (thought) or through effective action (according to the level of development). A learner who carries something out according to instructions or a model provided by someone is not, usually, an intellectually active learner.

No learning has an absolute departure point. Since the content to be learned may be new, it must necessarily be assimilated by the learner, and the content will be modified to a greater or lesser degree depending on the assimilation schemes at hand. As we said before, there is no similarity between specific objects unless there is similarity in the assimilation schemes which attempt to interpret them. In practical terms, this means that learners (defined by function of the assimilation schemes at their disposal), and not the content to be learned, are the departure point of all learning.

The properties of the content to be learned may or may not be observable to the learner. The very definition of observable is relative to the level of cognitive development of the individual rather than to his or her sensory capacities. Just as in the development of science certain facts were not observable because no interpretive scheme existed for them, in psychogenetic history there is a progression in observable data parallel to the development of the interpretive scheme of the individual. (The role of scientific theories is exactly parallel to that of assimilation schemes.)

Some examples may be useful:

A five-year-old girl is asked to find two sticks of equal length within a group of sticks. She already knows how to equate the bases to compare the ends (she places them perpendicular to the table with their bases resting on the surface in order to compare them); in a given moment, after multiple comparisons which consist of taking any one stick as the measurer and comparing it with another one, she faces a configuration of three in which the two on the ends have exactly the same length and the one in the middle is perceptively shorter.

Facing this configuration, she concludes that no two sticks have the same length. This girl does not have any perceptual defect, and her problem is not of a perceptual nature. She could not conclude equality because she proceeded exclusively by comparing proximal pairs. If we compare each stick in this trio with its immediate neighbor, the only thing we can observe is that they are unequal. The equality is not observable unless we modify the method of comparison.

In certain experiments of transmission of movement through apparently immobile intermediaries, the immobility of the intermediaries cannot be observed (it is denied as observable) due to a general idea which holds that an object can only transmit movement if it begins to move itself (if it becomes displaced). (Piaget and Ferreiro, 1972.)

In the terrain of scientific theories—and staying within the field of psychology—it is obvious that Freudian slips were not observable (interpretable facts) until Freud's theory provided us with interpretive schemes. By the same token, the apparently alogical responses of children were not observable (interpretable facts) until Piaget's theory revealed their full value, moving them beyond the category of pleasant family anecdotes into the realm of scientific data.

In Piaget's theory, objective knowledge appears as an end result rather than as an initial piece of information. The path toward this objective knowledge is not linear. We do not move toward it step-by-step, adding bits of knowledge one on top of another. We reach it through great global reconstructions, some of which are erroneous (with respect to the ultimate goal) but constructive (in the sense that they allow us to reach it). This notion of constructive error is essential. In associationist psychology (and pedagogy) all errors are alike. In Piagetian psychology it is essential to be able to distinguish those errors which constitute necessary prerequisites for arriving at the correct solution. The example we have given about regularization of irregular verbs is certainly an example of constructive error. It indicates the point at which children have discovered a rule for verb derivation but are not yet cognitively capable of dealing with general rules and the exceptions to those rules at the same time (for this reason irregular verb forms produced by adults appear unobservable). Piaget's work abounds with examples of such constructive errors. To cite one:

the judgments of numerical equivalence based on the equality of the borders between two sets (when the child judges that there is an equal number of elements in two rows of objects whose limits coincide, regardless of the fact that one has five, spaced apart, and the other seven, closer together) constitutes a notable progression beyond a previous stage in which there are no stable criteria to judge equivalence between two sets. Although these judgments lead the child to commit systematic errors, these errors are constructive, permitting, rather than impeding, later arrival at the correct solution.

In other words, children do not regularize irregular verbs "just because" or judge the equivalence between two sets by the equivalence of borders "just because." These are systematic errors, not errors due to lack of attention or memory. Our responsibility as psychologists is to try to understand them; the responsibility of educators is to take them into account and not to put them into an undifferentiated bag of errors. Identifying such constructive errors in the psychogenesis of conceptualizations about written language is one of the objectives of our work. Acceptance in pedagogic practice—which traditionally views error with dismay—of the need to allow learners to go through periods of constructive error is a long-term task demanding other kinds of efforts.

Finally, in Piaget's theory the comprehension of an object of knowledge appears widely linked to the possibility of the individual's reconstructing the object, having comprehended its laws of composition. Contrary to Gestaltist positions, Piagetian comprehension is not figurative but operative: it is not the comprehension of a composite form given as such once and for all but the comprehension of the transformations that generate such configurations, together with the invariants that belong to it. (For example, comprehending the relationships between the objects in a Euclidean space is equivalent to being able to reconstruct this space starting from its base coordinates and working with the resultant metric invariants.)

As we have noted, a pedagogic practice in accordance with Piagetian theory must not fear error (provided there is a distinction between constructive errors and those that are not constructive). In addition, such a practice must not fear forgetting. Forgetting in itself is not important; what is important is the incapacity to recover the forgotten content. If students memorize the multiplication tables without understanding the underlying operations, upon forgetting "how much 7×8 is," for example, they will be able to recover the forgotten knowledge only by asking someone who knows. If they understand the production mechanism of this knowledge, they will always be able to recover it on their own (through not just one but many ways). In the first case, students continually depend on others who possess knowledge and can impart it. In the second, they are independent learners, since they comprehend the production mechanism of this knowledge, and consequently are creators of knowledge.

There is a profound difference between the conception of the learner as a recipient of knowledge provided from without and the conception of the learner as a producer of knowledge. This is the difference which separates behaviorist models from the Piagetian framework.

Progression in knowledge is only attained through 'cognitive conflict', when the presence of an unassimilable object (in the wide sense of an object of knowledge) forces learners to modify their assimilation schemes or, in other words, to make an effort to incorporate what previously seemed unassimilable (and constitutes, technically, a 'disturbance'). In the same way that not every activity is intellectual activity, not every conflict is a cognitive conflict which permits a progression in knowledge. There are particular points in development in which certain matters, previously ignored, become disturbances.[1] In practical terms, it is not a matter of continually placing learners in conflictive situations difficult to withstand but of trying to detect the crucial moments at which they become vulnerable to disturbances and to their own contradictions, so that we can help them advance toward a new reconstruction.

We obviously cannot attempt to summarize Piagetian theory in this introduction. We only wish to indicate some points that we consider keys to approaching the application of this conceptual framework to a new area.

In summary, our objective is to demonstrate with concrete examples the relevance of Piaget's psychogenetic theory and of the developments in contemporary psycholinguistics to understanding the processes of learning about written language. We place ourselves above disputes over teaching methods in moving toward our final goal of contributing to a solution to the problems of written language learning in Latin America, so that the school system does not continue to produce illiterates.

General Characteristics of the Research

An investigation in the field of written language development for which there already exist numerous studies and publications may not appear novel. We can justify a new study, however, since the

---

[1] Authors' Note: For theoretical clarification of these problems we refer the reader to Piaget (1977). Particularly clear examples of cognitive conflict are found in Inhelder, Sinclair, and Bovet (1974).

double conceptual framework we have chosen—that of genetic psychology and contemporary psycholinguistics—permits us to address unresolved questions. If learning in this domain cannot be reduced to a series of specific skills that schoolchildren must acquire or to methodological practices carried out by teachers, we must account for the real process of constructing knowledge to overcome the reductionism of recent psychopedagogical postures. All theoretical approaches (and all pedagogical practice) depend on a conception of the nature of knowledge as well as an analysis of the particular object of knowledge. Our attempt to offer an explanation from another epistemological point of view, facing an old problem with new vision, justifies the effort. With this new focus, we present a series of investigations to examine the process of the construction of knowledge in written language. Our examination proceeds through: (*a*) identifying the underlying cognitive processes in written language acquisition; (*b*) understanding the nature of children's hypotheses; and (*c*) discovering the kinds of specific knowledge children possess when school learning begins.

Having introduced our theoretical departure point, it is necessary to clarify the principles we followed in structuring our experimental situations. Since our interest resides in discovering the construction process of the writing system, our goal in devising experimental situations was to help children make clear to us what writing is as they see it, what reading is as they understand it, what problems they pose, and how. This new focus demanded an adequate method. Neither reading readiness tests nor tests for evaluating school achievement served our purpose, as both refer to a problem area that does not concern us here. It did not serve our purpose to administer any test, because tests are based on an assumption about the learning process. Tests of the reading readiness kind rest on the assumption that certain linguistic aspects (such as correct articulation) and nonlinguistic aspects (such as visual perception and manual-motor coordination) of child behavior are related to the capacity for reading and writing. Case studies have revealed correlations between failure in reading and writing and parallel deficiencies in other domains. At the same time, it has been found that good achievement in the area of reading and writing is accompanied by success in other domains. This has led to establishing correlations between reading level and other aspects, such as corporal awareness, spatial and time orientation, left-right directionality, I.Q., and so on. This in turn is used to conclude that good performance in these other domains is a necessary and preliminary condition for written language learning. The principle underlying this belief is the supposed existence of a maturity for learning consisting of a series of specific skills measurable through observable behaviors. From one of the tests of greater distribution in Latin America, Lorenzo Filho's ABC, we find that before children can begin systematic learning they must possess a minimum level of maturity in visual-motor and audio-motor coordination as well as a good intelligence quotient and a minimum level of language (Filho, 1960). We do not believe, however, that one must start from the concept of maturity (sufficiently wide and ambiguous to include all unexplained issues) or from a list of aptitudes and skills. We are not interested in defining children's responses in terms of what they lack in skills or maturity. On the contrary, we are attempting to expose positive aspects of what they know. In each chapter of this book and in each analysis of the different levels of responses, this principle will reappear: child behavior is defined as a mode of approaching the object of knowledge (modes that come close to adult responses to lesser or greater degrees), a process that assumes a long road of construction. We are also not concerned with evaluating school achievement in terms of how many words children know how to write or how well they can decipher a text. On achievement tests, progress is measured according to the proposed model on which instruction is based. School advancement, then, is the result of assimilating a particular type of instruction. But the instructional model must not be confused with the underlying processes. If a distinction between method and process is necessary to avoid confusing the nature of the process with the proposed methodology, it is also necessary to distinguish between levels of conceptualization and correct responses. Measuring children's performance at a given moment in their learning not only presupposes a theory of the nature of the learning process but also hypothesizes about progress according to an ideal scale of achievement. Neither achievement nor predictive tests (based on an empiricist theory of learning) help resolve the kinds of problems we have posed here. Though we do use reading and writing tasks, our manner of instrumentalizing them is totally different.

The basic principles that guided the construction of our experimental design are:

1. Reading is not deciphering. Until now, psychology and pedagogy have viewed the learning of reading as an inevitable mechanism of establishing correspondence between oral language and written language. Only recently have some authors begun to defend other positions, manifesting that reading is not equivalent to decoding letters into sounds (Foucambert, Smith) and so cannot be reduced strictly to deciphering.
2. Writing is not copying a model. When writing is viewed as skills for reproducing graphic shapes or as a problem of acquiring

rules for transcribing oral language, the fact that writing is a conceptual task, as well as a psycho-motor task, is ignored. Even if the presence of models is necessary—insofar as they are required in any cognitive development—writing is not passive copying but active interpretation of the models of the adult world. Although far removed from conventional calligraphy and orthography, when children begin to write they produce visible marks on paper, putting into play their hypotheses about the very meaning of graphic representation.

3. Progress in literacy does not come about through advances in deciphering and copying. This third principle is a consequence of the first and second. If we understand the acquisition of the writing system as the product of an active construction, we assume the existence of levels of restructuring knowledge. Our objective is to study the construction processes independently of scholastic achievement. (It is understood that progress in conceptualization may or may not coincide with levels of scholastic achievement.)

The novelty of our viewpoint requires, then, an experimental situation, structured but flexible, permitting us to discover the hypotheses children put into play. Following the general approach of Piagetian genetic psychology, all tasks involve an interaction between the child and the object of knowledge (in this case, written language) in the form of a problem to be solved. From this interaction a dialogue develops between child and interviewer, a dialogue with the purpose of exposing the mechanisms of child thought. The experimental design includes situations of interpreting the alphabetic code as it appears in the daily world and situations of graphic production. In all the proposed tasks we introduce conflictive (or at least potentially conflictive) elements whose solution requires real reasoning on the part of the child. Details of the tasks will be presented in the corresponding chapters.

During the interview, always individual, the children's responses were recorded both by hand and on tape. Each subject was tested on the whole series of tasks in a room in the school or preschool he or she attended. The final protocol is the result of combining the written and taped versions.

The inquiry method we use, inspired by the clinical method (or method of critical exploration) developed by the Geneva school, explores the child's knowledge with respect to reading and writing activities. The kind of interview we use and the flexibility of the experimental situation permit us to obtain truly original responses—in the sense of being unexpected by an adult—and to elaborate adequate hypotheses for understanding their significance.

The analysis of the results presented in each chapter is fundamentally qualitative in nature, intended to discover and interpret
each category of response as well as to find successive levels of
development. These levels are relative to each of the proposed
tasks and do not assume comparability between tasks (for example, level 1 of one task is not necessarily contemporaneous to level
1 of another task). The quantitative references, when there are
any, are more for providing an idea about the frequency of a
specific kind of response than for making a statistical evaluation.
Obviously we exclude an evaluation in terms of correct or erroneous response, since our goal is to explain the conceptualization
processes of written language and consequently to understand the
reasons for children's so-called errors. We shall present, as examples, extracts of protocols illustrating the different kinds of responses. The transcription of the protocol maintains the language
used by the child in the dialogue.[1]

We began our study with a one-year semilongitudinal follow-
through. We randomly selected a group of thirty children of lower
class social background who were in first grade for the first time.
We interviewed them periodically, at the beginning, the middle,
and the end of the school year. We completed the experience with
twenty-eight of the initial thirty children. These children attended
two first grade classes in the same school. Both teachers followed
the same method of instruction and used the same beginning text,
but their different previous experiences led to differences in actual procedures. One of them had always taught at the primary
level and had taught first grade the year before. The other faced
initial instruction for the first time, having previously taught preschool. The method of instruction of reading and writing that was
used in this school was the so-called mixed method or word-type
(*palabras-tipo*) analytic-synthetic method (the most widespread
method in Argentina and in many other countries in Latin America). Instruction begins with words considered to be easy, such as
mamá, papá, oso (bear), *ala* (wing); in general, cases of duplicated
syllables or of the same vowel repeated in different syllables. These
words are broken down into smaller components and are recombined later. (The breakdown results in syllables represented by
consonant and vowel or vowels by themselves. The consonants are
combined with all the vowels to form new syllables.) Working with
a group of previously learned words (or, more appropriately, pre-

[1] Translator's Note: This statement, of course, refers to the original publication
in Spanish. The English translations of the children's responses result from the
difficult and imprecise task of conserving the original meaning, but as English-
speaking children would be most likely to express it. When a statement cannot be
translated without a certain change or loss of meaning, the original statement in
Spanish follows the approximate translation for purposes of clarification.

viously taught words) the teacher presents simple sentences including these words. This method upholds the principle of presenting one word at a time and not going on to the next until it has been learned. It emphasizes deciphering the written text, following the classic steps of moving from mechanical to comprehensive and finally to expressive reading. The children use a "reading book" (a beginning reader) and an exercise notebook (workbook). There is no uniform regulation in Argentina specifying the reader and many versions are allowed, the choice being the responsibility of the teacher. The type of handwriting used in initial instruction is lower-case cursive, the upper case being introduced in the middle of the year, and print being reserved for textbooks.

The population selected for this study came from the lower class. Among our reasons for such a selection was the accumulation of school failures in this critical school period among children of lower socioeconomic levels. We wanted, then, to discover before the fact how children become repeaters and how they end up with learning disorders. We also thought that lower class children were the ones who actually begin scholastic learning upon entering elementary school, while middle class children continue previously initiated learning. This occurs because, among other reasons, in Argentina there is an insufficient number of kindergarten/preschools and many lower class children do not have the opportunity to attend them.[1] The school these children attended was located in a section of the industrial belt of Buenos Aires. It received students from a working class suburb of surrounding *villas miserias* (makeshift quarters of precarious construction). The parents, for the most part, were unskilled workers or seasonal laborers. Of the thirty children in the sample, fifteen had attended preschool, seven were in a school situation for the first time, and the remaining six had attended, very irregularly, the last year of kindergarten/ preschool. Seventeen were boys and thirteen were girls. All were interviewed in the beginning, middle, and end of the year. The first experimental session took place during the first month of school; at that time the mean age of the group was 5.11. In the second session, at the middle of the year, the mean age was 6.3, and toward the end of the year, during the third session, it was 6.7. In addition to the specific experimental tasks, in each interview we administered the test of conservation of number (Piaget and Szeminska, 1952; Inhelder, Sinclair, and Bovet, 1974).

The results of this year-long investigation indicated two things: that the child's learning process may take paths unsuspected by

---

[1] Translator's Note: In Argentina, and throughout Latin America, elementary schools begin with first grade. Kindergarten/preschools are generally separate, voluntary, and private. They may have a two- or three-year program including children from ages three to five or four to five.

the teacher, and even lower class children do not start from zero in first grade. Six year olds already possess a whole series of conceptions about written language, the result of earlier experiences. In fact, the problem we posed was: at what point does written language constitute an object of knowledge? Our informal explorations indicated that around four years of age children spontaneously ask questions like "how do you spell?" or "what does it say?" at the same time as they solicit adults to read them stories or magazines. We do not wish to affirm that interest in written language commences at a specific chronological age. Quite possibly it constitutes a concern from a much earlier age (depending on individual children and their environmental conditions), but for practical research reasons we had to establish a starting point.

To find this out, we did a cross-age study with children from four to six years of age. To analyze the influences of the social class variable, we selected both a middle and lower class population in equivalent scholastic situations: all attended school.

The middle class sample was selected from children with professional parents (engineers, doctors, psychologists) to ensure the presence of books and willing readers within the family environment. At the other social extreme, the lower class children came from a section of the industrial belt of Buenos Aires. Although there is no record of a high degree of adult illiteracy in this zone, the occasions to participate in reading acts or of having available material written for children are fewer. Social differences in the home environment should, at least theoretically, influence the value placed on written language, a truly cultural object. We wanted to know how environmental action relates to children's hypotheses and knowledge about written language. However, it is impossible to evaluate the influence of social values through supposedly objective questionnaires designed to discover parents' reading activities. No survey can replace anthropological observation, but this influence can be evaluated on the basis of what children have been able to assimilate from their home environment. From an interactionist point of view, like that of the Piagetian conceptualization we adopted, knowledge is constructed through interaction between the knowing subject and the object to be known. A comparative study would allow us to account for environmental action through the ways assimilation takes place in children from different social classes.

The common denominator among the groups was school attendance. The four- and five-year-old children attended kindergarten/preschool and the six year olds attended first grade. In Argentina, kindergarten/preschool begins at four. This, then, was the youngest age to be considered. Reading and writing instruction begins in first grade. At the time we carried out this study, the Ministry of Education directed that the first month of school be dedicated to preparatory exercises (in general, exercises of visual-motor coordination, spatial orientation, and so on). We took advantage of this situation to question the six-year-old children before they received systematic instruction which began in the middle of the second month of school.

The population of the cross-age study was comprised of groups of 4-, 5-, and 6-year-old children, coming from the middle and lower class. The sample of middle class 4 and 5 year olds attended private kindergarten/preschools and the lower class 4 and 5 year olds attended kindergarten/preschools attached to public schools. The professional middle class of Buenos Aires tends to give great importance to preschool education and prefers to send its children to private kindergarten/preschools. We interviewed ten lower class 4 year olds—six boys and four girls—with a mean age of 4.8, twelve middle class 4 year olds—five boys and seven girls—with a mean age of 4.4, eleven lower class 5 year olds—six boys and five girls—with a mean age of 5.6, and sixteen middle class 5 year olds—seven boys and nine girls—with a mean age of 5.7. The sample of lower class 6 year olds was not complete. We began with a group of eleven from a highly marginalized social group (all inhabitants of *villas miserias*) but, for reasons beyond our control, we had to abandon this sample. (The area was next to a military camp and a coup d'état closed the zone to all visitors.) The results from this group are consequently incomplete, complicating the comparative analysis. Fortunately the results obtained from the previous longitudinal study, with a similar population, allowed us to compensate for the missing data. The mean age of this group was 6.4. The middle class 6-year-old sample was comprised of twenty subjects—fourteen of whom were boys and six girls—with a mean age of 5.11.[1] All 6 year olds attended public schools in various sections of the city. The lower class 6 year olds were at schools in the industrial belt. The middle class 6 year olds' schools were in the residential district.

In total six schools were involved. The interviews took place in the same room in the school and lasted twenty to thirty minutes. The type of interview and the experimental situation were the same for all the subjects of the cross-age study. The complete study presented in this book is the result of the analysis of data from a total of 108 subjects. The order of presentation of the data is the inverse of the order of collection. The objective of this presentation order is to be better able to follow the evolutionary line. The

---

[1] Authors' Note: In Argentina children may enter first grade at five if they will turn six during the school year. In general, the mean ages for the middle class are lower than those for the lower class.

analysis will be centered on the preschool age, with complementary data from the longitudinal study of six year olds who receive school assistance.

In the following we will abbreviate middle class as MC and lower class as LC.

II FORMAL ASPECTS OF THE GRAPHIC SYSTEM AND THEIR INTERPRETATION: LETTERS, NUMBERS, AND PUNCTUATION MARKS

Formal Characteristics a Text Must Possess for Reading to Occur

Not yet knowing how to read does not prevent children from having precise ideas about the characteristics a written text must have for reading to take place. When presented with different texts on cards and asked whether the cards are something to read (*sirven para leer*) or not something to read (*no sirven para leer*), children use two main criteria to make this decision: there must be a sufficient number of characters and a variation of these characters. The mere presence of graphic characters does not necessarily provide a readable text; if there are very few or if one is repeated many times the text is judged not readable by children. Children make this judgment before they are capable of appropriately reading the texts they examine.

Sufficient Number of Characters

We observe children using the number of characters as a criterion for judging whether something is readable by presenting them with cards, some with one letter, some with two letters (comprising syllables or whole words), some with three (also comprising syllables or words), and so on. The longest word contains nine letters. The cards are written either in printed upper-case letters or in lower-case cursive. We also present three cards with one numeral written on each. The syllables and words on some cards are patterned after the traditional combinations used in beginning reading/writing instruction (for example, *oso*[1], PAPÁ, PE, *pi*). Other cards have more difficult texts which children are less likely to recognize (for example, PERÍMETRO, *vacaciones, tra*).

The children work with fifteen to twenty cards. They must classify them according to our criterion but as they define it for themselves: "Look at these cards carefully and tell me if you think they

---

[1] Authors' Note: Italics indicate lower-case cursive; all caps indicate upper-case print.

all are something to read or if some are and some aren't." We questioned a total of sixty-three children with this technique.

The results allow us to distinguish those subjects who do not use any criterion to classify the cards from those who do. The first group are at what we could call level zero regarding this task. They respond in the following way: either all cards equally are something to read or one is and the next one is not, regardless of their objective characteristics (that is, they decide at random that one card is readable and from there they begin to alternate judgments, so that a card is readable if it is in the good pile but if it is changed to the other pile, then it is no longer readable). These children are not yet capable of discriminating within a graphic universe made up solely of letters and numbers. The interesting discovery is that very few children respond in this way: a total of nine, limited to the younger ages (2 four-year-old MC children, 4 LC children of the same age and 3 five-year-old LC children). The rest of the children (most of the four year olds, almost all of the five year olds, and all of the six year olds in both social groups) are capable of proceeding toward ordering this graphic universe in some coherent fashion.

The easiest criterion for an adult to utilize would certainly be the distinction between numbers and letters, and then the separation of print from cursive or letters from syllables and words. But this is not what children do.

The most frequent solution adopted by the children involves setting aside the cards with few characters (regardless, in many cases, of whether they are letters or numerals) because, according to these children, you can't read with few letters. We say "letters," but, of course, the label varies from child to child. The key number on which the child's decision rests tends to be three. For most of these children an example of print with three identifiable characters can be read, but an example with fewer than three characters becomes unreadable. For other children four characters are necessary, and some are satisfied with two. The fact that the majority of the judgments revolve around three is extremely important since, as we shall see in chapter 4, this renders unreadable the grammatical category of articles (which have two letters for the written representation of the singular determiners *el* and *la* [masculine and feminine singular forms of "the"] and for the indefinite article *un* ["a"]).

In many cases the children justify explicitly their use of the criterion of minimum quantity:

Gustavo (6 yrs., MC) demands at least three characters and he justifies this by saying that the cards in the group that are not something to read are there because "they have one word or two" (*tienen una palabra o dos*) while the others "have a lot, like four." (He uses "word" for "letter" or "graphic character.")

Juan Pablo (6 yrs., MC) also demands three, but he justifies this by saying simply that the ones that are not something to read "are too short" (*son muy cortitas*) while the others "are longer," even though he is capable of indicating among the not-something-to-read group that "some are numbers and some are letters."

Jorge (6 yrs., LC) requires a minimum of four characters. In order for a card to be something to read it must have "a lot of things, a whole bunch" (*muchas cosas, un montón*); for example he excludes a manuscript *m* "because it only has three."

To determine the minimum quantity the children require, it is not enough simply to observe which cards they include in each group; it is also necessary to know how they count the characters. In general, we do not encounter ambiguities with upper-case print, but with cursive characters the distinction between the end of one letter and the beginning of the next is a problem. An example is the cursive syllable *pi* which sometimes is considered to have three characters, sometimes four, but rarely two. In the same way, the cursive *m* has been considered to be three characters, and the cursive *p* is sometimes counted as two or three different characters. This is how the younger children explain themselves:

Lorena (5 yrs., MC) demands at least three characters and she points out that the cards which are not something to read are "just for making words" (*para armar una palabra nomás*) while in the something-to-read group the words "are already made" (*ya están hechas*). In other words, for a graphic representation to be a word, it must have at least three characters. (Lorena is not yet capable of reading a word like MAMÁ.)

Gustavo (5 yrs., MC) clearly indicates that "where there's just a couple (*unas poquitas*) it's not for reading (*no es para leer*); here there's not so much letters, there's two" (cards AS and SO).

Erik (5 yrs., LC) puts aside the cards with *f*, *e*, and *i* in cursive, saying that they are not something to read "because they only have one number." Then he has doubts about the cards with two and decides that there must be at least four until, finally, he settles for at least three.

María Paula (4 yrs., MC) rejects cards with just one letter saying, "that's not something to read one bit"; she is unsure of the cards with three because they are "a little bit for reading" (*un poquito para leer*), and she is sure of the ones with four: PELO is something to read "because it has about four numbers."

José Luis (4 yrs., MC) needs a minimum of three and he indicates that the cards in the something-to-read group are there "because there's letters; if there was two letters you couldn't read."

Mariana (4 yrs., MC) also requires three and she explains that the not-something-to-read cards cannot be read "because they're just one letter, but the others have lots of them." So, for example, she excludes OS "because there's two," but she includes *pi* in cursive "because there's a lot."

It becomes clear, from these examples, that the demand for a minimum quantity of characters has nothing to do with the labels the children may or may not be capable of employing. It does not matter if they call these characters letters, numbers, words, or things. The importance here is that the readability of a text appears to be associated with quantity.

Nevertheless, a noteworthy phenomenon occurs in some cases. A letter may receive different labels depending on whether it appears in the context of other letters (in which case it becomes something to read) or whether it appears by itself (in which case it becomes unreadable). For example:

Romina (4 yrs., MC) needs at least two characters for a card to be readable, and she explains that all the cards in this group "are letters," while the others (with only one character) are not readable because "they're numbers." It happens that in the not-something-to-read group there are both cards with one number and cards with one letter. Furthermore, there is a card in this group with the letter A, which Romina recognizes by name in other contexts. (In the something-to-read group she includes cards with such texts as LA [the feminine singular form of the article "the"] and FRUTA [fruit].)

This behavior should not be confused with that of giving number names to letters with similar graphic forms. L, for example, might be placed in the not-something-to-read group because it is identified as 7, and as such, recognized as a number. The same could occur due to the similarities between S and 2 or 5, between O and zero, and between E and 3.

Romina's case, however, is not one of graphic confusion but rather a conceptual issue.

Carolina (5 yrs., MC) puts UNO, DOS, *do, mamá* in the something-to-read group because "they're letters," and sets aside *e* (cursive), *j* (cursive), 7, SO, P, and TRA because "they're numbers." Then she changes her mind and takes TRA out of this group "because it's not a number or a letter" (*no es ni número ni letra*). What is happening here is that she begins to wonder whether a greater number of characters is needed. (In cursive *do* has three characters for her.)

Gladys (6 yrs., LC) calls "letters" the things that appear in a book but these same letters presented by themselves become "numbers." In her classification task she uses the criterion of quantity (at least three), and she groups the cards with three or more characters saying that they are something to read because "they're letters," while the cards with one or two characters are not something to read "because they're numbers."

We obtained the clearest evidence regarding this point from a five-year-old girl interviewed in Geneva: Sandra accepts as something to read (*bonne pour lire*) a card on which EA appears, and she says that it is something to read because "it's an *a* with an *e*" (*c'est un* a *avec un* e) but she rejects a card with E because "it's a number" (*c'est un chiffre*).

This tells us that even when a letter is recognized as such and, moreover, named appropriately, there is no guarantee that it will always be a letter. It depends on the context in which it appears. To an adult it seems obvious that a letter is always a letter, regardless of the context. For children this question is posed differently: the same graphic form may be one thing or another depending on the context. For something to be a letter it must be with other letters. Sandra does not have a perceptual problem; she has a conceptual problem, a good conceptual problem in the sense that it corresponds to a good question, a good conceptual query. Sandra is certainly right: a letter by itself does not constitute a written text, while a number by itself constitutes the expression of a quantity.

Of course, we could always take the easy way out by concluding that children confuse numbers and letters. But this would be overly simplistic and insufficient to account for cases like these where the confusion is illusory, since something is systematically "letter" if it appears with others and "number" if it appears by itself. There is no confusion, then, but rather a systematization different from the adult's.

Variation of Characters

For a text to be readable it is not enough for it to have characters identified as letters. It must have a certain number of characters, varying from two to four with three being the minimum in most cases. In addition to this criterion, there is another of great importance: if all the characters are the same, even though the amount is sufficient, the card will be judged not readable.

This becomes evident when children compare examples of upper-case print (MMMMMM, AAAAAA, MANTECA [lard]) with the same series in lower-case cursive. The number of letters (more than three) guarantees that the cards will not be rejected for insufficient characters; we use the letters *M* and *A* because they are among the first clearly recognized by children. The instructions for this task are the same as for the previous task (to decide what is something to read and what is not).

Only half of the four- and five-year-old children were questioned with this technique.[1] Of these, slightly more than half of the four year olds and two-thirds of the five year olds (of both social groups) explicitly affirm that reading cannot take place if all the letters are the same. They express this in the following ways:

Javier (4 yrs., LC) initially accepts the cards with repeated letters, precisely because they are letters, but then he rejects them "because they're the same letters; you can't, I tell you, they're the same; those ones are for reading, with the other letters." Javier manages to express here this complex thought: since they are letters, we have the raw material for a possible readable text, but only if other different letters appear as well.

Gustavo (4 yrs., LC) rejects the cards with repeated letters "because it has all the same."

Mariana (4 yrs., MC) rejects the series of cursive *m*'s "because they're all like that" and the series of cursive *a*'s "because they all are, too." The ambiguity of these explanations is clarified when she says the *manteca* card can be read "because they're not all the same like this one and this one" (the previous cards).

José Luis (4 yrs., MC) rejects the series of cursive *m*'s because "it's all messed up (*es un mamarracho*); it has little mountains and that's not how they make letters." He also rejects the series of cursive *a*'s because "it looks like a lake," and the series of printed *A*'s "because there's a lot of *a*'s and not much letters."

Romina (4 yrs., MC) also rejects the cards with the cursive *a* and *m* series because "it's all the same" (*todo igualito*) and she accepts *manteca* "because it's not all together, there's other letters too."

Rosario (5 yrs., LC) gives no reason for rejecting the cards with repeated letters and accepts *manteca* "because they don't have so many letters that are the same," likewise MANTECA "because it doesn't have the same letters, all the same letters."

Laura (5 yrs., MC) rejects the *A* series "because it says *a* all the time" (*dice todo el tiempo* a), and the *M* series because "it says em, em, em, em . . ." while she accepts MANTECA: "I don't know what it says but it's for reading" (*no se que dice pero es de leer*).

We have cited many examples to show that the justifications are always of the same kind. The rejection of cards with repeated letters does not depend on recognition of the letters in question, just as the acceptance of the cards with different letters does not depend on whether the child can read it. As Laura clearly says: "I don't know what it says but it's for reading." In other words, we

[1] Authors' Note: We currently have data from a larger number of subjects confirming extensively the results obtained here. The same phenomenon occurs in French.

have here a typical case of formal requirement preceding the initiation of written language instruction characterized by the sounding out of each graphic character.

The cursive *m* and *a* series have often been interpreted as being closer to representative drawing than to writing: "they're little mountains," "it's like the ocean," "it's a lake," "they're pictures." These are justifications given for rejecting specific cards. In not one case have children claimed that a card is something to read because it looks like a picture. All references to figurative drawing pertain to excluded cards. This allows us to assume that, from the age of four, in spite of marked differences in social background, children begin to establish a very important distinction between the graphic universe of representative drawing and the graphic universe of written language.

Other Classification Criteria Utilized

The two main classification criteria used by the children in this study are important because of their role in later development and also in quantitative terms. The criterion of sufficient number of characters is used by 57.41 percent of the total sample, but more frequently by the MC group (where the percentage remains around 70 percent for all age groups) than by the LC group (where the percentage becomes progressively greater from four to six years, ending up at around 60 percent of the six year olds). The criterion of variation of characters is used by 68 percent of the sample (remember that only half of the four and five year olds are included in this). The MC children use it somewhat more frequently than the LC (72.72 percent and 64.28 percent respectively), and in both groups we find a progression in the frequency of utilizing this criterion from four to five years.

Obviously, other possibilities for classifying the cards appear. One procedure that constitutes an intermediate point between level zero classification and using some systematic criterion is the utilization of cues for determining whether a card is readable or not. Only three LC children proceed this way: if they find some cue on the card which allows them to interpret it, the card is something to read, but if they find no cue it is not something to read.

Débora (4 yrs., LC) says the following are something to read: *papá* because it's "for papa" (*de papá*), *mamá* because "this one's for mama," O because "this one's for Christian," 7 because "this one's for my little brother who knocked out his tooth."

Atilio (5 yrs., LC) continually bases his judgments on the recognition of a single letter, and he claims that *fabuloso, dos, palo,* and *do* (all cursive) are something to read because in all of them "it says *oso* (bear), because it has this one" (the final *o*). PELO is something to read because "it's for papa" (the initial *P*), and MARAVILLA is too because it's "mama and Atilio" (mama for the initial *M* and Atilio for the final *A*).

Although the utilization of cues is not frequent in this classification task, it often appears in other situations.

Another alternative for classifying the cards is the distinction between cursive and printed characters. The important aspect of this response is how this difference is conceptualized:

Anabela (5 yrs., LC) groups the cards with cursive writing saying that "they're not for reading, these are for writing." In a separate group she puts the cards with printed characters and numbers saying that they are "for names and also for reading." Then, to complicate the situation further, she removes the cards with numbers saying that they're not for reading "because they're letters." Her reasoning is logical since the label she uses for the characters of a printed text is "numbers." So, on the cards that are something to read there are "numbers" (that is, printed letters).

Silvia (6 yrs., LC) groups the cursive cards and says that they are something to read because "they have letters"; in the other group she puts the cards with printed lettering, numbers, and some single letters, all of which are not something to read "because they don't have this" (that is, what the other cards have that she identifies as letters). We observe here that Silvia mixes the criterion of character type with that of minimum quantity.

Marisela (4 yrs., MC) affirms that the cursive texts are something to read "because they're letters: *a-e-i-o-u*", while the printed cards are not something to read but rather "for talking about letters (*para hablar de letras*), for counting." Trying to better explain her idea, Marisela gathers three cards: MAMÁ/PERÍMETRO/LA, lines them up and says "fifteen." She does the same with four cursive cards: *o/siete/kilo/pi* and says "*a-e-i-o-u*." (In the first case she has counted, correctly, the number of letters, while in the second case she has emitted the series of vowels which probably constitute for her the very definition of reading.)

From these examples it becomes apparent that the criterion of character type conceals a multitude of other considerations. It reflects the child's awareness of more than one kind of writing. But there is great variation in the way children conceptualize this fact. In at least two of the examples given (Anabela and Marisela) the distinction between cursive and print appears to be mixed with the distinction between numbers and letters.

Finally, a criterion that appears simple but rarely serves as the sole criterion is that of distinguishing letters from numerals. The utilization of this criterion requires not only a clear distinction between letter graphics and number graphics but also a rejection of the minimum-quantity-of-characters criterion, imposed so unyieldingly by the majority of children in this study.

Mariano (6 yrs., MC) achieves a solution by making three groups: one of single letters, which are not something to read; one of cards with at least two letters, which are something to read; and one of numbers which, according to Mariano, "don't go anywhere" (*no van en ningún lado*). The numbers are so markedly differentiated from the letters that the dichotomy is/is not something to read cannot be applied to them; they are something altogether different that cannot be defined by this dichotomous parameter.

The Relationship Between Letters and Numbers and the Recognition of Individual Letters

The relationship between letters and numbers evolves through three important conceptual stages. First, letters and numbers are confused, not only because they have marked graphic similarities but also because the fundamental dividing line that children attempt to establish at this point is the one that separates representative drawing from writing. (Numbers are written, as are letters, and they also appear in print in similar contexts.) During the next important stage the distinction is made between letters, which are used for reading, and numbers, which are used for counting. Numbers and letters can no longer be grouped together because they serve different functions. The third stage reintroduces the conflict: when children begin school (if not before) they discover that the teacher is just as likely to say "who can read this word?" as "who can read this number?" The idea that a number can be read, even though it has no letters, constitutes a real problem. This confusion can be resolved only when we realize that numbers are written in a system different from the alphabetic system used to write words. As Cohen (1958) indicates, "in all languages numbers are read ideographically." For people of different languages who use the same characters to represent numbers, there is no need to modify the writing system in order to read the numbers. The written numeral 8 does not have to change in any way in order to be read as eight, *ocho*, or *huit*, but we cannot move as easily from duck to *pato* or *canard*. It is possible that few teachers clearly understand that as they introduce children to written language they are confronting them with two totally different writing systems when they move from the math lesson to the reading/writing lesson.

Using varied information we determine where to place children among the different levels we shall propose. We consider their reactions to a printed text, to a group of small cards each with a single letter (upper-case print), the writing of their own name (done with pencil or by arranging mobile letters), or the recognition of their own name (when they are not capable of writing it themselves). Finally, we include the information derived from the card classification task we analyzed previously.

We normally begin this interview by suggesting to the children that we leaf through a book of children's stories. This allows us to counterpose a description or label for the pictures against a description for the print (simply by asking "what's this?" in reference to a picture and again in reference to the print). In this way, we detect the first label that a child is able to use reacting to a printed text, and we continue the questioning with this label. If the children use "letter" or "number" they receive neither approval nor correction. We attempt to understand the limits and the reasons for using the label, but we do not use an alternate term unless the children produce one.

Picture and Print

The majority of the children distinguish between print and picture by indicating that the picture is "for looking at" while the print is "for reading." When we ask why one can read the print, most of the children say "because there are letters," but a significant number of children—particularly LC children—say "because there are numbers."

No child has indicated the pictures alone as being for reading, but several have indicated text and picture together, as if they complement each other in allowing reading to take place. This does not necessarily mean that the text and the illustration are confused:

Ariel (5 yrs., MC) says that to read, "I read the pictures; I start here," and he shows the cover of the book. This does not prevent him from clearly explaining that the picture is "for looking at" and the print has "letters."

Jorge (4 yrs., MC) points to print and picture as being for reading "because they're the same; this is for reading (print) and this too (picture)," although he can tell us later that the text has "letters" which are "for reading" while the picture is "for looking at."

Fernando (4 yrs., LC) believes that print and picture are both used for reading and he explains the technical process of how one reads: "You know, with both eyes to look here (print) and over here (picture)." Fernando accompanies his statement with gestures to show us that since we have two eyes, we look at the text with one and the illustration with the other!

Roxana (5 yrs., LC) answers our question, "where is there something to read?" by responding, "here (print) and here (picture); this is to read (text) and there's where the pictures go (illustration); here's where you read, here, where the letters go."

Gustavo (4 yrs., LC) answers the same question by pointing first to the text, then to the large characters of the title and finally to the illustration saying, "and then you read me the picture." So we ask him if the picture can be read and he clarifies: "You can see, you can't read it. These are flowers but they're not letters, right?"

These examples show that print functions in a very specific way for these children: they know well that you read where the letters are, but the pictures can also be used for reading, as a support element. (In chapter 3, where we analyze specifically the relationship between print and picture, we will better understand the sense in which the picture is perceived as part of the reading material.)

Referring simultaneously to text and illustration as being the fundamental elements in an act of reading occurs much more frequently among LC children than MC children: around 25 percent of the LC children but just 7 percent of the MC children. The most dramatic difference—and certainly the one that has most repercussion on the children's scholastic future—is found among the six year olds. No MC child of this age points to both text and illustration as the agents for reading, while one-fourth of the LC six year olds do.

Nevertheless, as important as this difference may be, we must not forget the inverse of these percentages: around 75 percent of the LC children and 90 percent of the MC children have no doubts about this matter; they point only to the print as being for reading. Our question about where there is something to read even seems ridiculous to some, since the answer is overly obvious. As Romina (4 yrs., MC) says, to read you must look at the print "because if you don't, where will the letters be?"

Children who indicate the text exclusively as being for reading do not necessarily use the label "letters" for the graphemes of print. When asked why it is possible to read the text, a considerable number of children respond that it can be read because there are "numbers."

Erik (5 yrs., LC) says: "all this is the numbers for reading."

Anabela (5 yrs., LC) characterizes the text saying that "it's all writing," and when we ask her what is there in the writing, she responds, "what, what, the story, the . . . what the things say. They're numbers."

The LC children frequently apply the label "number" to letters with no significant difference across age groups (46 percent of the total LC sample). In the MC sample, very few children think that there are numbers in the text (a little over 10 percent, concentrated mostly among the four year olds).

To avoid confusion, we must clarify that we are referring to the label applied to the content of a printed text (a book of children's stories, in this case). For a child who says that such a text has letters, the same characters presented in isolated fashion in groups of two will not necessarily continue being letters.

In summary, while the LC children as a whole share with the MC children the possibility of distinguishing within the graphic universe between pictures, which are for looking at, and text, which is for reading, they are not as well off when it comes to distinguishing within nonrepresentational graphics (letters and numbers). Is this solely a matter of verbal confusion or is a conceptual confusion involved as well?

First, though, we must point out that some of the LC children seem not to have even reached the level we characterize as a simultaneous utilization of print and picture, although they distinguish between the two. Here are some examples, beginning with a six year old who does not appear to differentiate the properties of numbers (as graphic elements) from those of letters:

Silvia (6 yrs., LC): "to read, first you start to make the numbers. You have to learn. You have to make the numbers, then the letters."

Alejandro (4 yrs., LC): When we ask him where there is something to read he points vaguely at the page. We show him the picture and we ask him if you read that; he answers no but he is still unable to specify where there is something to read. We ask him if you have to look at the pictures in order to tell the story (*contar el cuento*), and he answers yes. Pointing to the text we ask him what it is: "to *contar*[1] the things, they tell you all the things" (*para contar las cosas; te dicen todas las cosas*). And when we ask him what one must do to *contar*, he counts the letters while saying, "one, two, eight, ten, nine, fourteen, seventeen, fifteen, seven."

Silvana (4 yrs., LC) says that to read one must look at the text where there are "numbers," but when we ask her where one must begin reading, she answers, "with a pen." We ask her to show us and she answers, "I write." So we ask her if we must write in order to read what is written and she answers yes.

These three examples are each very different, but together they give a kind of intuitive impression of the difficulties children must deal with. It is clear that in Silvia's case the difficulty resides in understanding the different functions of two school activities

---

[1] Translator's Note: *Contar* can mean either "to tell" or "to count"; the context does not allow us to be certain which meaning Alejandro is using here, if, indeed, he separates the two.

(making letters and making numbers) which seem very similar to her, and rightly so. With Alejandro the difficulties result from the ambiguity of the verb *contar:* one can *contar un cuento* (tell a story) and also *contar* (count) objects or graphemes. Both actions are quite different but the verbal denomination is the same. Finally, Silvana's problem is somewhat deeper: reading and writing are two actions not yet differentiated.

Also, reading and listening to a text read by someone are sometimes difficult to distinguish. In response to our question "what do I have to do to read?" Marcela (6 yrs., MC) answers, "you have to listen."

Letters: Recognizing Them and Being Able To Name Them

We move on to characterize the levels of recognition of individual letters and, particularly, the use of conventional labels to name them.

Level 1
At the most elementary level children recognize a total of one or two letters—particularly the initial letter of their own name— but do not use any letter names. In the same group are children who use number names for letters, but without consistency and not depending on graphic similarity between the number and the letter (as would be the case with the pairs E/3, L/7, S/2, S/5). One example will suffice:

Martín (4 yrs., MC) sporadically uses number names for letters: *F* is "three" (*el tres*),[1] *3* is "two" (*el dos*), *X* is "six" (*el seis*).

Level 2
Very close to the children at this elementary level are those who know some letter names, but who apply them inconsistently.

Débora (4 yrs., LC) knows the names of the vowels, which she uses for any letter, so that any consonant is called by the name of one of the vowels.

Marisela (4 yrs., MC) names letters the following way: *M* is "*i*," *L* is "*u*," *C* is "*el o*" (inappropriate article), *A* is "four" (*el cuatro*), *a* is "*e*," *e* is "six."

---

[1] Translator's Note: In Spanish both numbers and letters are usually preceded by a definite article when named. Since numbers are masculine and letters are feminine, the appropriate article for numbers is *el* and the one used for letters is *la*. Sometimes indefinite articles are used: *un* for numbers, *una* for letters.

Frequently vowel names alternate with number names:

María (6 yrs., LC) labels characters with number names and vowels, following graphic correspondence for number names, but without correspondence for letter names, so that *I* is "a one" (*un uno*), and *o* is "zero," but *M* is "an *e*" (*una* e), *P* is "a *u*" (*una* u), *A* is "a . . . an *e*" (*un . . . una* e).

Letters may be recognized by indicating who "the owner" of the letter is, that is, whose name it is the beginning of:

Carolina (5 yrs., MC): *C* is "ca for Carolina" (*la ca de Carolina*); *V* is "for Viviana" (*la de Viviana*); *F* is "I don't know whose it is."

Atilio (5 yrs., LC): *A* is "Atilio's" (*la de Atilio*); *T* is also "Atilio's"; *C* is "for *casa*" (*la de casa*); *P* is "for papá;" and *M* is "for *mamá.*"

Strangely enough, the most frequently recognized consonant is *Z,* as being "for Zorro" or even "Z for Zorro"; and several have called *N* "a sideways *Z,*" or "the *Z* for Zorro, only backwards." (Zorro is, at the time of this research, a very popular television cartoon character.) In this case, extrascholastic learning has permitted the last letter of the alphabet, one of the letters that appears least frequently in writing and one of the last to be introduced in school instruction, to become one of the first letters easily recognized.

Level 3
At a higher level we place the children who can recognize and name the vowels in some stable way (at least three of them) and who can identify some consonants, not only by relating them to some person or some name but by giving them a syllabic value derived from the name to which they belong.

Emilio (4 yrs., MC) knows some consonant names (*l* is "ele" and *T* is "te" [the letter names]) but for others he proceeds like this: *M* is "mi for Emilio"; *F* is "fe for Felisa"; *N* is "ni for Nicolás."

Carlos (6 yrs., MC): *C* is *"la ca"* for Carlos.

Gustavo (6 yrs., MC): *G* is *"la gu."*

Ariel (5 yrs., MC): *R* is *"la ri"* (the pronunciation is the same as the corresponding syllable of Ariel).

Marina (5 yrs., MC): *M* is "ma for Marina."

Level 4
At the fourth level are those who correctly name all the vowels and some consonants. Although they may continue at times to

mention a name which begins with the letter, the letter name is not derived from a syllabic value stemming from the person's name:

Laura (5 yrs., MC): *S* is "se for Silvia and Sarita" or "ese" (the letter name).

At this level we also place children who correctly name about ten different consonants. Obviously, each child continues to reveal a group of erroneously identified letters and this gives way to interesting assimilations.

Gustavo (5 yrs., MC) can name *G, S, N, Z, M, J, Y,* and others. But he has trouble with two of the letters of his own name: *V,* which is long *v* (*ve larga*), and *A,* which is short *v* (*ve corta*) (probably because it's like the *V* but cut off (*cortada*) by the horizontal line).

Level 5
Children at the highest level know practically all the letters of the alphabet by name and eventually are capable of giving both the name and the sound value or the different sound values that the same letter can represent.

Carlos (6 yrs., MC) knows all the letters by name and many by both name and sound value. For example, *s* is *"la sss . . . ese"*; *L* is *"la l, la ele."*

Miguel (6 yrs., MC) can name at least fourteen different consonants and says that *C* is *"la ca or la ce,"* admitting that "it has two names." His only errors are mistaking *K* for *R* and designating *s* as *"la se"* (the name for *s* in Spanish is *ese*).

Gabriela (5 yrs., MC) knows all consonants by name except *W* which she identifies as *Ñ.*

Rafael (5 yrs., MC) can name at least fifteen consonants and can separate the letter name from the sound value: *C* is "ca or ce; you can pronounce it ca or ce"; *H,* "you don't pronounce it at all; *che . . .* it's called something like that."[1]

This last level is represented exclusively by five- and six-year-old MC children: five of the seventeen MC five year olds interviewed are at this level, and seven of the twenty MC six year olds. The disparity between these and the LC children is quite apparent in this area.

At this point we must make some observations: (*a*) What we are

[1] Translator's Note: The Spanish name for *h* is *hache;* it functions as a silent letter in written Spanish when it is alone but it also combines with *c* to form *ch,* considered a letter and called *che.*

discussing here is socially transmitted knowledge, not conceptualizations that develop within children themselves. (It is not possible for children to discover on their own that *y* is called *i griega* or *w*, *doble v.*) (*b*) The specific knowledge of these children is restricted to printed upper-case letters, although it sometimes extends to lower-case letters. Very few are capable of naming cursive letters. This reinforces the extrascholastic nature of this knowledge, since cursive is the handwriting style used in schools in Argentina. (*c*) Knowledge of the letter names normally precedes knowledge of their sound equivalents in terms of phonetic value (as differentiated from syllabic values derived from particular names). This fact—traditionally considered a treacherous area in school learning—does not appear to cause confusion in any of the subjects studied. (*d*) The way children act while facing these graphic characters reveals a long practice of active exploration of this material. For example, some children know how to turn certain letters into others by transforming them in some way:

Mariano (6 yrs.) tells us spontaneously that "if I take an *M* and turn it upside down it's a *W*; if I turn an *A* upside down, it's an upside down *A* and *I* stays the same."

Alejandro (6 yrs.) explains that some letters "have two shapes, it's two in one," and he takes *A* as an example: "we take away the little stick and it's this one (*V*)."

Numbers and Letters

We indicated the reasons why children may initially confuse the graphic characters for numbers and letters, subsequently distinguish them clearly, and later puzzle over them again at a more sophisticated level of problem solving. A letter, recognized as such in the context of other letters (and even named correctly) can become a "number" when it is by itself. Finally we have indicated that the cursive-printing distinction can be mixed up with the letter-number labels.

This does not exhaust the problem of the relationship between these two graphic systems. We have had many cases of the label "number" applied to letters, but the reverse has never occurred (that is, the label "letter" has never been applied to numbers). This seems to indicate a psychogenetic precedence of numbers as graphic forms (an issue that would have to be studied in detail). We can speculate on some reasons for this: the graphic universe of numbers is more restricted than that of letters—we use ten different graphic shapes to compose all numbers, while we use twenty-six different graphic shapes (twenty-eight in Spanish, if we count *ñ* and *ll*)[1] to compose all words. In addition, the names of the graphic forms corresponding to numbers coincide with the words we use to count. (When we speak we do not use the names of letters, but when we count a series of objects we use the words, "one, two, three . . ." which also serve to identify the graphic forms of the numbers.)

There may very well be an initial stage of total indifferentiation between letters and numbers (as graphic elements). The following examples suggest this possibility:

Alejandro (4 yrs., LC) and *Liliana* (5 yrs., LC) never decide whether a text has "numbers" or "letters," although they show preference for the label "numbers."

David (5 yrs., LC) uses interchangeably letter names and number names. *P* is "*o*" at one point, but a little while later it's "four"; *A* is "*a*," but 2 is also "*a*" and *E* is also "*a*."

Fernando (4 yrs., MC) maintains that in a written text "there's numbers," but he labels isolated letters alternately "letter" or "number" (one is "letter" and the next one, regardless of which, is "number" and he continues in this way).

However, it is also possible to argue that this indifferentiation is only apparent and reflects the researcher's failure to uncover the system that the child may, at least sporadically, be able to use. For example, in some cases where we repeatedly had the impression of total indifferentiation, not only during the interview with the child but also upon reading the protocol and analyzing the data, we were able to discover later, through meticulous analysis, indications which contradicted these impressions.

One of the manifestations of unsuspected distinction discovered in some children consists of reserving the label "letter" for the characters of their own name, so that, in general, they use the label "number" for graphic characters, but if the characters belong to their own name (or are graphically similar and are taken for characters of their name) they become "letters." Walter and Anabela (5 yrs., LC) and Valeria (4 yrs., MC) proceed in this way.

It is highly exaggerated to speak of confusion when children use, in a regular and stable manner, number names to designate letters with shapes similar to numbers.

Gustavo (4 yrs., LC) uses a regular pattern for labeling numbers and letters, since *L* is systematically "one" (*el uno*), *S* is "five" (*el cinco*) and *G* is "six" (*el seis*).

---

[1] Translator's Note: In Spanish *ñ* is used to represent the medial sound in canyon and *ll* is used to represent a sound similar to the "y" sound in English (for example: La Jolla [La Joya]).

Evangelina (6 yrs., LC) uses the label "letters" but assigns number names to each one. However, she makes a subtle distinction: *R* "looks like a two," while 2 is "two" (*el dos*); it's not a letter but it is "a two." This is clearly a vocabulary problem, due to unfamiliarity with the names of the letters: saying that *R* looks like a 2 recognizes the similarity in shape, but this does not necessarily mean that *R* has been transformed into a number.

Letters are recognized more easily, in the beginning, as being "for" someone. The same is true with numbers:

Cynthia (5 yrs., MC) says that 9 "is Javier's number" and 2 "is Ramiro's number," that is, the number of the floor of the apartment building on which her friends live, or in terms of her own concrete experience, the elevator button she must press to get where they live. Cynthia cannot name these written numbers, but she recognizes them in function with their ownership relationships.

Diego (4 yrs., MC) says "my father is a nine; his name is Pablo," while he writes something that looks like a *P*.

These reiterated references to the names of people that the children know are characteristic of the MC children in particular and constitute an indication of different cultural patterns. MC children frequently observe the writing of the names of people they know, while this experience is not common to LC children.

Among the six year olds, the differences between MC and LC are dramatic (particularly regarding what school will demand of them): all of the MC six year olds except one appropriately differentiate letters from numbers, while only one of the LC six year olds does. In evaluating this difference we emphasize that we are analyzing the package of specific, socially transmitted knowledge with which six-year-old children officially begin the learning of written language. The inability to appropriately apply the labels "number" and "letter" to graphemes cannot be taken as an indication of conceptual confusion. On most of our historical monuments the date is engraved in what we call Roman numerals, but these numbers are actually letters utilized with numerical value. When letters replace numbers on a monument we consider it a sign of culture, but when a child does the same thing, we call it conceptual confusion. The absurdity of this reasoning becomes evident through historical comparison. No one would think of saying that the Romans conceptually confused numbers with letters because they used the letters of their alphabet to graphically represent numbers. They did this having learned it from the Greeks, who used the initial letter of the number names to graphically represent the numbers themselves (the letter *pi* for five since five = *pente;* the letter *delta* for ten since ten = *deka*).

Also in the Hebrew tradition letters are used to represent numbers. Since the era of the Maccabees (or perhaps earlier) the first nine letters have been used to represent the units, and to avoid confusion a kind of accent mark (the apex) is added, so that a letter with an apex becomes a number. The Greeks of the Alexandrian era did the same, utilizing the order of the letters to represent the order of the numbers, adding the apex as the only distinctive sign.

As much as it weighs against our lauded Western civilization, the utilization of special signs for numbers is not of Greco-Roman origin but of Hindu and Arabic origin. In Europe, the introduction of special number signs (that is, signs different from letters) is quite recent: their use became generalized in the thirteenth and fourteenth centuries, after they were adopted by mathematicians and Florentine merchants. Arabic numerals gradually came to take the place of Roman numerals, specifically because using special signs avoids confusing written words with mathematical notations (Cohen, 1958).

Historical reference is extremely fruitful: (*a*) to remind us of the late origin of certain cultural developments taken for granted today but which cost humanity tremendous intellectual effort, and (*b*) to avoid the ethnocentrism that inevitably occurs unless an effort is made at historical decentering. (For example, using different graphemes for numbers and letters was normal for various peoples of Asia when the great civilizations of Europe used, also normally, one system of signs.)

Distinguishing Between Letters and Punctuation Marks

A printed page has, in addition to letters and numbers (which appear at least for purposes of pagination), other elements which can easily be confused with letters: punctuation marks. The period, the question mark, and the exclamation point are the first to be introduced in initial school instruction. Children are exposed to the remaining punctuation marks through exploring a wide range of texts, not just beginning readers, and also through specific sociocultural transmission. Once again we encounter nondeducible, socially transmitted knowledge. The marks that accompany letters each have their own name, along with a function not always easy to identify. Question marks and exclamation points do not reproduce intonation, but the reader interprets them as signals for introducing specific intonation. The use of quotation marks, however, is not intrinsically linked to intonation: they are used for identifying a direct quote, for emphasizing a particular term, for replacing a complex expression, for introducing a term taken from another language, and so on. Blanche-Benveniste and Chervel (1974) summarize the problem in the following way: "The question mark is, without a doubt, of all the punctuation marks, the one with the best linguistic justification. The others are far from having such straightforward status: they do not in themselves symbolize prosodic characteristics, but rather, they simply replace prosodic signs. Since they cannot represent precisely certain kinds of silence or accent, the comma, semicolon, period, colon, exclamation point, dots and dashes have a logical use rather than a phonographic one. They contribute directly to meaning, and are similar to pictographic elements" (pp. 29–30).

At the beginning of our study we did not suspect that preschool children would be capable of distinguishing between letters and punctuation marks, but as we became aware of the enormous amount of specific knowledge six-year-old MC children have entering first grade, we decided to explore this area. Our results are only preliminary and are based exclusively on questions referring to a printed page (from a storybook). A strictly descriptive classification of the results allows us to distinguish the following levels:

Level 1
There is no distinction between punctuation marks and letters. The children use the same label for punctuation marks[1] that they use to designate numbers or letters. For example:

Ximena (4 yrs., MC) says that the marks ; ! - ¿ ? , ’   are letters, like the others.

David (5 yrs., LC) thinks that ? is a "number, six;" that — is a "letter, *o;*" that : are "letters, six."

Level 2
There begins to be a differentiation limited to periods, colons, hyphens, and three dots (that is, the punctuation marks made up solely of dots or one straight line). The children call these "dots" (*puntitos*) or "lines" (*rayitas*), but most of the punctuation marks continue to be identified as letters or numbers. For example:

Débora (4 yrs., LC) thinks that ; "is a letter, *u*" (*la* u), and that ¿[2] also "is a letter, *e* (*la* e), but that — "isn't a letter" and . . . is not a letter either, but "little dots."

Level 3
There is an initial differentiation which consists of separating two kinds of punctuation marks: those that have shapes similar to let-

[1] Translator's Note: The Spanish term for punctuation mark is *signo de puntuación.*
[2] Translator's Note: In Spanish the question mark precedes as well as follows the question. The preceding mark is inverted as ¿ .

ters and/or numbers and continue to be taken for them, and the rest, which are neither letters nor numbers, but the children have no idea what they might be. The marks still taken for letters or numbers are easy to imagine: ; is taken for *i*, ? for 2, 5, or S, and , for 6 or 9.

Level 4
There is a clear distinction between letters and punctuation marks. Only ; may persist as a letter due to its similarity to *i*, but all others are rejected as letters. The children at this level say that these marks are not letters, although "they go with letters." (Javier [4 yrs., LC] says, for example, that the comma "isn't a letter, it's with this letter," pointing to the letter preceding the comma, indicating that the comma is not a letter in itself although it can accompany or be part of a letter.) Many children say that "it's not a letter, it's something else," without being able to go beyond a description in terms of "sticks" (*palitos*), "dots" (*puntitos*), and so on.

Level 5
There is not only a clear distinction between letters and punctuation marks, but the children in this group also attempt to use differentiating labels and begin to distinguish function. In terms of labels, these children speak of "marks" (*signos* or *marcas*).

Marina (5 yrs., MC) says that ? is "the head letter" (*la letra de la cabeza*), that ! "is *la* i", and that : "are little dots, for the head, I think." The "head" letters are designated as such because "you think them but you don't say them."

Ariel (5 yrs., MC) says that — is simply "a line" and that its purpose is "to say . . . period, a period" (*punto, un punto*). But the period is simply "a dot" and it's used "because it starts someplace else."

Observing the distribution of these responses across ages and social groups we confirm that: (*a*) In the MC group there is a clear progression across ages, since the majority of the four year olds are at level 1 (no differentiation) while all of the five and six year olds are capable of some type of differentiation, and some reach level 5. (*b*) In the LC group, on the contrary, the evolutionary line is not so distinct: level 1 and level 2 responses are found across the three age groups, but none give level 5 responses. (*c*) The majority of the total LC responses are concentrated at level 2 (limited beginning of differentiation) while the majority of the total MC responses are concentrated at level 3 (initial differentiation).

In other words, most of the LC children are able to indicate that dots or lines alone do not constitute letters, while the MC children indicate, further, a global distinction between marks that go with letters and other marks which are identified as letters due to graphic similarity. If we consider only the six year olds, we note that upon beginning school instruction many MC six year olds have a clear idea that punctuation marks serve different functions (although they are not too clear about what these functions are), and none of them totally confuses punctuation marks with letters. However, some of the LC six year olds are still incapable of graphically differentiating letters from punctuation marks, and none of them arrives at giving these marks a specific label or at guessing about their function. Once again, the package of specific knowledge differs between the two groups: that of the MC group is testimony to extensive previous practice with texts and informants from which the LC children have not benefitted. School instruction, consequently, will not be the same for both groups (even though the same texts and methods are used).

Spatial Orientation in Reading

From left to right and from top to bottom: How does one know that this, and not some other pattern, determines the spatial orientation in reading? This is one of the most arbitrary characteristics of writing. It is not surprising to discover that preschool children do not know the correct orientation (in this case correct is synonymous with conventionally correct). It is not enough to know right from left and top from bottom on a page; some informant must have transmitted the appropriate information, either verbally or by having read to the child while following the words with a finger.

The most interesting information in this area comes from the four year olds. At this age—in both social groups—neither of the two conventional orientations is present. This can occur for three reasons: (*a*) because the child resorts to pointing at certain places above each line of print (at the center or at the margins) rather than following the whole text line by line, (*b*) because there is a marked tendency toward alternating, which consists of beginning the next page where the previous page leaves off (that is, if one page goes from top to bottom, the next page will start at the bottom and go toward the top), and (*c*) because there is also a strong tendency to go from bottom to top (going from near to far with respect to the reader).

Alternating the orientation from one page to the next can be reduced, among children four years and older, to alternating one of the two orientations while keeping the other constant:

Débora (4 yrs., LC) points at the first page from left to right and from top to bottom and to the second page also from left to right but from bottom to top. She maintains constant the lateral orientation but she alternates the vertical.

Valeria (4 yrs., MC) points at the second page from right to left and from bottom to top and then she goes to the first page where she also points from bottom to top but from left to right. She maintains constant the vertical orientation but alternates the lateral.

This alternating can also be employed in going from one line to the next (restricted to lateral alternation while maintaining the vertical orientation constant). In doing this the child points at one line from left to right, the next from right to left, and so on. In other words, the reading of a line of print begins where the previous line ends. A rather curious snakelike pattern results from this procedure. Even more curious is its coincidence with history: writing was done this way for some time in ancient Greece. This writing method has been called boustrophedon writing, because it brings to mind the way furrows are made in the earth with a plow pulled by oxen: "The direction of signs in writing varies greatly in the oldest Greek inscriptions, as it runs either from right to left or from left to right, continuing in boustrophedon fashion, alternately changing direction from line to line. Only gradually did the classical method of writing from left to right assert itself in the Greek system" (Gelb, 1952, p. 197).

The common directional tendencies mentioned above do not include all of the possibilities. Here are two examples of less common possibilities:

José (4 yrs., LC) traces a labyrinth over the central part of the text, followed by an outline of the surrounding edges, so that he explores the whole of the written territory (first its interior and then its borders) to end up at the starting point.

Ariel (5 yrs., MC) goes by page number: if the number is at the bottom he starts at the bottom and if it's at the top he starts at the top.

If we consider the distribution of responses by social group we confirm that: (*a*) The number of children who do not observe either of the two basic orientations is about the same in both groups (32.4 percent of the MC children and 36.6 percent of the LC children). This happens fundamentally because most of the four year olds fall into this category. (*b*) At the other extreme, the number of children who know both of the conventional orientations differs greatly between the two groups (almost half of the MC children—45.9 percent—and not quite a fourth of the LC children—23.3 percent). This is because the greater part of the MC six year olds fall into this group, while the LC six year olds are distributed at all levels without concentrating at any one.

This marked difference among the six year olds is evidence, once again, of the MC children's long experience with readers of texts, and not just with text exploration. There is nothing on a printed page that indicates where one must begin reading and where one must continue. To know this one must have witnessed acts of reading accompanied by specific gestural cues.

But children form their own ideas regardless of specific instruction. Among four year olds, this instruction appears to have no weight (either due to its nonexistence or to the child's inability to assimilate it), and yet some original ideas appear. The alternating orientation (from one line to the next or from one page to the next) seems to indicate not only children's uncertainty in this area but also their attempt to establish continuity in the act of reading, to avoid abrupt stops or jumps across spaces. If we end up at the bottom of a page it is most natural to begin the next page from where we leave off; if we finish a line at the right, it is most natural to begin the next line from there.

Final Observations

The data we have presented in this chapter indicate that long before knowing how to read, children are capable of dealing with texts in terms of certain specific formal characteristics.

We have chosen to begin with an analysis of this particular data in order to avoid from the start an overly simplistic view of children's development of notions relating to written language, a view which would see this evolutionary progression as a passage from the "concrete" to the "abstract." Our intent with this chapter is to caution the reader against such oversimplification.

We use the term "oversimplification" because the early appearance of something is often explained as being due to "concrete" content while the late appearance of other responses is due to a required "capacity for abstraction" or "abstract thought" or to "abstract content." If "concrete" and "abstract" are reserved for early or late acquisitions in the course of development, these terms become meaningless as a result. What we have here is a "pseudo-explanation" offered far too extensively.

Demanding either three letters or a variety of characters as the minimum for something "to be readable" is strictly a formal demand which has nothing to do with supposed "concrete" thought (not to be confused with "concrete operations" in the Piagetian sense). The apparently concrete nature of children's conceptualizations of written language (we emphasize *apparently*) is transmitted by their expectations relative to the representational content of a written text. This, in turn, is framed in a series of ideas, like the ones we have analyzed here, which are no less significant than the others.

Finally, it is useful to distinguish two types of phenomena, linked to each other but of different origin. The idea that reading cannot take place with fewer than three letters or that repeated letters do not provide readable material or that a letter by itself becomes a number are not socially transmitted notions. The first of these ideas is especially inconceivable as a criterion transmitted by an adult: an adult reads the article "a" (*el/la/un* in Spanish), the prepositions "of, on, to" (*de/en/a* in Spanish).

The criterion of variation of characters can stem from long practice with real texts where the norm is a variety of characters, but the limits of this demand are restricted to children. A French-speaking girl, for example, says the word *non* cannot be read "because there's the same one two times." Do teachers suspect this when they present beginning words such as *oso, ala, nene, mamá, papá* (English equivalents: mom, dad, see, too)? Do they imagine with the first two words that they are at the very limit (or below it) of acceptability based on number of letters?[1] Do they know with all these words that they are right on the borderline of the demand for variation of characters? These beginning words are the first introduced because they are considered easy, since they are short and present the same graphemes in repetition. At this point we must ask: easy for whom, easy from whose point of view, from whose definition of easy?

The number–letter–punctuation mark distinction and the recognition of standard spatial orientation in reading involve, on the contrary, socially transmitted, highly conventional knowledge. One can predict that children will differ substantially regarding this type of knowledge, since its development requires specific social conditions (accessible objects and informants).

The complexity of the phenomena we have analyzed makes a synthetic summary difficult. Some of this information is not new. For example, the confusion between letters and numbers has been indicated in the literature. It is one thing to point out this occurrence at a surface level and speak of confusion, but it is another to demonstrate, as we have done, that this confusion is only apparent in many cases. What appears as confusion is actually the child's systematization, operating from bases very different from the adult's.

Gibson (1970) introduces the first experimental results of Lavine, which are very close to ours in the sense of indicating the capacity for very fine discrimination in small children. Lavine (1977) studied discrimination possibilities of three- to five-year-old children responding to material made up of cards with pictures, geometric shapes, print in English (upper-case print and cursive),

---

[1] Translator's Note: In English many words used in beginning reading instruction have fewer than three letters: a, he, we, it, is, go, to.

Hebrew, Chinese, and also numbers. The instructions given required a dichotomous classification but on a basis different from ours. In this case the instructions were: "If it has writing on it, if it is writing, it goes in this box." Lavine's results show that from three years old the cards with pictures are rejected, while all the children accept as writing the examples in conventional written English. The cards with writing in languages unfamiliar to the children are more readily accepted than the geometric figures. Lavine concludes that the criteria children use to decide if something is writing include the following properties: linearity (contrasting with dispersed, nonaligned graphic forms), multiplicity (by contrasting an isolated graphic form and six aligned forms), and variety (by contrasting the same graphic form repeated six times and that form by itself).

Lavine contrasts singularity (one graphic form) with multiplicity (six graphic forms), while we work with all the points in between (two, three, four, and more). In terms of the instructions she gives, the criterion of multiplicity does not play an overly important role ("multiplicity was used as a criterion of writing only in the youngest group of children," says Lavine); but multiplicity plays a decisive role if the instructions change. As we have shown in this chapter, the number of graphemes is one of the most important criteria, among four to six year olds, in determining if a particular piece of writing is readable or not. The comparison between Lavine's results and our own shows how sensitive small children are to modifications in instructions as well as how capable they are of employing coherent classification criteria to graphic material long before they are able to read in the conventional sense of the term.

In this chapter we have not explored reading in a strict sense. We have not asked what writing represents to children, what meaning they attribute to a text. Our inquiry has referred exclusively to the conditions preliminary to reading: what the specific material is, the kind of objects with which it is possible to read, and the properties (abstract) that children require. In the following chapters we will approach the nature of written language as a symbolic object (what it conveys and how it conveys it) and its relationship to language itself.

III   READING WITH PICTURES

Written Language as a Substitute Object

In this chapter we approach the relationship between print and picture. To explore this we devised a task in which children must read written texts accompanied by pictorial illustrations. Illustrated texts are used traditionally in initial school instruction and also in children's books, comics, and the like. Furthermore, in the world surrounding children there are many printed materials which combine these two graphic elements (billboards, advertisements, and numerous objects of daily use). Our experimental situation is not artificial, since children, to lesser or greater degrees, see similar things in the environment. The presence of print-picture stimuli, so familiar in our culture, does not go unnoticed by children. The questions we raise are what conceptions do children have of the relationship between print and picture and how do they interpret this relationship. The objective of this chapter is to understand children's interpretations of the relationship between graphic illustrations and printed texts.

In children's own first spontaneously produced graphic representations, drawing and writing are undifferentiated. Gradually some lines acquire forms like drawings, while others evolve toward imitations of the most salient characteristics of written language (Lurçat, 1974). Are these common graphic roots evidence of similar conceptualizations? This is our fundamental question.

From a Piagetian perspective, drawing, as graphic imitation or material reproduction of a model, evidences semiotic function, understood as the ability to distinguish signifiers from signifieds. According to Piaget, semiotic function appears during the second year of life, continuing the initial sensory-motor actions at another level. Language, symbolic play, deferred imitation, mental imagery, and graphic expression involve semiotic function. Because of this children are capable of using differentiated signifiers, whether they be individual symbols or social signs (Piaget, 1951; Piaget and Inhelder, 1969).

Written language is also a symbolic object. It is a representation of something. Both drawing and writing—material substitutes for something which comes to mind—are later manifestations of the more general semiotic function. However, the two differ. Drawing maintains a relationship of similarity to the objects or occurrences it refers to; writing does not. Writing, as language, constitutes a system with its own rules; drawing does not. Both the nature and the content of these two substitute objects are different. At the initial levels we are concerned with whether the similarities or the differences prevail.

At four years old our subjects are capable of considering writing and drawing as substitute objects for reality. Books, very early, serve "for looking at" and for many, more specifically, "for reading." Children demonstrate behaviors imitative of reading acts such as holding the book in a certain way, particular body postures and eye movements, gestures of turning the page—accompanied or not by verbal formulations—that indicate a certain understanding of the nature of the reading behaviors they imitate. Print is seen as the carrier of some content; it suggests something. The questions "what does it say?" and "does it say something?" are accepted as pertinent to a text. Many of our subjects also differentiate between what are and what are not letters even before they are able to label them correctly.

Nevertheless, the problem of the relationship between picture and print persists. We must clarify just what writing—a symbolic object like drawing—constitutes a substitute for. What is its meaning and where does it come from? What does it represent within children's conceptions? The relationship between drawing and writing cannot be reduced solely to a common graphic origin. Even when children understand the different nature of these two objects, do they see them as similar upon interpreting them? Is the text accompanying a picture conceived of as a relatively close reproduction of the meaning of the picture?

Because our writing system is alphabetic, it has persistently been declared to represent speech sounds, to be the phonetic transcription of oral language. Sharing the opinion of other authors (Smith, 1971), we question this assumption. Raising the issue of the relationship between drawing and writing does not mean reducing written language to pictures. In psychogenetic development, written language maintains close links to both drawing and oral language, but it is neither the transcription of oral language nor a derivative of drawing. Written language constitutes a specific type of substitute object, the genesis of which we hope to uncover.

The tasks we devised to get at this issue consist of presenting children with large cards containing texts with pictures. For one task we present cards with one-word texts, for the other cards with sentences. We ask the children first if there is something to read, requesting them to indicate where and then to read what is written there. When necessary we ask the children to anticipate from the picture, and then to see if "it says" what they anticipate.

Word Reading Task

We use seven word-picture pairs, each composed of a one-word text (lower-case print in three cases, cursive in four) placed beneath a picture. The text-picture pairs are:[1]

Picture: a rubber ball. Text, in cursive: *ball* (*pelota*).
Picture: a cup of tea. Text, in print: **handle (asa).**
Picture: a tree (of nondescript species). Text, in cursive: *fig tree* (*hiquera*).
Picture: a teddy bear. Text, in cursive: *toy* (*juguete*).
Picture: a boat. Text, in print: **sailboat (velero).**
Picture: a traffic officer. Text, in print: **officer (agente).**
Picture: the profile of the face of a man smoking a pipe. Text, in cursive: *pipe* (*pipa*).

The texts correspond either to the name of the whole object (using common labels such as "ball," or less common ones such as "officer" or "sailboat") or to a part of the object (as in "handle") even though the whole object is represented. When the picture shows an example of a subcategory, the text may designate the main category (as in "toy"). In other cases the picture illustrates the main category while the text names a subcategory (as in "fig tree"). Finally, in one picture there are two objects and a suggestion of action (a man smoking a pipe) while the text consists solely of the name of one of the objects ("pipe"). The pictures do not always illustrate the texts exactly. This discrepancy contributes to a better evaluation of the children's hypotheses and helps us determine which of them decipher the text and which predict from the picture.

Sentence Reading Task

We use four picture-text pairs:

Card 1. Picture: a duck, static on a lagoon. Text, in cursive: *the duck swims* (*el pato nada*).
Card 2. Picture: a frog, static, peeking through some branches with flowers on them. Text, in cursive, composed of two lines differing in length: *the little frog went out* (*la ranita salió*) (upper line) / *for a stroll* (*de paseo*) (lower line).

---

[1] Translator's Note: To facilitate identification of the distinctive kinds of print presented to and produced by the research subjects, *italics* indicates cursive writing, **boldface** indicates lower-case print, and all caps indicates upper-case print. This distinction is maintained throughout the book.

Card 3. Picture, several elements: a boy rowing a boat toward an island where there are plants and animals, a sun in the sky, and some fish in the water. Text, in lower-case print: **Raúl rows on the river (Raúl rema enel río).**

Card 4. Picture: a dog running, with some cans behind him. Text, in upper-case print: THE DOG RUNS (EL PERRO CORRE).

The objective of both of these tasks is to discover children's hypotheses about written language when it is accompanied by pictures. In doing this we feel we can contribute towards understanding the role of pictures in relation to print throughout the developmental conceptualization process from its beginnings up to the intervention of systematic instruction.

The pictures on the cards come from popular children's magazines, to facilitate identification. Three alternate forms of writing occur in our texts: cursive, lower-case print, and upper-case print. This variation reflects the different kinds of print children may be familiar with.

We had observed, in general, that children expect print to contain the name of the illustrated object accompanying it. The word reading task is designed to evaluate whether this is true across ages. Likewise, it should enable us to differentiate behaviors reflecting text deciphering, or "sounding out," from those relying solely on predicting the text from the picture. The sentence reading task, on the other hand, should permit us to observe behaviors reflecting an initial consideration of text properties, including things such as noticing that a written sentence has parts, that these parts are distributed in an orderly fashion, that there are blank spaces between them, that each part is composed of smaller parts, and so on. How do children reconcile what they predict from the picture with the reality of text properties? The characteristics of the illustrations do not differ much from one task to the other. If the children focus solely on the pictures, they should give similar responses regardless of the text. Inversely, differences in responses could not be attributed entirely to the pictures. Finally, this same material should provide models for studying initial reading behavior, in the traditional sense of the term (beginning deciphering), in children who have begun school learning.

In the word reading task we use the one-word text to refer to the entire picture-text pair. For example, when we use the term "ball," we will be referring to the card on which that word appears with the corresponding picture. For the sentence reading task we use card 1 for the first picture-text pair (*the duck swims*), card 2 for the second picture-text pair, and so on.

Word Reading Task

The responses to this task can be classified in the following way: (a) Text and picture are not differentiated. (b) The text is considered to be a label for the picture; it represents the name of the illustrated object; text and picture are differentiated. (c) Properties of the text provide cues which confirm the predictions based on the picture.

Response Type A   Text and Picture Are Not Differentiated
In response to the question "where is there something to read?" the children in this group point as much to the picture as to the print. When asked to interpret ("what does it say here?"), they respond as if the question were "what is this?" and attribute the answer indifferently to either the print or the picture. Note these examples:[1]

Roxana (4 yrs., LC)
Show me where there's something to read.
What do you think it says?

(Shows picture.)

A ball (*ball*), a bear (*toy*), a boat (**sailboat**), a flower (**handle**).

Alejandro (4 yrs., LC)
Is there something to read?
And what does it say?

Yes (points to text).
The police (**officer**), the stuffed animal (*toy*), the trees (*fig tree*), the boat (**sailboat**), the man (*pipe*).

Where does it say man?
Where does it say boat?
It says boat in the picture?

(Points to picture.)
(Points to the boat in the picture.)
Yes.

The responses indentifying the pictures are clear: there is "a bear" or "the police." Alejandro, for example, initially shows the text as being something to read, but he ends up naming the items in the pictures. (Responding to the question "where does it say boat?" he points to the picture.)

The questions "where is there something to read?" and "what does it say?" are two different kinds of questions and merit separate analysis. Answering the question "where is there something to read?" requires an understanding of the activity called reading and a distinction between reading and looking. If it is true that one must look in order to read, certainly the reverse of this is not true (see chapter 5). At this level, the lack of differentiation be-

---

[1] Translator's Note: The subjects' original statements in Spanish are included in cases where they provide necessary information about how the child is or is not responding directly to the print.

tween picture and print presupposes a lack of distinction between the actions pertaining to each of these objects. However, the question "what does it say?" presupposes that it, indeed, says something.[1]

To know what it says, the meaning of the print must be found in the picture. Without the possibility of inferring it directly, the meaning is extracted from the illustration and applied to the text. The main characteristic of this level is the direct application of the meaning of one symbolic object to the other. First, the children identify the picture orally, and only then are they able to shift to the text.

Response Type B   The Text Is Considered To Be a Label for the Picture

Typical behavior at this level consists of explicitly "erasing" the article that goes with the name identifying the picture. For example:

Romina (4 yrs., MC)
What does it say here? *(fig tree)* *(higuera)*
A tree, it says tree. (*Un árbol, dice árbol.*)

María Paula (4 yrs., MC)
What does it say here? *(toy)* *(juguete)*
This is a bear, bear, it says bear here (pointing to text). (*Esto es un oso, oso, acá dice oso.*)

And here? *(pipe)* *(pipa)*
A man with a pipe, it says pipe. (*Un hombre con pipa, dice pipa.*)

Gabriela (5 yrs., MC)
What does it say? *(ball)*   I don't know.
What is it? (picture)   A ball.
What does it say? (text)   Ball.

Marcos (6 yrs., MC)
And what does it say here? **(handle)**   The cup . . . cup.

Facundo (6 yrs., MC)
And what does it say here? *(ball)*   I don't know.
What is it? (picture)   A ball.
What does it say? (text)   Ball.

Rosario (5 yrs., LC)
What does it say? *(ball)*   Ball.
How can you tell?   Because there's a ball.

These kinds of responses are similar to ones we encounter in the sentence reading task: in each case there is an explicit omis-

---

[1] Authors' Note: The research methods we use currently are much less suggestive, to avoid the suppositions implied in such questions.

sion of the article when referring to the text, which seems to represent the "label," or name of the object in the picture. María Paula differentiates between "this is a bear" and "it says bear here." Gabriela and Facundo say "a ball" when they must identify the picture, but they suppose that the text says only "ball."

A large number of children consider the text to represent the name of the pictured object (46 of the 60 four- to six-year-old children interviewed, that is, 76 percent of both MC and LC). We also obtain this kind of interpretation for the sentence reading task. Since the response does not change across diverse stimuli, we infer that the phenomenon we describe as "the text represents the name of the object" does not depend on the nature of the stimulus presented. Our hypothesis is that labeling constitutes an important developmental step in the conceptualization of written language.

Some of the children in this category have such strong convictions that they reject researchers' suggestions that the text might say a sentence and assert their hypothesis that only labels are written. This conviction persists even when faced with texts of several words. The following example illustrates this well:

Romina (4 yrs., MC)

What does it say? (*pipe*)	I don't know.
Do you think it might say "the man is smoking a pipe"?	Pipe!

(The same girl in the sentence reading task, using card 4)

What does it say?	Dog.
Or do you think it could say "the dog runs"?	No, it says dog.

It is evident that this child interprets written language as a way of representing names of objects. She does not consider the properties of the text. She attributes the name to the entire text, even when it appears in distinct parts. Although difficulty in considering text properties and attributing one label often appear together, there is a later developmental period when these two aspects become differentiated. The conception of print as a label for a picture continues but does not exclude the possibility of gradual focusing on graphic characteristics of the text. Comparing the responses given for these two experimental tasks (word and sentence) guides us toward the point at which this distinction appears. Since the illustrations are similar in both tasks (both have static images as well as ones that suggest action, with one or several objects represented), differences in responses must be attributed to differences in text properties.

Response Type C   Properties of the Text Provide Cues
                   Confirming Predictions Based on the Picture

At this level, consideration of the physical properties of print increasingly influences the kinds of predictions that children make from pictures and the kinds of hypotheses they formulate about what the print represents. We must consider two types of cues: continuity and length of text, and differences between letters.

The following are examples of how text length is considered explicitly:

Laura (5 yrs., LC)
What does it say? (*pipe*) (*pipa*)   *Papá.*
Could it say "Papa is smoking" (*papá*   No, because it's very small and
está fumando)?   doesn't fit (*es muy chiquito y no al-
                                         canza*).

Mariano (5 yrs., MC)
What does it say? (*fig tree*) (*higuera*)   I don't know.
Could it say tree or do you think it   Tree.
might say "the tree has leaves"?
Why?   Because it's short and there's only
                                         tree (*es cortito y hay árbol solamente*).

The justifications "it's short" or "it's very small and doesn't fit" that Laura and Mariano use to reject sentences demonstrate a clear consideration of formal characteristics of print. These same children accept a sentence for interpreting a text with blank spaces between words. Obviously none of these children reads the text in the traditional sense of the term, but still they are able to infer that one of its properties, spatial length, is directly related to the length of the utterance attributed to it.

Focusing on individual letters as cues demonstrates consideration of the text in terms of more specific properties than length. Letters are particular characteristics that differentiate one text from another and that support a particular interpretation and eliminate other possibilities. This is the first step toward stability and conservation of meaning. Consider these examples:

Carlos (6 yrs., MC)
What does it say? (*toy*) (*juguete*)   Bear (*oso*).
Does it have the letters of bear (*oso*)?   No, I don't think so.
And it says bear?   No.
And here what does it say? (*pipe*)   Papa.
(*pipa*)
Where?   Papa, but here it doesn't say it be-
                                             cause there's an *i* and an *a* (*pero acá
                                             no dice porque está la* i . . .*y la* a.)
What does it say, then?   . . . Pipe!

Martín (6 yrs., MC)

What does it say here? (*pipe*)	I don't know.
What is it? (picture)	A pipe.
And what do you think it says?	I don't know.
If you look at the pictures you can't tell?	No!
What do you have to do to know what it says?	You have to know how to read!

Diego (6 yrs., MC)

What does it say here? (*toy*) (*juguete*)	Bear . . . toy bear, because it can't be bear (*oso . . . oso de juguete, porque oso no puede ser*).
So what does it say?	My little bear (*mi osito*). Oh, I don't know what it says. In all of them I do (the other cards) but not here.

These are some examples of the beginnings of a search oriented toward confirming predictions. As Carlos says, if the letters of "bear" are not there, it can't say bear. At this level predictions based on pictures give way to a process of searching for confirmation in the text. Martín is quite clear in this sense: you can't tell just from looking at the pictures. There is finally a conciliation between hypotheses about what the text represents and consideration of its properties. The text is no longer entirely predictable from the pictures; one must have cues from within the text that confirm what is predicted.

Sentence Reading Task

Our primary concern is to understand what relationships children establish between picture and print. One of the questions we pose is: what role does the picture play? The following are examples of children's responses:

Emilio (4 yrs., MC)

What does it say? Show me.	*Card 3* Boat and sun (pointing to text) and a cow and a sun and a tree (pointing to picture).

Epifanio (6 yrs., LC)

	Card 3 Boy goes catching fish. (*Nene anda cazando pescado.*)
Where?	Here, fish (*pescado*) (pointing to part of the print) . . . trees, flowers, Bambi (pointing to picture).

Marcela (6 yrs., MC)

	Card 2 Here it says frog (*rana*).
Where?	(Points to picture.)

And here? (text)
And here? (second line of text)

(Corrects herself and points to text.)
Flower (*flor*).

Jorge Luis (4 yrs., MC)

Or, "the boy is in the river"?

Card 3
A little fish.
. . . with a little boat and over here
an anchor (pointing to picture).

The preceding examples show that these children think that one can go back and forth between picture and print without having to differentiate the two symbol systems. In fact, many children begin their interpretation with the text but, feeling this is incomplete, look to the picture to fill in what is missing (Emilio, Epifanio, and Jorge Luis). Marcela, however, points first to the picture, then corrects herself and points to the text as a result of the researcher's intervention. For all of them, it is possible to continue reading from the text to the picture and vice versa. The common denominator is the fluidity in going from the writing to the drawing. One might suppose that text and illustration are confused in these cases, that if the researcher asks "what does it say?" the children understand it as "what's in the picture?" Our data indicate an initial developmental point at which both text and picture are considered readable. Does this mean that children treat print as if it were picture? Our analysis does not lead us to this conclusion. We believe children are able to go from one system to the other without fundamentally modifying the act of interpretation because print and picture form a complementary whole. Both are part of a closely knit unit and together express a meaning. To interpret the text, one can look to the pictures for the information not found in the print.

Relying on pictures to make predictions about the text is not restricted to the kind of examples cited but is also found in more advanced responses. What is typical about these examples is that the interpretation can be attributed as much to the drawing as to the text.

The linguistic form as such does not seem to intervene in this process, even when the vehicle for interpretation is oral language. Language is required by the experimental situation but is not essential to the act of comprehension in the child. It might surprise an adult that children are capable of moving from one symbol system to another without discriminating fundamental differences in the nature of each. Adults are too well trained in expressing written symbols through their spoken equivalents. This is not the case for the children we have studied. For them, initially, writing does not seem to be a transcription of oral language.

In this context what role does the picture play? What is the role of the text and what relationship exists between the two? In examples such as the ones cited, it is hard to determine whether the child is referring to the text or to the picture. Does this reflect a methodological problem or the fact that for children at this level text and illustration form a unit that does not need to be separated? We are inclined to think that the boundaries between the two are still weak, that they are complementary representations of the outside world.

The ways children interpret our questions demonstrate conceptualizations prior to actual reading. One might consider that these children do not read, in the strict sense, but what is reading at its very beginnings? If learning to read is a process, then there must be different levels in this process and different forms of reading. What, then, are the different forms of initial reading?

Let's consider some additional examples:

Fernando (4 yrs., MC)
Is there something to read here?
And here, is there something to read? (text)

Card 3
Yes, here (points to picture).
It says that a boy is rowing and there's little fish under the water and an animal called . . . there's a deer watching the boy row.

It says all that?
(Nods in agreement.)

Liliana (5 yrs., LC)
Here, what do you think it says?
Where?
What does it say there?
Here it says frog (first line) and here? (second line)
Where does it say flower?
This says frog (first line) and here? (second line)

Card 2
To read a frog (*para leer una rana*).
(Points to first line.)
Frog (*rana*).
Yes, and a flower (*una flor*).

Where does it say flower?
Here (picture).
A letter for reading (*una letra para leer*).

Once again, in Fernando's case, the picture is included as something that can be read. In fact, he does just that: he reads from the picture, or, rather, he interprets the picture and attributes his interpretation to the text. What Fernando relates is a description of the illustration, but how he relates it merits special consideration. He begins his utterance with, "It says that . . .". In this example we find similarities to small children attempting to read story books. What happens when four year olds try to read a story? They infer the content from the picture. Their postural attitudes, how they hold the book, and where they look imitate the adult act of reading. This imitation does not end here. There is a certain style in what children say, certain words, intonational patterns, and gestures that indicate that the intent is reading. Obviously, for this to take place, children must witness reading acts, must have readers accessible, and must be read to. In other words, they must have examples to imitate. Of course there are differences in Fernando's case, but the similarities are enough to show that this is one of the first indications of reference to the text (simulation of the act of reading), even if the print is not separate from the picture.

Liliana's case illustrates another kind of conceptualization. For Liliana, like Fernando, both picture and text can be read. The way these two children go back and forth from print to picture shows, again, how it is possible to move from one to the other to support the interpretation. The function Liliana thinks the text serves is to read what is in the picture. Her expression "to read a frog" tells us that, according to her, text and picture form a union with different functions closely linked together. The picture can be interpreted. The text serves to read what the picture represents. In this case, as in many others, the expectation is that the text corresponds to the picture; the object represented in one is also represented in the other. This is one of the simplest ways of understanding the relationship.

At this point we raise two questions. Can the text be interpreted without the illustration? To what extent does the print, interpreted from the picture, retain the same meaning when it is by itself or with a different illustration? It is clear that the text does not provide meaning directly at this level. It is also evident that print still has not acquired the degree of stability and conventionality necessary to conserve a given meaning. One might suppose that a particular text could be read differently depending on the picture that goes with it.[1] Underlying this issue is the understanding of written language as an arbitrary system of signs. What is evident, though, is the complexity of the construction of written language, with the intervention of many factors.

We have discussed the similarities in the cases of Liliana and Fernando. But there are also differences. For Fernando the text is used to describe the picture, but for Liliana the print is considered a way of labeling the pictured object. These two ways of considering the text will go through an evolution, but it is basically the latter case that we encounter time and time again in this experimental situation.

If the text relates to a description of all elements in the picture, the meaning is expressed through the whole of the description. The elements composing the picture may be ordered by the child

[1] Authors' Note: New research studies we are doing show that at this level a particular text placed below different illustrations changes meaning based on the illustration. So, for example, the text "lion" placed below a giraffe will say "giraffe."

through the act of interpretation. This does not require that these elements be understood in an exact order or specify where to start and where to end. If, however, print is understood as a way of labeling an object (or a picture representing an object), then a kind of ordering begins to develop. (This ordering is still not a conventional one but, rather is motivated by the picture.) The ordering relationship still does not involve a correspondence between graphic and sound segments but between a written form and certain objects.

In view of these examples we must reexamine all angles of the relationship between picture and print. Where is the boundary line separating one from the other? How are the relationships understood and the characteristics of each conceived? Which elements are thought to be in correspondence? And, fundamentally, what does written language represent?

We can state some basic conclusions: (*a*) it is clear that written language constitutes a substitute object for these children, as does drawing, but including writing in the same category as drawing does not help us to understand its genesis; and (*b*) we know that the written text suggests something, is conceived as being an intermediary for something, but we still must resolve the problem of what print represents.

We propose a developmental progression defined in the following terms:

1. Picture and print are not differentiated. The text is entirely predictable from the illustration. The text represents the same elements as the picture. Picture and print constitute a unit which cannot be separated.
2. The print is differentiated from the picture. The text is treated as a unit independent of its graphic characteristics. The text represents either the name of the illustrated object or a sentence associated with the illustration, but in both cases the interpretation is attributed to the text as a unit.
3. An initial consideration of graphic properties of print emerges. The text continues to be predictable from the illustration.
4. Children search for a one-to-one correspondence between graphic and sound segments.

This classification attempts to account for all factors involved in reading with pictures, from the process of differentiating print and picture, to the consideration of graphic characteristics, and, finally, to the relationship between text discontinuity and segmentation of attributed utterances.

Response Type 1   Picture and Print Are Not Differentiated
The examples given previously fall into this category. Here is one more:

Roxana (4 yrs., LC)	*Card 1*
Show me where there's something to read.	Here (points to picture).
And here, what do you think it says? (text)	A little duck (*un patito*).
Show me.	(Points to end of text.) A little duck.
Or could it say "the duck swims" (*el pato nada*)?	Yes.
Show me how it says that.	The duck swims in the water (*el pato nada en el agua*).
Where do you start?	Over here (points to picture).
And here? (text)	Little duck swims in the water (*patito nada en el agua*).

This example clearly illustrates that the text is predicted from the picture. The prediction is oriented toward a certain relationship between the print and the object in the picture. The two most significant aspects in this category are: for all these children it is possible to read the picture as well as the text; and most of them begin by labeling the object in the picture, but they also accept a sentence.

Another interesting point is that these children maintain the same response despite different stimuli. These differences are in the print on the cards: some are in cursive, others in printing. There are also differences in the illustrations: some represent static figures, while others contain several elements and suggest action. In summary, what is typical of the responses at this level is the assumption that the text represents what appears in the picture or, more accurately, what children are capable of isolating from the picture, regardless of characteristics of print such as spacing, number of lines, length, and cursive-print distinctions.

Response Type 2   Process of Differentiating Picture and Print

Response Type 2a   Print Is Considered To Be a Label for the Picture

Valeria (4 yrs., MC)	*Card 1*
	A chick (*un pollito*).
Where?	(Points to all of text.)
Or could it say, "the duck is in the water" (*el pato está en el agua*)?	No. Just duck (*pato solo*).

Gabriela (5 yrs., MC)

What do you think it says?

Card 4
A dog.
Dog.

These examples introduce us to the second level of development. The first difference we perceive is a differentiation between the reference made to the illustration and that made to the text. Valeria anticipates "a chick" from the picture. But on rejecting the researcher's suggested sentence she affirms: "no, just duck," meaning "it could only say duck." She herself, while responding to card 4, states that in the text are "names." Gabriela says "a dog" referring to the picture, but when she refers to the text she says "dog." What is the difference? She has "erased" the article.

The hypothesis of these children gives us a clue to understanding the process: the text retains just one of the potentially representable aspects, the name of the object, and leaves out other such elements. The direct correspondence between the print and the illustrated object continues here. The novelty of this level is that the text corresponds to the name of the object (picture), not to the object itself.

What is the significance of erasing the article? Is it a specific response to this task or does it constitute a constant interpretation that, at this level, is applied to an extensive series of stimuli? The child expects to find the name of the object represented, whatever the reality of the graphic notation. This kind of response also appears in the word reading task.

The text receives the attribution of the name of the illustration; it is a name-sign. Picture and print are linked to the enunciation of the name. Consequently, the text is treated as a unit, without regard for the specific properties that differentiate it from others. The picture is recognized by the relationship between its parts, but the verbal identification corresponds to the name of the whole, not to the parts (a duck, for example, has a head, body, legs, but in totality is a duck). Since it is this global identification of the illustration that determines the meaning of the text, the text itself is treated as a whole which cannot be broken into smaller units. Consequently, the name is attributed to the whole text and read globally without attention to the particulars of the graphic notation (spacing, length, type of characters).

Although the examples we have shown of this level are quite similar to those of the first level (both demonstrate a dependency of the print on the picture), they indicate progress toward greater differentiation: the name is not confused with the picture. The systematic erasing of the article, explicit in many of the examples cited, appears to be the first indication that the print is differentiated from the picture: what is written is the name, the verbal label corresponding to the object.

The following responses are the result of carrying this hypothesis to its ultimate consequence: each picture suggests a name, each name is attributed to the text regardless of its graphic characteristics.

Romina (4 yrs., MC, previously cited) says for card 1 "duck" (*pato*). For card 2 she responds: "toad (*sapo*) . . . I don't know. It's a frog (*rana*)"; for card 3: "little fish" (*pescadito*); and for card 4: "dog" (*perro*) (rejecting the proposal of a sentence for this last card and reaffirming that it says dog).

Carolina (5 yrs., MC) responds: "little duck (*patito*), toad (*sapo*), boat (*barco*), dog (*perro*)," for each card respectively. When asked how she knows it says toad she answers "because there's a toad."

Sandro (6 yrs., LC) responds: "duck, frog (pointing at both lines of print), boat, dog," giving a name for each card.

Juan Pablo (6 yrs., MC) also says: "duck, toad, boat, dog." When asked "how do you know it says duck here?" he affirms "because there's a duck here."

There is no need to present more examples. This type of response appears at different ages and in both social groups studied. Carolina, like Juan Pablo, justifies the enunciation of the name by pointing out the presence of the object in the picture: "because there's a toad." The children at this level reject proposals of sentences, reaffirming their hypothesis that only names are written, while these same suggestions are easily accepted at earlier levels. Also, the responses are justified by the presence of the object in the picture. At later levels the presence of the picture alone is not enough to predict the text.

For the children at this level the differences between various kinds of graphic notations, the properties of the text itself, are not relevant. That is, they are not assimilable or interpretable stimuli. To the contrary, all situations are treated the same way. The text is seen as a unit to which one attributes another unit: the name, a unit of meaning.

Response Type 2b   Print Represents a Sentence Associated with the Picture

In the following examples the starting point is the sentence. The sentence, like the name, constitutes a whole. And, as with names, the sentence is attributed to the text as a whole, regardless of its graphic properties.

Favio (5 yrs., LC)
What does it say?

Where?

Where?

And here?
Do you think it says "dog"?

Where does it say that?

Erik (5 yrs., LC)

Where?

Mariano (6 yrs., MC)
What does it say?

Card 1
The duck is going around in the water (*el pato anda paseando por el agua*).
(Points to whole text.)

Card 3
The boy goes in the boat (*el nene anda en el bote*).
(Points to whole text.)

Card 4
I don't know.
No. It says the dog is running (*el perro está corriendo*).
(Points to whole text.)

Card 3
The fishes go around in the water (*por el agua andan los pescados*).
(Points to whole text.)

Card 3
The boy is in the boat (*el nene está en el barco*) (pointing to whole text).

In these three examples, the sentence is attributed to the whole text. It is also important to note that the vocal emission is made all at once with no pauses. These two facts indicate that the mechanism put into play by these children is very similar to the one used in the cases of single names. The children proceed toward a global correspondence between the utterance, suggested by the picture, and the text. The lexical unit used in the previous examples and the syntactic unit used in these examples are simply two different departure points.[1]

Between the conception that only a name is written and the one that supports a sentence there are intermediate variants which lean toward one or the other of the two responses. They consist of enunciating the name of the main figure in the picture without a preceding article but with the addition of a "complement" to this name. This usually results in a complete but grammatically unac-

---

[1] Authors' Note: These different departure points may be due to the different interpretations of the question "what does this say?" This question might be interpreted as "what is written?" or as "what can be read?" To the degree that print is not conceived of as representing language itself, this distinction is very important. What we suppose, based on our data, is that those who interpret the question "what does this say?" as "what is written?" propose just the name, while those who interpret it as "what can be read?" propose a sentence. Obviously, the research procedure does not allow us to firmly establish this interpretation which nevertheless concurs with cases we analyze later.

ceptable sentence due to the article missing from the noun phrase. Aside from erasing the article, some of the children pause between the initial enunciation of the name and the complement added to it. In terms of how the enunciation matches the text, this varies: they either point to all the text or to some part of it without precision. The following are examples:

Mariana (4 yrs., MC)
And here? What does it say?
Where?

Card 3
Boy is rowing (*nene está remando*).
(Points to whole text from right to left.)

Machi (5 yrs., MC)

Where does it say that?

Card 4
Dog running (*perro corriendo*).
(Points to whole text from left to right in an imprecise manner.)

Cynthia (5 yrs., MC)
And here, what does it say?

Card 3
Boy fishing (*nene pescando*).

Carolina (5 yrs., MC)

What was that? Boy . . .

Card 3
Boy . . . with a sailboat to the beach . . . to the jungle.
Taking a boat to the jungle.

Pablo (5 yrs., MC)

Where?
Or could it say "the duck is in the water" (*el pato está en el agua*)?

Card 1
Duck (*pato*).
(Points to whole text.)
Little duck, is in the water (*patito, está en el agua*). (Points to whole text.)

Card 3
Boy is in the boat (*nene está en el bote*). (Points to whole text.)

Card 4
Dog went for a walk (*perro salió a pasear*). (Points to whole text.)

These responses fluctuate between two hypotheses: from the naming hypothesis they retain the erasing of the article; from the sentence hypothesis, the fact that the name is not sufficient. Trying to take both into account, they remain in between. It is as if initially they base their response on one of them—producing the noun with no article—but they immediately remember the other possibility and feel obliged to complete the enunciation. Perhaps this completion comes from a consideration of the length of the text. These same children never produce sentences for the word reading task. Why do they produce them here? If the picture were the determining factor, then we would have to find differences between responses to static illustrations (cards 1 and 2) and those which suggest action (3 and 4). Even though sentences are produced more frequently for card 3, they are also given for cards 1 and 4.

Pablo's case is quite interesting because he starts by giving the name of the object, then he accepts the researcher's suggested sentence but reformulates it in terms of his own hypothesis: he erases the article so that the final sentence is compatible with both the name and the sentence hypotheses. In level 2a responses, the children reject proposed sentences. Here they accept them, integrating the two. The phenomenon of pointing to the whole text without precision indicates that, as in preceding categories, here too a unit is conceived in its totality and attributed globally.

Carolina is also an interesting example. For cards 1 and 4 she gives a name. For card 2 she gives two names, one for each line, and for card 3 she gives a name with a completing sentence. Her case introduces us to the next level. To what can the differences in her responses be attributed? What we have seen in all the examples cited is difficulty considering the text in terms of its constituent parts. Carolina, on the other hand, starts to take the properties of the text into account. When there is only one element in the picture and only one line of print (as in cards 1 and 4) there is no problem, but when more segments appear in the text (as in card 2 with two lines of print or in card 3 where many segments appear together with many elements in the picture), a differentiation becomes necessary.

Response Type 3   Initial Consideration of Some of the Graphic
                   Properties of Print

This category of response is, without question, the most original. In the previous ones, the discontinuity of the text does not, in itself, impose segmentation of the utterance. Each situation is treated in the same way. However, the properties previously ignored come to be considered at later periods of development. How, then, are graphic differences in texts conceived? The characteristic children react to first is the presence of two lines of print in card 2 (the little frog went out / for a stroll). The next is the appearance of several segments in a line together with several objects in the picture (in card 3).

In terms of conceptualization of written language, the hypotheses of children in this third category are the same as in previous ones: print represents the name of the object in the picture or a sentence associated with the picture. What differentiates this category from the preceding one is a consideration of the graphic properties of the text. There is, then, continuity in the conceptualizations but discontinuity in the way of considering the formal properties of the text. We will maintain the previous classification by first discussing the naming cases and then the sentence ones.

Response Type 3a   Print Is Considered To Be a Label for the
                    Picture

How does one reconcile the name hypothesis with a quantitative appreciation of two lines of print? Here are some attempted solutions:

Sandro (6 yrs., LC)

Card 2
Frog (*rana*) (points to first line).
Frog (*rana*) (points to second line).

María (6 yrs., LC)

Rana (without pointing).
Where?   *Raanaaa* (points to first line, elongating her emission).
                            Rana (points to second line, short emission).

María Eugenia (4 yrs., MC)

Ra- (points to first line) *na* (second line).

Jorge Luis (4 yrs., MC)

There's a frog and I don't know.
What could it say?   Frog (*rana*) (points to first line).
                            Little frog (*rana chiquita*) (second line).

Carolina (5 yrs., MC)

Toad (*sapo*) (points to first line).
And here? (second line)   I don't know, because I don't know what it is (referring to picture).

Gladys (6 yrs., LC)

Toad (first line).
Flowers (second line).

These six examples illustrate how the name supposition is maintained while the child offers solutions to the problem of finding more than one line of print. If the name is attributed to the text and is matched to the first line, the second line is "left over."

For Saundro, María, María Eugenia, and Jorge Luis there is just one name even though there are two lines; but Carolina's and Gladys's solution is different: since there are two lines there must be two names. Gladys succeeds in solving this conflict, but Carolina finds nothing else in the picture to name. Let's examine each of the examples in detail. Sandro repeats the same thing for each line, matching the same attribution twice to account for the spatial organization of the text. María does something a bit different. Considering the length of the lines, she elongates her emission for the upper line and shortens it for the lower one. María Eugenia also produces a phonic differentiation, but through syllabic segmentation. Jorge Luis's solution is particularly noteworthy. He also offers the same interpretation for both lines but differentiates them based on one of the text's characteristics, as if he believed that the print were directly related to what it represents: line length varies with size of object (this is consistent with the supposition that some of the qualities of the referent appear in the text). This last example overlaps with the proposals of Carolina and Gladys; they also believe that each line represents different elements of the picture.

The discontinuity of the lines has become evident: for each line, a response. But the nature of the responses vary: for some two successive repetitions of the same name (there is still no clear conception of a necessary repetition of graphic characters for an identical meaning); for others a phonetic differentiation which does not affect the meaning; for the rest two names, one for each line. Even though the children at this level do not account for the number of smaller units in the text, they are able to consider the larger units—number of lines. Their responses reflect a progression from previous levels where children attribute just one meaning for each case regardless of differences in the text. The children we have just cited face the conflict between the unit of meaning and the diversity in the lines of print. How does one reconcile the two? This lack of coordination between the meaning unit and the discontinuity in the graphic notation causes our subjects to vacillate between the two, but they do not manage to consider both at the same time. Either the meaning is retained (by modifying certain characteristics of the utterance that do not affect it) or new meanings are introduced in accordance with the graphic discontinuity. The result produces either sound transformations of the same word or juxtaposed names.

It becomes clear that graphic diversity constitutes a disturbance with respect to the name hypothesis. The responses the children give are rehearsals for overcoming this conflict, but they cannot yet arrive at a stable solution. Conserving the unit of meaning requires integrating the juxtaposed names into larger units (to link them through thematic units); transforming the graphic discontinuity into sound discontinuity requires utilizing some type of segmentation (María Eugenia provides us the first example of this type).

Card 3, which has several elements in the picture, presents a special situation in which children can consider text segments within one line. At this level, the name hypothesis is maintained, but attributing as many names to each of the graphic segments as there are isolated elements in the picture is novel. This attempt at establishing a correspondence between parts of the text and object names often provokes surprising responses.

Here are two examples:

Leonardo (5 yrs., LC)

Card 3
Fish (*pescado*), boat (*barco*), boy (*nene*) (points from right to left, without specifying).

Where? Let's see . . .

Fish (*pescado*) (points to **río**), bo-oat (*bar-co*) (points to **el en**) and boy (*nene*) (points to **rema**) . . . and . . . tree (*árbol*) (points to **Raúl**).

Or could it say "the boy rows in the river" (*el nene rema en el río*)?

Boy rows in the river (nene rema en el río) (points from right to left to **río el en**), fish (*pescado*) (points to **rema**), and tree (*árbol*) (points to **Raúl**).

Valeria (4 yrs., LC)

Card 3
Fish (*pescado*).

Where?

(Points to **Raúl**.)

And here? **(rema)**

Water (*agua*).

Anything else?

Yes, fish (*pescado*) (points to **en**), boy (*nene*) (points to **el**), boat (*barco*) (points to **río**).

Or could it say "the boy rows in the river" (*el nene rema en el río*)?

No.

What does it say?

Water (*agua*) (for **Raúl**), fish (*pescado*) (for **rema**), boy (*nene*) (for **en**), boat (*barco*) (for **el**), tree (*árbol*) for (río).

When we describe this level as "consideration of the characteristics of the text," we are referring to some characteristics. Which characteristics are most relevant? In the responses to both card 2 and card 3 we see a quantitative estimation of the text, in the first case in terms of lines and in the second in terms of smaller graphic parts. The two subjects cited search the picture for objects to name, attempting to find those that are spatially closest to parts of the text. They stop their search when they come to the end of the text. There is a consideration of the graphic properties of the text in terms of the number of parts. Valeria, for example, names one object for every graphic unit she finds in the text. Leonardo presents us with another case of syllabication, as we saw earlier with María Eugenia, but of greater interest. He syllabicates when he finds two text fragments which are too small, joining them from a meaning point of view and separating them in his utterance. Obviously, there must be elements to name in the picture, but even without these elements children find pertinent solutions when they make a quantitative estimation of the graphic units. This is what the same children do in response to card 2:

Leonardo
What does it say?
And here? (Points to the rest of the text.)
Let's see.

Toad (*sapo*) (points to *ranita*).
Flowers (*flores*).

Flowers (points to *la*), toad (points to *ranita*), flowers (points to *salió*), flowers (points to *de*), toad (points to *paseo*).

Valeria

Where?
And here? (*ranita*)
And here? (*salió*)
And here? (second line)

Frog (*rana*).
(Points to *la*.)
Flower (*flor*).
Another flower.
These flowers (points to the flowers in the picture which she has not yet used).

These are typical solutions to the conflict between the children's hypotheses and the reality of graphic notations. At this level children are capable of taking into account some graphic properties of the text. However, the graphic differences between segments are still ignored; consequently, the same name can be assigned to different places and different strings of letters can receive the same meaningful interpretation.

Returning to the case of card 3, the most interesting moment is when children begin to use the parts of the text in attempting to account for the multiplicity of elements in the picture. When they initiate their effort to make a name correspond to each text segment, a new problem arises: which label for which segment? In the examples already cited this problem is resolved according to the order of enunciation. But there are cases where the position of the elements in the illustration is utilized, placing each name below the corresponding picture. Here are some examples:

José (4 yrs., LC)

Card 3
Boat (*bote*) (points to **en el río**).

And here? (the rest)

Tree (*árbol*). Boat . . . tree (points to text from right to left).

Atilio (5 yrs., LC)

Card 3
Little fish (*pescadito*) (points to **Raúl**).
Boy (*chico*) (points to **río**).

Anything else?

Boat and sun (*lancha y sol*) (points to the center of the text).

Both children point to the part of the text closest to the picture. José works from right to left, anticipating two names for a text with five parts. His solution consists of joining the three smaller units and the two larger ones, a division resulting in two equal parts. Atilio utilizes the spatial order with respect to the illustration, trying to place each label directly below the picture; the result is nonlinear. He anticipates four names for five segments, ending up by placing one of the names on the two smallest segments (**en el**). (Grouping the smaller segments, treating them as if they were one, is a resource which Leonardo also uses.)

In summary, the characteristic response of this level is attributing various names to the text and taking into account certain graphic features. The name hypothesis is not abandoned but, rather, is accommodated to the reality of word boundaries and line divisions. There should be as many labels as parts of text. This results in juxtaposing elements of the same category, in this case names. Even if the text has been differentiated from the picture, it continues in large measure to depend on it. What children suppose to be represented in writing are names, and only those of the objects in the picture. Any kind of utterance other than names is excluded. Leonardo, although he does not reject the sentence, returns to the system of juxtaposed names. Reading, for the subjects at any of the levels we have seen, means putting two systems into correspondence, systems different from each other but very closely related. Initially, the correspondence is a global comparison between picture and print, without considering the particularities of the text. Later, these properties begin to emerge and a global comparison is no longer sufficient. Language intervenes as an intermediary between the two systems, but not as an independent element. Print represents the names of the objects in the picture. Names, of course, are elements of language, but we cannot conclude that children conceive of the written text as representing language simply because they suppose that names appear in print.

The best possible correspondence at this level is reduced to a quantitative relationship between directly perceivable units: graphic segments and the names of the elements in the picture. However, the text possesses a linear order. The parts are ordered. What is the meaning of this order and how does one discover it? At this level the linear order of the text can be matched to the illustration if the elements in the picture lend themselves to a linear ordering. This solution is used by Valeria and Leonardo, who order the pictures according to the order of the text (even when the conventional orientation of writing has not yet been acquired.)

Response Type 3b   Print Represents Sentences Associated with the Picture

What kind of solution will children who respond with sentences offer for the reality of graphic segmentation? Observe the following possibilities:

Favio (5 yrs., LC)

Card 2
The frog is out strolling (*la rana está paseando*) (points to second line).
The frog is looking at the flower (*la rana está mirando la flor*) (points to first line).
This one (second line) has to be as long as this one (first line, referring, evidently, to the difference in length between the two lines).

Gustavo (5 yrs., MC)

Card 3
Here it says "the boy rows and the little fish go around in the water."

All together, how was that?

The boy rows (*el nene rema*) . . . (points to **en el río**) the little boat (*el botecito*) . . .
No, the fish are under the water (*los pescaditos están por abajo del agua*) (points to the rest of text).

These responses are just as interesting as the previous ones and they suggest similar processes. The difference can be explained in terms of the unit chosen as the departure point. When one begins attributing names, the graphic segments receive as many name-units as necessary. On the other hand, if one chooses a sentence unit, then two sentences may be produced and matched respectively to two lines of print (as Favio does), or one line of text may be divided in two and a sentence matched to each part (as Gustavo does). In each of these two cases, the children tend to maintain the integrity of the chosen unit. Favio's case is curious in another sense because as he attributes two sentences—units of the same value—he demands equality in the length of the lines. Evidently, this difference in length disturbs his hypothesis of equality in meaningful attribution.

Once again we pose the question: are print and picture differentiated? Yes and no. Yes, in the sense that the forms are not confused. When these children are asked "where is there something to read?" they all point to the print with no mistakes and differentiate an act of reading from an act of looking. However, the relationship between picture and print is conceived in such a direct sense that the children expect to see the same elements represented in each of the symbol systems. Both picture and print lend themselves to an interpretive component. Do the children suppose that the interpretation given to the illustration can be attributed entirely to the text? The data lead us to sustain the hypothesis we expressed previously: the child is operating at two levels—one is the actual reality of what is drawn and the other, what the drawing suggests; one thing is what appears and the other is what it means. Consequently, the text may be considered through two aspects: what is written and how it can be interpreted. The data we present in subsequent chapters gives credit to this hypothesis, as do the further examples elicited from the task we are analyzing here.

Response Type 3c   Differentiation between What Is Written and
                    What Can Be Read

Adults understand that everything we say when we read is written. To what degree is this assumption shared by children? The responses at this level are much like those discussed under 3a. The novelty here is that children attribute only names to the text and proceed, later, to a reading which includes these names as integrative elements of a sentence.

There are two variants of this type of response: (*a*) the child matches one or two names to the text and then reads a sentence, and (*b*) the child anticipates a sentence but only attributes one or two names to the text.

This new kind of response is highly instructive. It is in between the name hypothesis and the responses adopting the sentence form. Neither our procedures nor the stimuli presented change to the slightest degree and yet these children understand differently the question "what does it say here?" Note these examples:

Roxana (5 yrs., LC)
What does it say here?

And here? (Points to *salió*, the excluded part.)
It says toad-flower (*sapo-flor*)?

Let's see.

Didn't you tell me that it said "the toad is with the flowers"?

Erik (5 yrs., LC)
What does it say here?
Where?
How do you know?
Then where does it say duck?

What does it say?

Card 2
Sa- (points to second line) *po* (toad broken into syllables) (points to first line, excluding *salió*, because the difference in length bothers her).
Flower (*flor*).

No, it says: the toad is with the flowers (*el sapo está con las flores*).
Saapo (points to second and first line, still leaving out *salió*).
Floores (points to *salió*).
Yes.

Card 1
Duck (*pato*).
(Points to whole text.)
Because the duck is swimming.
Here (points to *nada*) and here the water (*el agua*) (points to *el pato*).
Duck is in the water (*pato está en el agua*).
The duck is in the middle of the water (*el pato está metido en el agua*).

Diego (6 yrs., MC)
And here?

Card 1
The duck, the duck goes down a stream (*el pato se va por un arroyo*). Here (points to *pato*) it says duck (*pato*).

And here? (Points to *nada*.)
So, all together?

Stream (*arroyo*).
The duck falls in the stream (*el pato se cae al arroyo*).

We chose to show only a few examples so as not to slow down the reader, but this type of response is quite frequent among our subjects. One thing is what figures in the print, another what can be read from this print. One can begin, like Erik, by anticipating the name and then, using the picture to justify his prediction, give a second name. In the end, according to Erik, what can be read is a sentence. We note that in the last two examples cited, the children offer more than one version of their final reading. Erik says first "duck is in the water" and then says "the duck is in the middle of the water." Diego says first "the duck goes down a stream" and later "the duck falls in the stream." This kind of response reflects a new form of differentiation: on one hand, what the text says and, on the other, what can be interpreted, leaving the possibility of variable results. In other words, the written text represents the names but not the relationship between them. The reader uses these names to read a sentence, giving the text an interpretative component which does not necessarily appear in written form.

Response Type 4 Search for a One-to-One Correspondence
               between Graphic and Sound Segments

The decisive step leading to a different conception of written language appears to be the possibility of breaking up the utterance so that the breaks correspond to parts of the text. We have previously emphasized the importance of focusing on the type of linguistic unit the child is operating with. The breaking up will give different results depending on whether the focus is on the word or the sentence. Continuing with the order we have established, we shall start with the responses of children who attribute names to the print. Before beginning an analysis of the data, we must point out that these children's syllabic hypothesis relates primarily to their conception of written language and not so much to the reality of the notation. If we say that children at this point can break up a name into syllables, this does not mean that they attribute a conventional and stable representation to each syllable. What matters here is not the details of the notation but the mechanism that is put into play.

Response Type 4a   Print Is Considered To Be a Label for the
                    Picture; a Correspondence Is Established
                    between Syllabic Segments of the Name and
                    Graphic Segments of the Text

Segmenting a name into its constituent elements leads all the children studied to syllable division. The procedure they use consists of matching a syllabic to each written part. This correspondence continues evolving toward the establishment of rules that imply restrictions, order, and so on. Syllabication also has antecedents in behaviors that correspond to prior levels. The following evidence provides an understanding of the evolution of syllabication.

   We characterize the first cases of syllabic division as syllabication without correspondence.

Marisela (4 yrs., MC)	*Card 2*
What does it say?	The little toad (*el sapito*).
Let's see, how?	*El-sa-pi-to.*
José (4 yrs., LC)	*Card 2*
	Flo-res (flowers).
Where?	(Points to *salió*).
Ximena (4 yrs., MC)	*Card 4*
	Pe-rro (dog).
Where?	(Points to whole text.)

   Common to these three examples is syllabication used without establishing correspondence with graphic segments. We consider these reactions to be behavioral cues of the act of reading rather than attempts at actual reading. These children produce an enunciation, which is different from one that might be produced in natural speech, to give the impression that they are reading. Syllabication without correspondence is an imitation of the reading act that does not take into account objective characteristics of the text. The proof that syllabication is not used for interpreting graphic segments is the lack of relationship between the emission and the pointing. When asked to show where, these children point to the text but without repeating the emission simultaneously as they point. Ximena says "*pe-rro*" and then indicates the text without speaking. José does the same. For these subjects the syllabicated form of the emission is not the result of having placed it in correspondence with objective qualities of the text. They are two separate actions: one, reading the text globally, even though this reading is syllabicated, and the other, locating what has been read. In other words, syllabication is not yet an instrument for comprehending print. In order to be such, it must evolve from global correspondence to one-to-one correspondence. The beginnings of

matching syllables to graphic notation can be characterized by a
syllabication which corresponds to text boundaries.

Javier (4 yrs., LC)

And here? (second line)
You say *sa . . .po?*
And here?

Card 2
Sa . . . po (toad) (points to the first
line from left to right making the
first syllable coincide with left part
and the last with the right).
(No response.)
No, *sapo.*
Sa . . . po (repeats previous procedure).

Rosario (5 yrs., LC)
What does it say?

Let's see.

Card 3
Boat (*barco*), *bar . . . co* (making her
emission coincide with pointing
from left to right).
Baaarcooo (while running her finger
along the text, she makes her emission last as long as the text).

Walter (5 yrs., LC)

Let's see.

Card 1
Duck (*pato*).
Paaatoo (syllabizing without very
marked breaks while pointing to the
text).

These three examples differ from the preceding ones in that
the pointing act is made to correspond simultaneously to the verbal emission, elongating the enunciation of the word to coincide
with the spatial extremes of the text. However, there is still no
relationship between graphic units and sound segments. Only the
text boundaries are matched to the emission boundaries, leaving
the correspondences in between the boundaries unresolved. This
results in a word segmentation that is not of a uniform type but,
rather, consists of syllables elongated or shortened to coincide with
the pointing act.

Two issues arise with respect to graphic segments: the possibility of achieving breaks in the enunciation and consideration of the
number of parts. Syllabication is one means of breaking up the
emission, but without relation to the parts of the text.

The examples that follow correspond to level 4 and show solutions to both issues: breaking up the utterance and correspondence between all parts. Even when there is a conflict between the
number of graphic pieces and syllabic breaks, two available resources are utilized: repeating some segment of the emission or
grouping the graphic parts in such a way that they coincide with
the syllabicated segments. Accommodating the utterance to the
text or the text to the utterance are two manifestations of the

same intent: to overcome the conflict of a quantitative difference between the terms to be related.

Martín (5 yrs., MC)	*Card 3*
What does it say here?	*Pes-ca-dos* (fishes).
Where?	*Pes-* (points to **Raúl rema**) *-ca-* **(en el)** *-dos* **(río).**
	Card 2
What does it say?	Toad (*sapo*).
Let's see . . .	*Sa-sa-po* (matching them to the three pieces of the first line).

These examples show how the same child can give both kinds of responses. The solution Martín finds to account for the three parts of *la ranita salió* is a common one. A variant of this is repeating the vowel when the name attributed to the text has only two parts (for example, *pa-a-to,* or *pe-e-rro*).

Within this category we will also consider children who, respecting the properties of the text, take into account the length of the parts that make it up. For them not all parts of the text have the same value, but certain restrictions pertaining to two-letter fragments are established. (Such fragments do not have a sufficient number of letters and therefore are not considered readable.) Either these graphic parts are not assigned an oral correspondence or they are joined to the larger unit that follows them. So, for example, María Paula (4 yrs., MC) says for card 1: *"pa-to"* (duck) (matching the first syllable to *el pato* and the second to *nada*). Rosario (5 yrs., LC), whom we cited earlier as providing an example of syllabication matched to the boundaries of the text, points only to the larger graphic parts (*pato* and *nada*) leaving out the smallest (*el*).

All of these examples show the possibility of breaking up the utterance so that the graphic segments are accounted for. Considering graphic parts in quantitative terms also appears in some of the level 3 responses, especially in the 3a type (juxtaposed names). What is the difference between these two kinds of responses? We believe the difference is that upon achieving the use of syllabication, the pieces of the text are considered to be part of a meaningful unit (for example, Martín) and not discrete units which can stand by themselves (Leonardo or Valeria, level 3a). The syllabic resource shows the beginnings of an equilibrium between integrity of meaning and graphic segmentation.

Response Type 4b   Print Represents Sentences Associated with
                    the Picture; a Correspondence Is

Established between Segmentation of the
Utterance and Graphic Parts

We will now analyze the responses attributing a sentence to the text. The problem of segmenting the utterance and the necessity of establishing correspondence appear this time with respect to sentences.

The segmentation some children arrive at consists of matching the name and then, separately, the complete sentence. What is curious about this response is the possibility of utilizing simultaneously these two forms of conceptualization. Analyzing these examples, it becomes clear that name and sentence are treated as two units.

Rosario (5 yrs., LC)	*Card 2*
	Sa-pi-to (little toad).
Where?	(Points to first line.)
And here? (second line)	The little toad jumps (*el sapito salta*).
Let's see . . .	*Sa-pi-to* (matching this to the three fragments of the first line).
And "jumps"?	. . .
Gustavo (5 yrs., MC)	*Card 4*
	Pe-rro (dog) . . . here it says runs (*corre*), the dog runs (*el perro corre*) (points to CORRE). Here, I don't know (indicates EL PERRO). Here, dog (*perro*) (points to CORRE) and here the dog that runs (*el perro que corre*) (points to EL PERRO).

These cases are good examples of the procedure described above: on one hand, the name; on the other, the sentence. This results from the difficulty children have in segmenting the sentence. The name can be isolated if it is placed outside of the sentence itself.

Some children attribute a sentence, segmented into two parts, to the text. This level of response goes beyond the limitations of the preceding ones in admitting the possibility of dividing the unit. The result is a separation into two parts. Note the following examples:

Javier (4 yrs., LC)	*Card 4*
	The dog wants to eat (*el perro quiere comer*).
Where?	Dog (*pe-rro*) (points to CORRE) wants to eat (*quiere comer*) (points to EL PERRO).

And the whole thing together?	The dog (*el perro*) (points to CORRE) wants to eat (*quiere comer*) (points to EL PERRO).
Diego (6 yrs., MC)	*Card 4* Dog running (*perro corriendo*).
Where does it say that?	The dog (*el perro*) (for EL PERRO) is running (*está corriendo*) (for CORRE).

Both Javier and Diego use the same procedure (although the reading order varies). They match one part of the utterance to one part of the text and the other part of the utterance to the rest of the text. This results in a grammatical division between subject and predicate.

In some cases the child attributes a sentence to the text, dividing the utterance into three parts. We find this kind of response only for card 3, because of its text characteristics. It does not appear for cards 1 or 4 (there was no example for card 2) because of the difficulty of considering a two-letter fragment (the written form of the article) readable. Cards 1 and 4 present three parts, but one of these parts is too small to receive an oral correspondence. However, the text on card 3 has five parts and, although two are small, grouping solutions may be used to solve this conflict. This leaves four parts, or possibly three, to consider.

It is pertinent to consider again the issue of breaking up the utterance. Segmentation of a unit involves conceiving the internal parts of the unit. With an oral enunciation, which parts can be broken up? Or, to state it differently, which elements of the utterance have a written representation? We see in the preceding examples that the break corresponds—at the syntactic level—to a division between subject and predicate. Breaking up the utterance into three parts requires conceiving three representable elements: grammatically, the subject, the verb, and the object. Recognizing parts, which together form a whole, does not necessarily mean that these parts will be considered in order. They may be attributed to any of the graphic pieces.

Let's look at the next example that corresponds to this level:

María Isabel (6 yrs., MC)	*Card 3* Fishes (*pescados* [noun]).
Where?	Here (points to **rema**).
How do you know it says that?	Because the *m* is there (points to the *m* in **rema**).
And here? (**en el río**)	Boy (*nene*).
Where?	*Ne-ne-e* (matches these three segments to **en el río**).

And here? **(Raúl)**
All together?

Fishes (*pesca* [verb]).
No, here, boy (*nene*) (for **rema**), here it says fishes (*pesca* [verb]) (for **Raúl**) and here it says fishes (*pescados* [noun]) (for **en el río**).

(Researcher repeats the child's oral rendition in left-to-right order while pointing to the words.)
Fishes boy fishes? (*Pesca nene pescados?*)
Let's see . . .

No, the boy fishes fishes (*el nene pesca pescados*).
The boy (*el nene*) (for **Raúl**) fishes (*pesca*) (for **rema**) fishes (*pes-ca-dos*) **(en el río)**.

María Isabel begins by attributing two nouns, fishes and boy, and then the verb, fishes. This procedure is not new. We find it among the children who believe that only names are written and add on the action relationship as an interpretative component. María Isabel also starts out with the names first. This fact confirms continuity in procedures. But the progress at this level lies in understanding the relationship in written form, independently of the terms that it relates. However, these isolatable elements are still not ordered. The difficulty seems to consist of accounting for, simultaneously, the segmentation of the utterance, the order of the parts, and the properties of the text. María Isabel begins proposing attributions that would result in, following conventional reading order, this utterance: fishes (verb) fishes (noun) boy. Later she corrects herself and proposes: fishes (verb) boy fishes (noun). Only when she moves to the oral terrain, through the researcher's probe, do the syntactic restrictions that lead her to the correct order appear: the boy fishes fishes. In this way she arrives at a solution to the segmentation of the utterance (three represented elements), the order (from left to right), and consideration of the properties of the text (three breaks for the larger segments and syllabic breaks for the smaller ones).

Developmental Progression of the Results Obtained from the Sentence Reading Task

We summarize the responses grouped in the four preceding levels in the following paragraphs.

- Print and picture are not differentiated; the two constitute a unit. It is possible to move from one to the other since they are conceived as different forms for representing the same meaning. The text is directly related to the picture.

- Later, we note a process of differentiation between print and picture. The utterance associated with the picture is attributed to the text; this utterance is not analyzed according to the sequence of the segments that make it up but is attributed globally, independent of graphic segmentation. This kind of response produces two variants: either the name of the object or a sentence related to the illustration is represented. An alternative solution, mediating between these two hypotheses, consists of attributing the name without an article but with a complement.

- Next, we note an initial consideration of some of the graphic properties of print. To each part of the text the child attributes an oral unit belonging to the same category (names or sentences). An intermediary option between juxtaposed names and juxtaposed sentences consists of attributing names and then reading a sentence, respecting the distinction between "what is written" and "what can be read."

- Finally, we observe the search for a one-to-one correspondence between graphic and sound segments. When a name is attributed to the text, the segmentation results in syllabic breaks. When a sentence is attributed, the breaks are syntactic (subject-predicate, subject-verb-object).

- At all levels, the meaning of the text can be predicted from the picture, but while the prediction is absolute in the initial levels, at later points cues are needed to verify what is predicted.

- In differentiating between what is written and what can be read, the thematic content is predicted rather than the text itself. This results from an interpretation departing from the written thematic elements.

- Ultimately, through considering the properties of the text in terms of segmentation, length, and cueing letters, a reading of all graphic parts is achieved. Only three children among the entire sample (1 five and 2 six year olds) arrive at a correct reading when dealing with upper-case, printed characters. However, some of the problems we have alluded to still persist. This example will show how the conflict regarding length of written parts and segmentation of the utterance persists, in spite of knowing how to read.

Martín (6 yrs., MC)	*Card 4*
What does it say?	*El-pe-rro-co-rre* (deciphering the text and breaking up syllabically what he reads).
Where does it say *perro*?	Here (points to PERRO).
Where does it say *corre*?	Here (CORRE).
And here? (EL)	*El perro.*

If we consider the different types of responses to both tasks (word reading and sentence reading) in comparative terms, we observe a correlation between the two. The children who give more advanced responses for one task also give them for the other. Inversely, the less evolved responses coincide for both situations. Specifically, the children who give type 4 responses, or a combination of types 3 and 4, for the sentence reading task give type C responses, exclusively, for the word reading task. While they are able to make sound segments correspond to graphic parts in the sentence reading task, in the word reading task they either consider length of text or look for letters with cueing value to confirm their prediction based on the illustration. (This is true for 14 subjects: 7 six year olds, 4 five year olds, and 3 four year olds.)

The subjects who produce type 3 responses, or alternate between types 2 and 3, for the sentence reading task give type A and B responses for the word reading task. That is, they fluctuate between considering the text as a label for the picture and giving a sentence that describes the picture. In order to interpret this fact, one must recall that the type 3 responses (specifically, type 3c) are characterized by discrimination between what is written and what can be read. The sentences may be due to criteria that correspond to the concept "can be read," while the labels may be explained by "what is written." Sentence responses for the word reading task generally appear when the children accept a countersuggestion from the researcher. However, we have confirmed that this fluctuation between name and sentence is typical of type 2 and 3 responses. (This is true for 26 subjects: 14 give type B responses for word reading, 6 six year olds, 3 five year olds, and 5 four year olds. Twelve subjects give type A and B responses for word reading, 2 six year olds, 8 five year olds, and 2 four year olds.)

The children who give type 2a responses for sentence reading, that is, those who think that what is written is the name of the illustrated object, give type B responses for word reading. (This is true for 10 subjects: 5 six year olds and 5 five year olds.) Finally, the subjects classified in category 1 for sentence reading are in category A for word reading. That is, the back and forth movement between picture and print appears in both situations. (This is true for 9 subjects: 2 six year olds, 1 five year old, and 6 four year olds.)

If we consider this relationship from another point of view, all the subjects who give type C responses for word reading belong to category 4, or alternate between 3 and 4, for sentence reading. The subjects who give type B responses for word reading are in categories 2 or 3 for sentence reading, except for five subjects who give type 4 responses for this task. And, finally, the subjects in category A for word reading alternate between categories 2 and 3 or give type 1 responses for sentence reading.

The importance of this comparison is that it demonstrates a clear relationship between the responses to these experimental tasks because:

- Consideration of the formal properties of print and correspondence with sound segments is the final step in the developmental progression established here.
- The confusion between text and illustration occurs regardless of the stimulus presented and constitutes the initial step in this progression.
- The conception of print as a label for the picture constitutes an important moment in the child's conceptualization, although it can appear with more or less advanced behaviors; the labeling behavior can occur independently of consideration of text properties or may coincide with the beginning of such consideration.
- The fluctuation between type 2 and 3 responses show the different focuses that children employ, depending on whether they are accounting for what is written or what can be read and also on their consideration of the characteristics of the graphic notation.

Considering the distribution of responses across our sample we note a great concentration at types 2 and 3 of sentence reading and at type B of word reading, which indicates that these are typical responses for four to six year olds. The small percentage of responses comprised of types 1 and A could be interpreted as delayed development from earlier levels, while types 4 and C responses introduce subsequent levels.

Considering the distribution of responses across cards for the sentence reading task, we can confirm a concentration of type 2 responses for cards 1 and 4 and of type 3 responses for cards 2 and 3, while the greatest frequency of response 4 corresponds to card 4. The type 1 responses remain more or less constant for the different cards.

This distribution relates to the following factors:

- The text property that is most evident in our experimental task is the separation into two lines. 56.36 percent of the type 3 responses correspond to card 2 (*the little frog went out / for a stroll* [*la ranita salió / de paseo*]).
- When many elements appear in the picture, there is a tendency to consider the text in terms of its parts in order to reconcile the number of objects in the picture with the number of parts in the text. 42.30 percent of type 3 responses correspond to card 3 (*Raúl rows on the river* [*Raúl rema en el río*]).

- However, if the illustration presents only one object to which the print may refer, the possibility of considering the text in terms of its parts is lessened. There are greater difficulties in making the number of parts correspond to elements represented in the picture. This is concretely the case for cards 1 and 4 (*the duck swims* [*el pato nada*]; THE DOG RUNS [EL PERRO CORRE]).
- If the children are capable of achieving a correspondence between graphic and sound segments, the presence or absence of elements in the illustration does not matter much. Even though the children continue to think that what is represented in writing relates to the picture, what they match to the parts of the text is a particular segmentation of the utterance. The greater percentage of type 4 responses for card 4 can be explained by the presence of the specific type of graphics (upper-case print), more familiar to the middle class six-year-old subjects. They, for the most part, are the ones who achieve type 4 behaviors.
- We can also confirm a constant distribution of type 4 behaviors for cards 1, 2, and 3.
- This constancy holds for type 1 behaviors as well, for the different cards, with a slight increase for card 3 because of the more complicated figures in the picture.

Although the frequency of responses varies in relation to the different cards, all the response types appear for all four cards. From this we conclude that although characteristics of text and illustration may influence responses, many responses are produced totally independent of both print and picture. This conclusion is most important because it shows that the responses are more directly related to children's conceptualizations than to the characteristics of the stimulus presented.

The First Grade Child's Concept of Reading

The data presented in this chapter (together with all the data we collected) supports our affirmation that children possess conceptualizations about the nature of written language long before the intervention of systematic instruction. These conceptualizations are not arbitrary but possess an internal logic, making them understandable from a psychogenetic point of view. Our hypothesis is that conceptualization processes, independent of the school situation, determine to a large degree the final results of school learning. These results will differ greatly between students who begin schooling at level 1 of this development and those who begin at level 3 or 4. Evidently, the latter are the ones in better shape for receiving systematic instruction, while the former will have more difficulty reconciling adult proposals with their own hypotheses about written texts.

The four year old's conceptions are oriented toward predicting the meaning of what is written from the picture (or from adult information in other situations). These predictions become gradually more appropriate in terms of the graphic notation until, finally, the text, utilized as a source of information, provides cues for verifying the cognitive predictions. We are concerned with systematic instructions in terms of specific methodological practices because we believe that none of these practices allows for the natural processes of conceptualization, although some respect them more while others impose adult conceptions from the start. In addition to factors related to conceptualization levels, there are some determined by children's social background. The influence of the social factor is directly related to the degree of contact with written language. It is evident that the presence of books, readers, and writers is greater in the middle class than it is in the lower class. It is also clear that almost all middle class children go to pre-school/kindergarten, while lower class children have less opportunity to ponder written language.[1]

If we put together all the factors which would tend to have a negative influence—conceptualization level, methodology, and social class—the probabilities of being successful at learning written language are, obviously, very few. It is a widely recognized fact that there is a high incidence of school failure and that these failures occur especially in the beginning years of school.[1]

To better analyze the causes of these failures, we followed a group of very poor children from the beginning to the end of first grade schooling. Our objective was to study the cognitive processes they put into play, as well as the hypotheses they develop as instruction advances. For this reason we interviewed the children at the beginning, the middle, and the end of the school year.[2]

The experimental task used for this purpose includes, among other things, the problem of the relationship between picture and print. Using a similar procedure, we introduce more complex variations since many of the children are at an advanced level in their learning. At the beginning of the year we present the word reading task, identical to the one we use with the preschoolers. Around the middle of the year, we interview the subjects with two cards from the sentence reading task: card 1 (*the duck swims* [*el pato nada*]) and card 2 (*the little frog went out / for a stroll* [*la ranita salió / de paseo*]), and we introduce two new cards, composed of the same

---

[1] Translator's Note: These statements refer specifically to Argentina and may or may not apply to other places.

[2] Authors' Note: Obviously we are aware of the presence of factors external to schooling that are involved in failures, but we believe that there are also internal factors—directly related to the external ones—that stem as much from the conception of learning as from the objective purposes the school hopes to achieve.

illustration and different texts. The two texts read: *it's a nice day* (*es un lindo día*) and *the girl is sitting* (*la nena está sentada*), both in cursive. The illustration (the same for each of the two texts) shows a boy and a girl sitting on a bench next to a tree in a plaza. At the end of the year, we introduce two different cards, again, both written in cursive. The picture-text pairs are the following: (*a*) Picture: a duck stepping on a stick. Text: *the* (female) *duck steps on the stick* (*la pata pisa el palo*). (*b*) Picture: a monkey hanging from the branch of a tree, eating a banana. Text: *the monkey's hand has fingers* (*la mano del mono tiene dedos*).

These four new texts present greater difficulties since children are less likely to find the anticipated words from the pictures, or they find them in unexpected places. First we will analyze the responses to the word reading task. Remember that this task was used only at the beginning of the school year.

Word Reading Task

The types of responses can be classified according to the same criteria used for the preschool children, although the quantitative distribution may not be the same. That is, one group of children offers responses of confusion between picture and print, another conceives of the text as a label for the illustration, and the third group considers text properties to confirm the prediction made from the picture. The quantitative distribution of responses is the following: 10 percent at level A, 66.66 percent at level B, and 23.33 percent at level C. In other words, children beginning school have criteria for conceptualizing written language that correspond to the three levels analyzed.

At this age, however, children evidence more uncertainty about predicting the text's meaning from the picture. The reason for this uncertainty is that the relationship between picture and print is conceived in a different way. The children anticipate the text but clarify that they do so based on the picture, as if they are not totally sure of what they anticipate. María Laura, for example, after giving names for all the written words, clarifies, "maybe it's the picture" (*quizas que es el dibujo*). Another reason for this doubt comes from the text itself or, rather, from the cues it provides for confirming predictions. Walter anticipates "bear" (*oso*) for *toy* (*juguete*) but then corrects himself: "no, it doesn't say *oso* because the O's not there."[1] We also find this kind of behavior among the preschoolers. This is the moment the child moves from looking for meaning in the picture to looking for it (or confirming it) in

---

[1] Authors' Note: The capital letter in the child's dialogue indicates use of the letter name.

the text. Let's look now at what happens once instruction has begun.

Sentence Reading Task

After various attempts to organize these responses we finally achieved a classification that considers both the final response and the process leading to it. For each case we will give corresponding examples so our criteria may be understood.

Response Type 1   Divorcing Deciphering from Meaning

Response Type 1a   Meaning without Deciphering
The children in this group look at the picture for meaning and respond with a name, or juxtaposed names, and occasionally with a sentence. In some cases—certainly the more interesting ones— they try to account for some of the properties of the text, making pauses in their emissions correspond to recognizable breaks in the text (spaces between words). The pauses come between words (when the response consists of juxtaposed names) or between syllables of a word (when the response consists of just one name). As they respond these children point to the parts of the text with their finger while they match a sound segment to each one. In this way, for example, three different children give these readings for the text *the duck swims* (*el pato nada*):

   Child 1: duck (*pato*), water (*agua*), flower (*flor*)
   Child 2: *pa-ti-to* (little duck)
   Child 3: *pa-m-to* (The *m* sound is introduced as a neutral sound, made through closed lips, in order to be able to break the word *pato* [duck] into three parts.)

These responses do not differ from those we observe in preschool children. Without resorting to deciphering, the children predict the meaning of the text from the illustration and achieve, in the best of these cases, consideration of some of the properties of the text (number of parts).

Response Type 1b   Deciphering without Meaning
These children do not look for meaning in either the picture or the text. They limit themselves to deciphering (sounding out) isolated elements by identifying individual letters or by constructing meaningless syllables vaguely sustained by the text. Here are examples of these two variants:

Text: *it's a nice day* (*es un lindo día*)
u, n, la, l, i, la, n, la, d, i, la, a."

Text: *the girl is sitting* (*la nena está sentada*)
"ei, se, los, es, is, lo, so."

Of course the children who produce this kind of reading are incapable of telling us the meaning of what they have read; they are involved in pure deciphering totally void of meaning, an end in itself. Not one preschool child responds in a similar way. This is, without a doubt, a product of schooling.

Level 1c   Attempt at Relating Deciphering and Meaning
This is actually an intermediary between categories 1 and 2 of this classification. The children in this group look for meaning in the picture, but then justify their response by looking in the text for cues confirming their interpretation. In general, they predict just one name, probably because of the difficulty in finding these support cues. The following examples are from two different children:

Text: *the little frog went out / for a stroll* (*la ranita salió / de paseo*)
ra-na (frog), "because it is has an *A*," pointing to the last *a* of *ranita*.

Text: *the duck steps on the stick* (*la pata pisa el palo*)
pa-to (duck), "because it has a *T*," pointing to the *t* of *pato*.

We are already familiar with this kind of response because we find it with the preschool children. (See type c responses to the word reading task.)

Response Type 2   Conflict between Deciphering and Meaning

Response Type 2a   Primacy of Deciphering
The children at this point are capable of predicting the text meaning from the illustration, but they know that the text is not entirely predictable from the picture. They opt, then, for sounding out to find the precise meaning, but they lose the meaning in the process, trapped by the demand for exact deciphering. In extreme cases, these are children who appear to read correctly, since they make no mistakes in deciphering, but they do not have the slightest idea of what the text means. Here are two examples of responses to the same text: *it's a nice day* (*es un lindo día*):

    Child 1: "es un-en-li-o-di-da"
    Child 2: "es un li-n-d-do d-i-a"

When we ask these children the meaning of what they have just read, they answer, "I don't know." This is another typical product of schooling.

Response Type 2b   Primacy of Meaning

The departure point here is similar to the preceding one (2a), but in this case the children continue to search for meaning. The final response consists of a sentence or a complex nominal phrase resulting from the integration, to varying degrees, of elements obtained through deciphering. In general, there is elimination and/or substitution of certain deciphered fragments which remain impossible to integrate into a coherent whole. It is important to observe, with respect to the next subcategory (2c), that these children do not distinguish between what the text says (textually) and what it means (consecutive interpretation). The following example illustrates this point:

Text: *the monkey's hand has fingers* (*la mano del mono tiene dedos*)
"*la ma-no de-l mo-no* (the monkey's hand), *la mano del mono tie-ne* (the monkey's hand has), *ti-ne* (nonsense) *de-do, dedo* (finger); *la mano del mo . . .* (the monkey's ha . . .) *ti-ne-dos . . . tinedos . . . tinedo* (nonsense). *La mano del mono tinedo.*" (Final reading: the hand of Tinedo the monkey.) When asked "what does that mean?" this child responds, "Tinedo is the monkey's name."

Response Type 2c   Fluctuation between Deciphering and
Meaning

In the case of the two preceding variants (2a and 2b) the same child may shift from deciphering to meaning in the same session, when moving to a new text. In this variant (2c), the fluctuation between deciphering and meaning takes place within the same text; the child attempts to overcome the conflict but does not truly achieve an integration of meaning and deciphering. These attempts at reconciliation, which continually fail, lead to varied results.

The child may begin to sound out while looking for meaning in the text, only to fall into pure deciphering, resulting in part of the text being deciphered and comprehensible and the other, deciphered but incomprehensible. An example of this is "the monkey's hand di-de-dos (nonsense)" (*la mano del mono di-de-dos*) for the text *the monkey's hand has fingers* (*la mano del mono tiene dedos*). In this case, the child is unable to give any interpretation for the text.

In other cases, children resolve this conflict by adding meaning, retaining the distinction between what the text says (textually) and what it means (consecutive interpretation). As an example we will use extracts from a long protocol of one child (same text as the previous example):

> *La mono* (ungrammatical gender agreement between the feminine definite article and the masculine

	noun for monkey) *de di-ne de-do* (of di-ne [nonsense] finger).
What does it mean?	That the monkey is peeling a banana (*el mono está pelando una banana*). (Interpreting from the picture.)
(Suggests new attempt.)	*La mono de-l moto ti-ne de-do* (the [feminine] monkey [masculine] of the [masculine] motorcycle [feminine] ti-ne [nonsense] finger). No! *Motoneta* (motor scooter).
What does it mean?	The monkey is riding a motor scooter (*el mono está andando en motoneta*). (This time independent of the picture.)
What does it say here? (*dedos*)	*D-e-do-s* (finger). *La mono* (the [feminine] monkey [masculine]) . . . *do* (nonsense) *motoneta* (motor scooter) *di-ne* (nonsense) *de-do-s* (fingers).
What does it mean?	A monkey that's telling the birds to be quiet (*un mono que está diciendo que se callen los pajaritos*). (This interpretation does not come from the picture but from the interpretation of fingers (*dedos*) as "*de-do-s*," which brings to mind the silence gesture of putting the finger to the mouth and going "shhh."

Finally, we observe conflicts centered around the grammatical agreement between the article and the noun: the noun is predicted from the picture and the article is deciphered. The prediction of the noun is supported by multiple cues in the text but does not derive from it, while the article is read through deciphering. The children find themselves facing contradictory results, but they invest the same confidence in their prediction that they have in their sounding out. Consequently, they do not modify their final result, even though they are aware of its incongruity, as the following example shows:

Text: *the duck steps on the stick* (*la pata pisa el palo*)

	. . . *la* (the—feminine) . . . *pato* (duck—masculine) . . . *pisa* (steps on) . . . *el* (the—masculine) *pa-ol* (nonsense word).
How is it, then?	*La . . . pato . . . pisa el pa-lo* The [feminine] duck [masculine] steps on the stick).

Do you say it like that?   No, *el pato.*
And here? (text)   *La pato pisa el palo.*

Response Type 3   Coordination between Deciphering and Meaning

In this category we include the cases that arrive at a correct response, although this response is not always reached immediately. To the contrary, the children tend to go through a long process before arriving at the final result, including all intermediary points between slow processes of coordination, immediate self-corrections, and readings that are correct on the first attempt. The defining criterion for placing a response in this category is that the child manages to coordinate deciphering with the search for meaning, without rejecting either one at the expense of the other. The most interesting variants we have observed are the following:

(a.) Elimination and reintegration of a text segment, with both the elimination and the reintegration resulting in acceptable sentences. For example:

Text: *the little frog went out/for a stroll (la ranita salió/de paseo)*

	La rana sa-le pa-sea (roughly: the frog goes out goes strolling).
What does it say then?	*La rana pasea* (the frog goes strolling).
What does it say here? (*salió*))	*La rana sa-lió pa-se-o* (roughly: the frog went out stroll); *la ra-ra-na salió de pa-se-o* (correct reading except for repetition of the first syllable of *rana*).

(Here, as in all cases of syllabicated reading, we took the precaution of verifying whether the child understood what he was reading. The reading of little frog [*ranita*] as "*ra-ra-na*" is an attempt to match the length of the emission to the length of the written word, but the child's interpretation corresponds simply to "frog" [*rana*].)

(b.) Integration of a part of the text not recognized during initial deciphering resulting from consideration of the meaning of the sentence. For example:

Text: *the monkey's hand has fingers (la mano del mono tiene dedos)*

	La mano dell moono ti-ene, ennne deedos (systematically sounded out with elongation of certain vowels and

consonants and segmentation of the verb *tiene* [has]).

La ma-no dell mo-no mo-no (the monkey's monkey's hand), *deedos* (fingers).

What do you think this says? (*tiene*)

(Thinks for awhile, and, without more deciphering, exclaims:) *Tiene!*

How is it all together?

La mano del mono tiene dedos.

(c.) Correction of the reading is based on judgments of grammaticality. The initial procedure is similar to that of the last two examples cited for 2c, but in this case the children manage to modify their reading by referring to their own internal grammar. For example, they would move from *la palo* (ungrammatical structure) to *el palo* (grammatically appropriate) or from *las patas pisa* (the ducks steps) to *las patas pisan* (the ducks step—grammatical, but the text has no plural markers) and finally to *la pata pisa* (the duck steps).

Considering the evolution of each child in our sample during the course of the year in terms of these categories, we can assert that:

- All children who continue to give type 1 responses (divorcing deciphering from meaning) throughout the year remain at the preoperative stage of cognitive development throughout the year, except for one child (five children in all).[1]
- All those who give type 3 responses (coordination of deciphering and meaning) by the middle of the school year are simultaneously in the intermediate or fully operative stage (three children in all).
- All children who achieve type 3 responses by the end of the school year are by that point in the intermediate or fully operative stage, except for one child (fifteen children in all).
- All who succeed in giving type 3 responses pass previously through type 2 responses (conflict between deciphering and meaning), except for one child (fourteen children in all). In addition, it appears necessary for children moving from type 2 responses to pass through type 2c responses (fluctuating between deciphering and searching for meaning in the same reading act) before arriving at type 3 responses. This is true for eleven of thirteen children.
- The difference between response types 2a and 2b, on one hand, and type 2c, on the other, turns out to be important for the

[1] Authors' Note: We evaluated operative level with the test of conservation of number. We used this systematically with the school-age children and occasionally with the preschoolers.

children who remain in type 2 behaviors throughout the year. If we accept, as our data indicate, that 2c behaviors constitute a progression with respect to 2a and 2b, we can see that these children, even though they remain at type 2, progress within this category. They give type 2a and/or 2b responses at the middle of the school year and type 2c toward the end of the year.

· This same kind of progression shows up in the passage from type 1 behaviors to type 2 behaviors: those who advance through the year from type 1 to type 2 behaviors respond only according to types 2a or 2b.

From these observations we conclude that the classification we have established represents a developmental ordering of the responses. We are not saying that all children go through these phases, but in the children we have studied, who have received a kind of reading instruction that gives first place and prerequisite status to deciphering, progress—when it happens—follows the stages we have described.

Comparing this data to that obtained from preschool children, an imposing conclusion emerges: the phenomena of divorcing deciphering from meaning and of rejecting meaning at the expense of deciphering are school products. They are the consequence of reading instruction which forces children to forget meaning until they have mastered the mechanics of deciphering. On their own, children are not inclined toward such dissociation. Before entering school, all of them, whatever their level of reading (judged by adult norms), start from the supposition that print can be interpreted through oral language. And children apply the totality of their linguistic knowledge with respect to their oral language: they eliminate ungrammatical constructions as well as those void of meaning.

In spite of this initial divorce, which has all the characteristics of an artificial product, the progression we have described comes about when children try arduously, with both difficulty and distress, to connect the deciphering technique they are learning with their own linguistic knowledge, which allows them to make both corrections and predictions on the text. The passage—apparently obligatory—through conflict before arriving at real coordination suggests an evolution similar to that observed in other cases of cognitive construction (Inhelder, Sinclair, and Bovet, 1974).

A very important point we wish to emphasize is that, despite the fact that school practice does not reinforce either predictions or self-corrections (the former because they are identified as simply guessing at random and the latter because the teacher is the one who corrects, without providing sufficient time for the child to perceive an incongruity and attempt to pinpoint it), progress always occurs relative to the need to overcome a conflict. The conflicting results that stem from deciphering, on one hand, and meaningful predictions and grammatical judgments, on the other, are a disturbance which can be overcome only by a process of coordination. Those who reach this point, in spite of school practice, are the ones who have not abandoned the search for meaning (linguistically transmittable) in the text. The others have remained in the initial divorce, without receiving the help that the school should provide.

IV READING WITHOUT PICTURES: INTERPRETING THE PARTS OF A TEXT

The Separation of Words in Writing

In this chapter we discuss two different but closely linked problems. One involves the ways children deal with unillustrated texts accompanied by an adult's utterance. Our question is: with an orally read text, will children be able to establish a correspondence between the parts of the utterance and the parts of the text? To state it differently, starting from the oral reading of a written sentence, will children be able to match the words in the enunciation to the segments of the text (the written words)? This issue may not seem to be of great significance, but it is extraordinarily complex and provides an unsuspected wealth of information.

The other problem is: in writing we use not only letters and punctuation marks but the additional graphic element of blank spaces. Groups of letters separated by blanks correspond to the words we emit. It appears very simple, and yet it is not.

In determining when graphic symbols are written together or separately, written language adopts a definition of "word" that is not a linguistic definition. For example, in different parts of the Spanish-speaking community "the day before yesterday" may be written as *anteayer, antier,* or *antes de ayer,* using one written word or three written words with no change in meaning. The writing system determines that *guárdamelo* (keep it for me [imperative]) is one word but *me lo guardas* ([you] keep it for me [indicative]) is written as three. To repeat an action I say that I must *hacer lo mismo* (do the same) or *hacerlo de nuevo* (do it again), and here the written segmentation is not the same even though the pauses in the utterance occur at the same points. This is far from a strictly Spanish phenomenon: how does one know, for example, that "himself" is one word in written English when "him" and "self" actually constitute two words?

The blanks between the words do not correspond to actual pauses in oral language. They separate elements of highly abstract character, which are resistant to a precise linguistic definition and termed words in written language.

In contemporary linguistics the term "word" has been replaced by technical terms such as morpheme, moneme, or lexeme. Although the word unit may have an intuitive status which seems clear to the speaker, this unit resists rigorous linguistic analysis. Saussure (1966, p. 105) avoided considering the word as a concrete unit of language because of its complex and ambiguous nature: "to be convinced, we need only think of French *cheval* (horse) and its plural form *chevaux*. People readily say that they are two forms of the same word; but, considered as wholes, they are certainly two distinct things with respect to both meaning and sound." If we take the intuitive definition of word as the association of a meaning to a specific sound pattern, we immediately run into several difficulties. In terms of meaning, it is clear that different kinds of words (nouns, verbs, articles, prepositions) carry very different kinds of meaning. Also, units smaller than the word transmit certain meanings (like the plural *-s*). There are also difficulties in terms of sound pattern. Taking verbs as an example: *cantamos* ([we] sing) or *cantaré* ([I will] sing) could be thought of as two different words or as two occurrences of the same word.

It is easy to have the impression that our way of writing is natural, but writing has not always been done in this way. The convention of word separation was adopted recently in the history of writing systems.

Cohen (1958) points out in a discussion of Latin that "connecting lines between letters appeared frequently in the lower case; before the reform of Charlemagne these connections even appeared between words, but this begins to disappear toward the end of the eighth century; however, it is only in the eleventh century that words are almost always separated appropriately" (p. 348).

Other written languages (such as Arabic and Hebrew) have special forms for letters coming at the end of words, facilitating recognition of word boundaries even when blank spaces are not employed. In ancient Ethiopian writing (fourth century) words were separated by two superimposed dots. In Sanskrit words were not separated, but the end of a word not terminating in a vowel could be marked by a special sign for a consonant with no vowel (a sign called *virama,* meaning pause or rest).

Words were not separated in ancient Greek writing either.

Although some ancient inscriptions have a mark of separation between the words, they appear unseparated in most cases, leaving readers with the task of discriminating the boundaries on their own. . . . Separation by spacing is found more frequently in short documents of daily life addressed to people with little education. Sometimes periods or commas were used to avoid possible confusions. The use of spacing became generalized in the seventh century, but even in the ninth and tenth centuries it was common to use spacing only between long words. For Greek, as for other languages, the habit of separating or not separating words in writing must be considered in relation to the realities of pronunciation: we know . . . that in Greek the words were linked together . . . continuity (in writing) had a reality for the reader (Cohen, 1958, pp. 245–246).

Our procedure for studying this problem is to write a sentence in front of children and then read the sentence with normal intonation while pointing to the text with a continuous gesture. We use only transitive verbs and simple nominative phrases comprised only of a noun, with or without an article. We use the following sentences: [1]

PAPÁ PATEA LA PELOTA (DAD KICKS THE BALL) (upper-case print).
la nena come un caramelo (*the girl eats a candy*) (cursive). Alternately: *la nena compró un caramelo* (*the girl bought a candy*) or *la nena comió un caramelo* (*the girl ate a candy*) (also in cursive).
elosocomemiel (*thebeareatshoney*) (alternately in printing and cursive, but without spacing in either case).
EL PERRO CORRIÓ AL GATO (THE DOG CHASED THE CAT) (upper-case print). [2]

After reading the sentence once aloud, we ask the children where they think the words that make up the sentence are. For example, working with PAPÁ PATEA LA PELOTA (read without pausing between words), we ask: "Where did I write *papá*? Where did I write *pelota*? Where did I write *patea*? Where did I write *la*?" Of course we vary the order of the questions, but we always begin with one of the nouns. We also ask the inverse of these questions. We point to a part of the text and ask what is written there. [3]

The task appears easy. Since the text is written and read in front of the child (and repeated several times, if necessary, to avoid forgetting) it would seem obvious that each word of the utterance should correspond to a segment of the written sentence, following the spoken order. We write the sentence in front of the children, instead of presenting it to them already written; they witness the act of writing and the left-right order, a necessary precaution since nothing assures us that the child already accepts this conventional orientation (see "Spatial Orientation in Reading" in chapter 2).

We are not interested in the child's ability to decipher the given

---

[1] Translator's Note: The sentences all have a subject-verb-object structure which corresponds directly to the word order in their English translations.

[2] Translator's Note: The verb *correr* in Spanish usually means to run but due to the characteristics of both subject and direct object, in this transitive context it becomes to chase.

[3] Authors' Note: We are currently continuing our research with other kinds of sentences, studying in particular ones with intransitive verbs, copulatives with adjectives, negatives, and so on.

text, but his ability to deduce what should be written in each segment, using the information at hand (written text and adult's oral reading, in addition to the child's own linguistic knowledge). However, this is a surprisingly difficult task due to children's conceptualizations about what is written, or what they expect to be written.

Here are two extreme examples (both typical) demonstrating the tremendous differences that occur:

Mariano (6 yrs., MC)	PAPÁ PATEA LA PELOTA
	(DAD KICKS THE BALL)
Where does it say *pelota?*	(Points to PATEA LA PELOTA but corrects himself immediately.) No! Here it says *pelota* (LA PELOTA), and here *papá* (PAPÁ PATEA). *Papá patea la pelota* . . . (repeating to himself). No! Here *papá* (PAPÁ) and here *patea* (PATEA).
Where does it say *la?*	(Reflects, saying to himself) *la patea . . . a la pelota* (he kicks it . . . the ball) (points to LA).
Facundo (6 yrs., MC)	PAPÁ PATEA LA PELOTA
Where does it say *papá?*	(Points to PAPÁ PATEA.)
Where does it say *pelota?*	(Points to LA PELOTA.)
Where does it say *patea?*	(Shakes head, "no.")
Where does it say *la?*	(Shakes head, "no.")

We purposely chose examples of two children of the same age and social class to analyze the differences. Both begin by dividing the written text in two parts, locating the nouns in relation to the order in which they are uttered: *papá* for the first two segments, *pelota* for the last two. Starting from their shared initial focus, Mariano continues searching for a correspondence between the segments of the text and a possible segmentation of the utterance, utilizing a method common to various children and seemingly quite efficient. He repeats the sentence to himself while attentively observing the text. With the aid of this method, Mariano is able to locate the verb. The search for the article, however, must be suggested by the researcher. (This happens in many cases for reasons we will analyze later.) Mariano finds the article by repeating a fragment of the sentence to himself and, curiously, after going through a pronominalization (*la patea . . . a la pelota*) (he kicks it . . . the ball).

Facundo, on the other hand, seems to consider the search process over once both nouns have been located and he denies that the article or the verb are written. (The meaning of this denial is not clear from this one example, but we will attempt to clarify it later.) These two examples demonstrate the extreme differences that can be encountered in response to an apparently simple task. This simplicity, however, is illusory. The crucial problem is determining which elements of a sentence are represented in writing from the child's point of view.

It seems so obvious to literate adults that when we write we transcribe what we say, we can hardly imagine it being otherwise. Yet the problem is valid. When we say "we're going to write this sentence," what exactly do we write? A simple sentence, like the ones we have presented, constitutes an intonational unit, the qualities of which are not transcribed. We can enunciate this sentence in a loud voice or in a whisper, and these changes in volume are not transcribed. We can stress a certain thematic element of the sentence (for example, *papá*, to indicate that he, and not someone else, kicked the ball) and this particular emphasis is not represented in the text. The transcription retains all the emitted words but represents them uniformly, regardless of the syntactic value, the semantic importance, or the informative value of each. For example, an oral sentence has predictable or easily reconstructible parts, a distinction eliminated in the transcription, which gives as much emphasis to articles, conjunctions, and prepositions, as it does to the elements that contribute the essential content of the message.

At the syntactic level, we are tempted to draw an analogy between children's expectations and the processes of reduction used in writing a telegram. A telegram written as "Arriving Saturday train" is read by the recipient as "*I am* arriving *on* Saturday *by* train" (or *we are* if more than one person is known to be coming). The omitted words do not interfere with comprehending the message because they are reconstructible based on the common linguistic knowledge of sender and receiver.[1]

In the same way, we can read *papá patea pelota* as *papá patea la pelota*, since we know that *pelota* is a feminine noun and takes the feminine article (*la*).

That children do not expect to find all the words of the oral message transcribed is an extremely important observation because it indicates a different conception of written language. The text suggests an oral emission but does not determine it entirely (in the same way that the text of a telegram suggests a complete sentence without reproducing it entirely.)

[1] Authors' Note: Obviously a great number of factors intervene in determining the essential elements of a message. The presuppositions common to both communicating parties are particularly important. For example, the word "train" might be superfluous if it were known that this were the mode of travel or the only possible travel access; "Saturday train" might be sufficient if the sender's intention of arrival were known by the receiver, and so on.

If this is true, which words of a sentence do children expect to see represented in writing? The following experimental data allows us to show a psychogenetic progression which, in an initial approximation, can be characterized as follows: only nouns are represented, nouns and verb are represented, and articles are also represented.

To better understand this progression, we will analyze it in inverse order, beginning with the cases closest to adult conceptions. Then we will return to the developmental sequence, indicating the ages at which the different conceptualizations appear.

Response Type A   Everything Is Written, Including Articles

Children who share adults' basic assumption about written language (all emitted words are written) give, of course, correct responses to the experimental task, but they may give them at the end of a long process. It is the characteristics of this process that we analyze here.

Cases like Mariano's are particularly interesting because one can follow with great detail the process leading to the correct response. Mariano is able to locate all the words of the sentence through a process of deduction and not by deciphering the text. He could have identified only the word *papá* (in a global, nonanalytical sense). For the rest of the sentence, the location of the words among the ordered parts of the text is achieved without using deciphering, working exclusively by matching ordered segments (sound with visual). Mariano's reading process is radically different from the one imposed in the classroom. And Mariano is not the only example of his kind, although he belongs to a group that has few representatives among the four to six year olds in our study. Here are other examples:

Isabel (6 yrs., MC)

la nena come un caramelo (the girl eats a candy)

Where does it say *caramelo?*
(Points to *la,* but corrects immediately and points to *caramelo.*)

How did you figure out it was there?
Because I thought about it. I said it to myself and I figured it out.

Where does it say *la nena?*
(Points to *la nena.*)

What does it say here (*come*)?
Come.

And here (*un*)?
I don't know.

Can you say it all together?
La nena come caramelos (the girl eats candies).

I wrote *la nena come un caramelo.*
Oh, then here it says *un* (points to *un*).

What does it say here (*caramelo*)?
Caramelo.

Where does it say *nena?*
(Points to *la nena.*)

Where does it say *come?*
(Points to *come.*)

What does it say here (*la*)?
Ne-

And here (*nena*)?	*na.*
Do you say *ne-na?*	No, *nena.*
Do you remember how the whole thing goes?	*La nena come un caramelo.*
Say the whole thing but pointing.	*La (la) nena (nena) come (come) ca- (un) ramelos (caramelo).*

Isabel is quite explicit and she gives us several clues for under-standing the kind of work children like her do with the written text. Repeating the sentence to herself allows her to correct her first mistake quickly. ("I thought about it. I said it to myself and I figured it out.") In her first oral repetition the indefinite article disappears (a frequent occurrence), but when she hears the orig-inal sentence again she deduces (as she indicates with the "then" she utilizes) the location of the indefinite article in the text. The rest of the protocol must be analyzed in another context, because it exemplifies a frequent procedure that interprets the smallest segments of the text (in this case, the transcribed articles) as pieces of something larger, as incomplete fragments of writing. These pieces are matched to syllabic segments of words (that is, to parts of a greater whole).

The same Isabel, for the sentence ELOSOCOMEMIEL (THEBEAREATSHONEY)—without objecting to a sentence writ-ten with no blanks—does the following:

Where does it say *oso?*	(Points to EL.)
Where does it say *miel?*	(Points to MI.) No, here (MIEL).
Where does it say *come?*	(Points to ME.)
Is that written okay like that, all to-gether without separating?	Yes.
Where does it say *miel?*	(Doubts for a minute, then points to COME.)
Where does it say *oso?*	(Points to ELOSO.) *Miel* here (COME); *oso* here (ELOSO). No, here it says *miel* (MIEL) because here it has to say *come* (COME).

It is clear in this case that correctly locating the parts of the sentence does not depend on being able to read (in the traditional sense of the term). The strictly deductive character of this process is emphasized once again when Isabel asserts "here it has to say *come.*" In truth, it has to say that for someone who supposes that writing replicates, in a left-right spatial order, the temporally or-dered units of the utterance. Although Isabel can give responses of the highest level, she is indecisive about the article, as can be seen in the case of *la nena come caramelos.* Here it is even clearer as the end of the interview about ELOSOCOMEMIEL (THEBEAREATSHONEY) indicates:

Show me each one.	*El oso* (ELOSO), just *oso*, *come* (COME).
And where's *miel?*	(Points to MIEL.)
Is it all right all together like that?	Yes. It doesn't matter that it's writ-
It doesn't matter if it's written like that?	ten all together.

The explicit shift from "*el oso*" to "just *oso*" indicates clearly the general difficulty we find in the level immediately preceding this one. The "it has to say" referring to the verb is not automatically generalized to the article.

Isabel gives a true example of deduction without deciphering, but some of the children interviewed on this task are capable of using deciphering. The problem is knowing how and when they use it. Some resort to deciphering only in problematic moments, as a possible alternative but not as the main method. Others utilize deciphering as an initial strategy, but they subordinate it to judgments of grammaticality (a strategy we rarely observe in the subjects who have learned to read in school by the traditional method, which imposes deciphering as the only valid strategy—see "Reading in the First Grade Child" in chapter 3). Miguel, for example, presents both kinds of behavior in two different situations. Faced with cursive writing, he only uses deciphering at problematic points; faced with an upper-case text, the only writing form he feels sure of, he uses deciphering but subordinates it to his grammatical judgments. Here are the two examples:

Miguel (6 yrs., MC)

	la nena compró un caramelo
	(the girl bought a candy)
Where does it say *nena?*	(Points to *nena.*)
Where does it say *caramelo?*	(Points to *caramelo.*)
Where does it say *compró?*	What?
(Repeats question.)	(Points to *un*, corrects, points to *compró.*)
Why do you think it's not here (*un*)?	*Un* (points to *un*).
How could you tell?	I guessed.
Yes, but how?	I looked.
What did you look at?	The letter *U . . . un.*
How did it go all together?	*Una nena compró un caramelo* (a girl bought a candy).
Say it to me and show it to me.	*Una (la) nena (nena) compró (compró) un (un) caramelo (caramelo).*
Where does it say *una?*	(Doubts, then points to *la.*)
EL PERRO CORRIÓ AL GATO	(THE DOG CHASED THE CAT) (Before the researcher reads the sentence, Miguel begins to decipher.) *El p-e, el pe, el pe . . . rrr-o, el perro,*

Look carefully (CORRIÓ).

co, co . . . rrria, el perro corría (the dog was running).

Co-rrr-o, el perro corro (the dog [I] run)? No! It can't be *el perro corro!*
Co-rr-e ([he] runs), *co-rrr-i-a* ([he] was running), it can't be *corría* because it's an *O. Corriendo* (running or chasing), *el perro corriendo l-a, al gato!* (The dog chasing the cat.)

How does it go all together?

El perro corría al gato. (The dog was chasing the cat.)

In the first situation Miguel uses deciphering (made difficult by the cursive writing) merely as an auxiliary. Deciphering is used only to locate one of the articles but does not prevent changing the definite article to the indefinite article in the subject of the sentence (he locates *una* in *la* in spite of having utilized the *u* as a cue in locating *un*). Miguel's deciphering in the case of the second sentence is especially interesting. The conflict between the predicted verb tense and the identification, through deciphering, of contradictory cues is finally resolved in favor of the initial prediction, after going through an attempt at reconciling this conflict (*corría* [third person singular, past imperfect]; *corro* [first person singular, present]; *corre* [third person singular, present]; *corría;* *corriendo* [gerund—equivalent to -ing form in English]; *corría*). The choice of the past imperfect verb tense is not random but responds to the use of verb tense to mark aspectual values (Bronckart, 1976; Ferreiro, 1971). The imperfect is, in fact, the ideal tense for this sentence, since it places the action in the past while implying a continuous and unfinished action. (Semantically, to run or chase does not indicate the result of the action but its process; in this sense, the use of the imperfect is more normal. The opposite would be the case if the lexical choice were "caught" or "trapped.")

In summary, the supposition that the article is written does not depend on being able to decipher the text. To the contrary, deciphering is used as an auxiliary resource, subject to the learner's assumptions and judgments of grammaticality.

Response Type B   Everything Is Written, except for Articles

In this category we are looking at responses that move progressively away from adult assumptions. Here the children are able to locate all the parts of the utterance in the various written segments, except for the articles. After some examples we will analyze the reasons why children may think that articles are not written.

Isabel (6 yrs., MC)

Where does it say *pelota*?
Where does it say *papá*?
Where does it say *pelota*?
Where does it say *patea*?

How did it go all together?
Where does it say *pelota*?
Where does it say *patea*?
What does it say here? (PELOTA)
Should we leave it in or take it out?
It doesn't say anything?

Alejandro (6 yrs., MC)

(Reads sentence.)
Where does it say *pelota*?
How do you know?
Where does it say *patea*?
Where does it say *papá*?
What's this? (LA)
Where does it say *pelota*?

So what does it say here? (LA PE-
LOTA)
What does it say here? (PAPÁ)
Here? (PATEA)
Where does it say *la pelota*?
What does it say here? (LA)

Cynthia (5 yrs., MC)
Where does it say *pelota*?
Yes, but where's *pelota*?
Where does it say *patea*?
Where does it say *papá*?
What does it say here? (LA)

I wrote it because the whole thing
says, "*Papá patea la pelota.*"

PAPÁ PATEA LA PELOTA
(DAD KICKS THE BALL)
(Points to PATEA.)
(Points to PAPÁ.)
(Points again to PATEA.)
(Points to LA PELOTA.) *Pa-tea* (one
syllable for each word).
Papá patea la pelota.
(Points to PATEA.)
(Points to LA.)
I don't know.
I don't know. Take it out.
It doesn't say anything.

PAPÁ PATEA LA PELOTA
I don't know how to read. But here
it has to say something because the
letters it has here, I think them.
(Correctly names each written let-
ter.)
(Points to PELOTA.)
Because I know the letters.
(Points to PATEA.)
(Points to PAPÁ.)
It's part of *pelota*.
(Points to LA PELOTA.) Here, *pe-*
(LA).
Here, *pe-* (LA) . . . No. This (LA)
doesn't mean *pelota*. We'll take it out.
Papá.
Patea.
(Points to PELOTA.)
That says . . . I bet that's part of
something, of some name . . .
That's a part that means the goal.

PAPÁ PATEA LA PELOTA
Papá patea la pelota.
(Points to PELOTA.)
(Points to PATEA.)
(Points to PAPÁ.)
I don't know. *Papá patea la pelota*
. . . (repeats sentence to herself,
following the text with her finger
from left to right). What is this,
anyway? (LA) Why did you write it?
(Proposes that researcher rewrite
the sentence on the other side of the
paper.)
Without making a mistake, can you

	put it here right? But don't make any mistakes!
(Rewrites sentence.)	*Papá patea la pe . . .* What is this? (PELOTA).
What is it?	. . .
Paula (4 yrs., MC)	PAPÁ PATEA LA PELOTA (Repeats sentence correctly.)
Where does it say *papá?*	(Points to PAPÁ.)
Where does it say *pelota?*	*Papá . . . pelota,* here (PATEA).
Where does it say *patea?*	*Papá* (PAPÁ) *patea* (PATEA) *la-pelota* (PELOTA).
What does it say here? (LA)	I already told you, you can't read with two letters!
Why did I put it?	Don't put it like that . . . so far away from the other ones (indicates with a gesture that this piece should be joined to one of the larger pieces next to it).
What did it say all together?	*Pa-pá-pa-te-a-la-pe-lo-ta* (without pointing).
Where does it say *papá?*	(PAPA)
Where does it say *pelota?*	(PELOTA)
Where does it say *patea?*	(PATEA)
Does it say *la* somewhere?	Here, here (points to all the *A*'s in the text).
All together how does it go?	*Papá patea la pelota.*
(Covers part of sentence leaving visible PAPÁ PATEA.) What does this say?	*Papá patea.*
(Covers other part leaving visible LA PELOTA.) What does this say?	*Pelota.*
(Leaves visible only LA.)	That doesn't say anything.

These four examples are representative of this response category. Being able to locate the article as an independent fragment must be carefully differentiated from being able to repeat the uttered sentence correctly. These children assert over and over that the text says *papá patea la pelota,* but this does not make them suppose that the article is written. In an act of reading the article appears—because we shift to the oral level, and children know well that the utterance without the article is ungrammatical—but this in no way guarantees the inference that the article must also appear in the written text.

We will formulate this problem from another perspective. Instead of asking why the article might be eliminated from writing, we shall ask why it should be included. In other words, we will adopt the child's point of view and suppose that we must justify the inclusion of the article and not its omission.

What we said before about the highly predictable elements of the oral emission, comparing it to the processes of text reduction in writing a telegram, is, in principle, applicable here. It is not necessary to write the article since it can be predicted from the noun; once the noun is written, the writing of the article becomes superfluous, since it goes with the noun. This could be one reason, but there are others.

Suppose that children share with us a nontechnical definition of writing summed up as follows: "what we write are words," "we write the words we say." The problem resides in knowing whether children share our definition of "word."

Fortunately, we have data from a recent study by Ioanna Berthoud (1976) on children's notion of "word." This study was done in French, but it shows evidence of developmental characteristics found in other languages, especially those close to French in terms of structure. Berthoud presented to children of different ages an oral list of words including nouns, verbs, adjectives, conjunctions, and articles. The children were asked whether each thing they heard was a word or not. Children ages four through seven systematically rejected articles, prepositions, pronouns, and conjunctions from the class of words. Children of the same ages, when asked to count how many words were in an orally presented sentence, systematically omitted the articles (or counted them together with the following noun). Herein lies one of the keys to this issue. If articles are not words, there is no reason for writing them given that we agree that what we write are, indeed, words.

The difficulties with articles stem, also, from graphic considerations. If the article is not a word, then there is no reason to write it, but, also, the written form which corresponds to the article is too small; it does not have the minimum number of letters children require for something to be readable (see chapter 2). Paula is particularly clear on this issue. When asked what the segment corresponding to the article (LA) says, she openly responds: "I already told you, you can't read with two letters!" In the other examples presented, the children tend to utilize the larger written parts—those having more than two letters—and they have trouble assigning a value to the smaller segment when asked to do so. This is common across children. Isabel uses LA as a syllabic fragment of *patea;* Alejandro uses it as a syllabic fragment of *pelota.* Cynthia finds no way to interpret it and asks, frankly, "What is it? Why did you write it?" Paula tells us, "It doesn't say anything."

Isabel and Cynthia, who initially have difficulties with the segment LA, end up accepting it but then have problems with the next segment (PELOTA). Why does this happen? The answer is clear (not from these examples alone, but in view of all our data). According to the analysis of the oral utterance children at this level make, there should only be three written parts in the text and not four (since, from their perspective, there is no reason to write the article). This is why they always end up with a piece left over. This leftover piece will generally be the written element with the fewest letters, since they all consider first the written parts having more than two letters. Eventually the leftover piece may be the last segment, when the quantity-of-letters criterion is momentarily put aside and the main criterion is the matching of two sequential orders (that of the utterance and that of the writing).

The basic point is that the children expect to find three written parts and the text has four. This creates a conflict which may be resolved in various ways: asserting that the leftover part says nothing; proposing to take it out; joining it to one of the larger pieces so that it can be read; or giving it a syllabic value.

The solution of interpreting two-letter segments as syllabic segments is particularly instructive and merits special attention. We have encountered it for each of the sentences we use. For example, in the sentence *la nena compró un caramelo* (*the girl bought a candy*) or *la nena come un caramelo* (*the girl eats a candy*), the problem is duplicated. Both the definite and the indefinite articles are handled in the same way. Different children give different syllabic interpretations of the two-letter segments. For example: *"ne-na"* for *la nena,* *"co-me"* for *come un,* *"ca-ramelo," "cara-melo"* or *"unca-ramelo"* for *un caramelo.*

The syllabic interpretation joins the small segment to the larger one immediately following it or, less frequently, to the one preceding it. This generally occurs along with a correspondence between the syllables in their orally uttered sequence and the ordered parts of the text, but it does not always happen this way. Emilio (4 yrs., MC) thinks, like Alejandro, that LA is a part of PELOTA, but while Alejandro reads, *"pe-lota"* for LA PELOTA, Emilio reads *"lota"* (not a word) for LA and *"pelota"* for PELOTA. His attributions result in *"papá patea lota pelota."* But Emilio reads the whole text, from left to right continuously, as *"papá patea la pelota."* This does not prevent him when reading by fragments from saying *"lota"* for LA, since it is part of *pelota.*

In the previous cases, syllabic interpretation of the two-letter segments leads inevitably to syllabically interpreting the larger fragment it is linked to, so that only by joining the two do we end up with the complete written representation of the corresponding word. For Emilio, *pelota* is written completely in one segment (the correct one, in this case), and he attributes an incomplete syllabic fragment to LA. He attributes a syllabic fragment to a two-letter unit of print but not to any of the larger units. At Emilio's age, a syllabic fragment can be any syllable, regardless of the order of emission. This phenomenon relates directly to the responses of some children (see "The Child's Own Name" in chapter 6) who propose a syllable for a visible part of their own written name, but may propose the first syllable, when only the last is visible. Returning to the fundamental problem, we note that one aspect of the process is recognizing that a word has parts, components forming a whole, and another is ordering those parts. The basic logical activities of segmenting and ordering are in no way alien to the comprehension of written language.

To summarize the characteristics of this response category, the problem of the article as a written word appears to be a double one: metalinguistic (if articles are not considered to be words, there is no reason to write them), and graphic (you can't read with just two letters). The reading of a sentence with articles is not problematic in the sense that all children produce them in a continuous act of reading. The problem arises when we attempt a correspondence between parts of the text and parts of the utterance. In the tasks we use, the problem arises immediately because children expect to find three written parts where the text has four. Interpreting the leftover piece syllabically appears as one, and perhaps the most interesting, way to resolve this conflict. We also see this leftover problem in other kinds of responses, with different characteristics.

Response Type C   Both Nouns Appear Independently in Written Form, but the Verb Is Linked to the Whole Sentence or the Whole Predicate

The responses at this level are extremely interesting, and difficult to present, because they move considerably away from adult expectations. We begin by examining some cases in which the child manages to locate the verb in an independent way, but only after serious difficulties. (These cases are really intermediary ones between levels B and C.)

Gustavo (6 yrs., MC)	PAPÁ PATEA LA PELOTA (DAD KICKS THE BALL)
Where does it say *pelota?*	(Points to PELOTA.)
Where does it say *patea?*	(Points to LA.)
Where does it say *papá?*	(Points to PAPÁ.)
Say it all together.	*Pa-* (PAPÁ) *pá* (PATEA) *patea* (LA) *lapelota* (PELOTA).
Again!	*Patea* here (PATEA), *patea la pelota* (points to PATEA LA PELOTA with a continuous gesture).
Marina (5 yrs., MC)	*la nena compró un caramelo* (*the girl bought a candy*) (Repeats sentence correctly.)

Where does it say *la nena?*

Where does it say *caramelo?*
(Repeats sentence.)
Where does it say *compró?*
What does it say here? *(la nena)*
Where does it say *compró?*

Before you told me that *compró* is here. *(compró)*
Where does it say *caramelo?*
Where does it say *un?*

(Points word by word from left to right.)
How does it go?

(Points to each word as before.)

You show me!

Rosario (5 yrs., LC)
(Reads sentence.)
You say it and show me!

Once more.

Is *papá* written there?

All of it says *papá?*
Is just *papá* there?
Is *pelota* written there?
What else is written there?
What else?
Where's *papá?*
Patea?
La pelota?
And here? (PELOTA)
In that part itself it says *papá patea la pelota?*
What does it say there?
Let's see. Here? (PAPÁ)
Here? (PATEA)
Here? (PELOTA)

It says *la nena* here (*la nena compró*).
All this says *la nena,* and all this says *el caramelo* (*un caramelo*).
(Points to *compró un caramelo.*)

I think here (*compró*).
La nena.
. . . *un caramelo* (completing the sentence to herself while looking at the text).
Yes.

(Points to *un caramelo*)
I think here (the accent mark on the final *o* of *compró*).
Ne-na-com-pra-le (girl buy . . .) (one syllable for each word).
(Goes again through text from left to right and finishes utterance): *unca-ra-me-me-lo* (a candy).
Ne-na-compra-un-caramelo (girl buys a candy).
Ne- (*la*) *na* (*nena*) *compra* (*compró*) *unca-* (*un*) *ra-* (*car*) *melo* (*ramelo*).

PAPÁ PATEA LA PELOTA

Papá (PAPÁ) *patea* (PATEA) *la* (LA) *pe* . . . (PELOTA).
(Stops, confused, as if something were missing for a complete reading.)
Papá patea la pelota (points correctly to each word).
Yes. Here (points to whole sentence).
Papá patea la pelota.
(Points to PAPÁ.)
(Points to PATEA.)
Patea (points to LA).
La pelota (points to PELOTA).
(Points to PAPÁ.)
(Points to PATEA.)
(Points to LA.)
. . . *Papá patea la pelota.*
(Gesture of negation.)

. . .
Papá.
Patea.
La pelota.

Here? (LA)	. . . *La pelota.*
Say it and show me.	*Papá patea la pelota* (points correctly to each word).
(Same child)	*la nena come un caramelo* (*the girl eats a candy*)
You say it and show me.	*La nena (la) come (nena) ca- (come) ra- (un) melo (caramelo)* (leaves out indefinite article *un*).
Again!	*La nena (la) co- (nena) me (come) ca- (un) ra- (caramelo)* . . . (Stops, confused because there's no segment left with which to finish the sentence.) *La nena (la) come (nena) ca- (come) ra- (un) melo (caramelo).*
Is *la nena* written there?	Yes (points to *la nena*).
Is *caramelo* written there?	(Points to *come un*).
What does it say here? (*la nena*)	*Nena.*
And here? (*come un*)	*Caramelo.*
And here? (*caramelo*)	. . .
Where does it say *la nena*?	(Points to *la nena.*)
And here? (*come un*)	*Caramelo.*
And here? (*caramelo*)	*La nena come un caramelo.*
Let's see. Here? (*la nena*)	*Nena.*
Here? (*caramelo*)	*Come caramelo.* (eats candy).
Here? (*un*)	. . .
Here? (*la nena*)	*La nena.*
Here? (*come un*)	*Caramelo.*
Here? (*caramelo*)	*La nena come caramelo.* (*the girl eats candy.*)
Say it and show me.	*La nena (la) come (nena) ca- (come) ra- (un) melo (caramelo).*

These three examples, different in various respects, are similar in one essential aspect: the difficulty of conceiving that the verb might appear in an independent written segment. All these children locate the verb when reading the whole sentence continuously, but when identifying each of the parts and assigning a verbal translation to each, there is a definite disharmony between the continuous reading and the reading of isolated fragments. In the previous section we saw how the article, included in the continuous reading, disappears when it comes to interpreting parts. Let us examine how the value assigned to each segment of the text changes entirely when shifting from the whole sentence to each of its parts.

Gustavo finds a stable placement for both nouns, at either end of the text, but he places the verb alternately in one or the other of the two remaining fragments and immediately completes it by adding on the object ("*patea, patea la pelota*"). We cannot be sure to what point Gustavo believes that the verb can appear independently in writing, or that it can but only when joined to its direct object complement. Gustavo also works with syllabic segmentation of the utterance, searching for a correspondence between syllables and parts of text. The other two children we cite here do this to an even greater degree.

Marina carries syllabic segmentation to its ultimate consequence, finding herself obligated to go through the text a second time to complete the sentence. (Curiously, where the syllabic segmentation coincides with the article, Marina joins it with the first syllable of the following noun, coming up with *"unca"* instead of *"un-ca,"* even when this forces her to repeat one of the following syllables in order to achieve a successful one-to-one correspondence: *"ra-me-me-lo."*) Marina begins by dividing the text in two, matching a noun to each part. When asked about the verb she begins to doubt; she shifts from clear affirmation ("it says *la nena* here," "all this says *el caramelo*") to expression of possibility ("I think here") when she must locate the verb. And in any case, this verb is not an independent element because she immediately completes the researcher's question, "Where does it say *compró?*" by supplying the object of the verb, *un caramelo.*

Rosario shares with the previous two children the difficulty of assigning a precise value to each part, and she also uses the resource of syllabic segmentation. Clearly, these children work towards a successful one-to-one correspondence but without considering other properties of the text fragments such as length or number of characters. Rosario attributes several times the syllable "ca" to a four-letter fragment and "ra" to a two-letter fragment, with no apparent conflict, just as she repeatedly proposes *la nena* for the small fragment beginning the text. In other words, she is only concerned with the one-to-one correspondence, ignoring the physical properties of the objects placed in correspondence. She attends only to the possibility of matching each element of one series sequentially to each element of another series (a visual series and a sound series in this case) without resulting in missing or leftover elements.

Rosario is original with respect to the other two children in proposing a rather curious solution for two different sentences. She places both nouns and the whole sentence in the leftover fragment. (Many other children adopt this procedure as well.)

But we return to the problem of locating the verb. In the procedure we used at first we asked directly "where does it say . . . ?" a rather suggestive inquiry because it assumes that in some place it says *patea,* for example, given that the whole text says *papá patea la pelota.* That question did not turn out to be suited to our purposes, and we had to substitute a less suggestive one: "does it say *patea* somewhere?" Only with an affirmative response would we go on to ask "where?" Even when using the initial suggestive procedure, we find children with enough conviction to tell us, "No, it doesn't say that." Marcela (6 yrs., MC), for example, when asked where the verb in one of the written sentences is, responds, "No, it's not there," and finds no contradiction between this negation and the affirmation that the text "says" a complete sentence.

Obviously, once we substituted the question "does it say . . . somewhere?" for "where does it say . . . ?" we began to use this form of questioning systematically for all parts of the sentence. We then discovered other, even more surprising facts, which we will go on to later.

Before discussing clear-cut cases in which the isolated verb is never located, we will present a unique variant of locating the verb, not in the conjugated form appropriate to the utterance but in the infinitive. Only two children (4 and 5 yrs., LC) in the study use this variant, but we consider it of great enough interest to analyze it here.[1]

José uses this procedure systematically for each sentence presented to him, translating *patea* to *patiar* (dialect variation of the standard infinitive *patear*), *come* to *comer* (for two different sentences) and *compraron* to *comprar*. The following is the protocol of one of these sentences:

José (4 yrs., LC)

	la nena come un caramelo
	(*the girl eats a candy*)
	(Repeats sentence correctly.)
Is *nena* written there?	Yes (points to *un caramelo*).
Is *caramelo* written there?	Yes (points to *la nena come*).
Is *come* written there?	Yes (points to *come*).
Where does it say *nena*?	(*caramelo*)
Where does it say *caramelo*?	(*un*)
Where does it say *come*?	(*come*)
And here? (*la nena*)	. . . I don't know.
You say it and show me.	. . . (hesitates).
What does it say here? (*caramelo*)	Here it says *ne-na* (first syllable for *un*, second for *caramelo*).
And here? (*la nena come*)	*Comer* (infinitive of *come*). *Comer caramelo . . . la nena comiendo caramelo* (to eat candy . . . the girl eating candy).
How does it go?	*La nena come caramelo* (the girl eats candy).

[1] Authors' Note: In our current research we have encountered more cases of transforming the verb to the infinitive, and this probably indicates an intermediary response between the hypothesis that the verb does not appear in written form and the one which supposes that the verb is written in its conjugated form.

Where does it say that?	(Points to *la nena.*)
And here? (*come*)	*Comer.*
Comer or *come*?	*Comer.*
How does it go all together?	*Nena come caramelo* (girl eats candy).
I wrote *la nena come un caramelo.*	*Come un caramelo* (eats a candy).
So what does it say here? (*come*)	*Comer.*
Is *un* written there?	. . .
Does it say *un* somewhere?	No.
Caramelo?	(Points to *la nena.*)
Nena?	(Points to the rest.)
How does it go all together?	*Nena come caramelo* (girl eats candy).
Nena come caramelo or *la nena come un caramelo?*	*Nena come caramelo.*

Working on this sentence, as with the other sentences, José encounters difficulties that an adult would not easily suspect. He begins, like many other children, matching both nouns to the whole text (one part for each), as if he were not aware of the blank spaces between the written parts. Obviously, these blanks constitute a disturbance that José initially tries to ignore but then attempts to deal with (as we can see when he produces "*ne-na*" through syllabic segmentation). We note that José works with the text from right to left, in spite of having seen the text being written from left to right. This occurs with many children and relates to the difficulties of recognizing conventional directionality in print (see "Spatial Orientation in Reading" in chapter 2).

José also places the verb stably in the central part of the text only when he enunciates it in the infinitive form, and he holds firmly to this form. When asked if he means to say *comer* or *come,* he opts for the infinitive, a choice he reiterates even after hearing and repeating the original sentence. José does not seem disturbed by locating the verb in the infinitive while he gives a complete reading of the text, without the articles but with the verb in its original conjugated form.

In summary, the written representation of the verb in its most stable form as an infinitive can be compatible with an oral reading of the verb in its conjugated form with corresponding grammatical inflections. This finding is no less surprising than realizing that the absence of an article from a written sentence is compatible with a continuous reading in which the article appears.

This phenomenon reinforces our previous interpretation: print is not seen as an exact reproduction of an oral text but as the representation of some essential elements of the oral text. Consequently, not everything is written. The written text suggests an oral act which can be constructed from the elements indicated in writing. Instead of the mirror image of written language (that is, writing as a mirror image of the oral act, reproducing it in complete detail), children offer a different conception: written language consists of a series of cues regarding the essential elements of the oral message; on the basis of these elements one constructs the message.

All the sentences we use share one constant: the enunciation of two terms and of a relationship between them (for example, "girl" and "candy" linked by the relationship "eat").[1]

In a certain sense, José's interpretation approximates a purely logical representation of the content of the message, something like $R (a, b)$, that is, as a symbolic representation of the terms a, b linked by the relationship R. As a logical representation rather than a phonological or grammatical one, the correspondence between the order of uttering the terms and the order of writing them disappears (or is minimized). $R (a, b)$ or $(a) R (b)$ are conventional variants receiving the same interpretation: a has relationship R with b; or a is in relationship R with respect to b; or there exists a relationship R between a and b.

We will clarify this point further with another example. How do we read a mathematical string of writing? For example, $4 + 2 = 6$ can be read as "four plus two equals six," "four and two are six," "six is the result of adding two and four," "the addition of two and four gives the sum of six," and "four and two, added together, make six." There is an infinite number of possible readings for the same written text. We can begin reading the sentence with the result, one of the terms, or the operation itself without having to modify the written text. (From a pedagogical point of view, it is interesting to note that first grade instruction introduces the writing of a precise relationship, addition, which permits multiple equivalent readings, and the writing of much less precise relationships, such as those expressed by verbs, which permit a single reading.)

In the sentences we use, the words have a pragmatically oriented relationship and their written order does not alter the meaning of the relationship: "girl eat candy," "girl candy eat," and "candy girl eat" always indicate the same actor-object relationship.

One might argue that, if this were true, children would produce continuous readings corresponding to the different possible enunciation orders. But this does not happen. In ordering the meanings attributed to the text, practically any order is possible (both nouns and then the verb; the verb between the two nouns; from left to right or from right to left following the order of the

[1] Authors' Note: This is a pragmatically oriented relationship, since for this pair of terms only one can be conceived of as the agent. In other words, the meaning of the relationship is already given. Later we will see what happens with sentences where the indicated relationship is not pragmatically oriented, or is so oriented to a much lesser degree, as in the case of "the dog chased the cat."

researcher's questions). When we shift to the oral domain the syntactic restrictions come into play. Only at the oral level must one respect the customary order of the utterance (subject-verb-direct complement). This difference between restrictions on the oral text and restrictions attributed to the written text leads us to suppose, once again, that print is seen as representing some of the characteristics of the message (in this case, its logical structure), facilitating the shift to oral expression but not reproducing it in its entirety.

The following are clear-cut cases demonstrating difficulty in conceiving that verbs can be represented independently in writing; that they can have the same autonomy at the representational level as nouns have. This central notion leads to many response variants. A frequent variant is locating both nouns at very distinct places and assigning the verb to another segment but linked inseparably to its direct object complement (in the sentences we use, this means attributing the entire predicate to one text segment). This variant may coexist or alternate with another which tends to segment the sentence into two parts, locating the subject in one and the predicate in the other. (Since the subject in our sentences always consists of just one noun, we cannot distinguish between the subject-predicate interpretation and the "both nouns but one of them accompanying the verb" interpretation.) Consider these examples:

Pablo (6 yrs., MC)

la nena comió un caramelo
(the girl ate a candy)

Where did I write *la nena?*	(Hesitates, then points to *caramelo.*)
Where did I write *caramelo?*	(Points to *la nena.*)
What does it say here? (*comió*)	*Comió un caramelo* (ate a candy).
And here? (*caramelo*)	*La nena* (the girl).
Here? (*comió*)	*Comió caramelo* (ate candy).
Does it say *un* somewhere?	I don't know.
How does it go all together?	*La nena (caramelo) comió un caramelo* (points to the rest from right to left).

Silvana (4 yrs., LC)

la nena come un caramelo
(the girl eats a candy)
(Repeats sentence correctly.)

Does it say *nena* somewhere?	Here, here, and here (points to the first three words).
Does it say *caramelo?*	Here (last two words).
Does it say *come* somewhere?	(Points to *nena.*) Here.
Show me and tell me how it goes.	(Points to text from right to left without speaking.)
How does it go?	*Nena* (girl) and *caramelo* (candy) (without pointing).
Where does it say *nena?*	(Points to *la* and *come.*)
Where does it say *caramelo?*	(Points to *un caramelo.*)

And here? (*nena*)	*Compró el caramelo* (bought the candy).

(The interview is repeated immediately with identical results.)

It would be easy to multiply these examples, because many children adopt this strategy, with any of the sentences. Javier (4 yrs., LC), for ELOSOCOMEMIEL (THEBEAREATSHONEY), places *oso* at the beginning, *miel* at the end, and for the middle says *"está comiendo miel"* (is eating honey).

Another variant consists of uttering the verb during a continuous reading but without pointing, while pointing at each of the nouns (without separating them from the articles, of course). Finally, a further variant consists of locating the verb and the object in the same piece of writing, which, again, means supposing that the verb is not represented in an isolated and independent fashion.

The final two examples show how these variants may be applied alternately by the same child working with the same sentence (reinforcing our hypothesis that they are alternative response modes for the same problem).

Javier (4 yrs., LC)	*la nena come un caramelo* (*the girl eats a candy*) (Repeats sentence correctly, but pointing from right to left.)
Say it and show me again.	*La ne-na* (*caramelo*) *está comiendo* (is eating) (*un compró*) *caramelo* (*nena la*).
Where does it say *la nena*?	(*caramelo*)
Where does it say *caramelo*?	(*un*)
Is *come* written there?	Yes. Over here (points again to *un*).
And here? (*come*)	*La-ne-na* (*la nena come*, one syllable for each word).
But here, just this part (*come*) . . .	*La nena está comiendo caramelo* (the girl is eating candy).
And here? (*nena*)	Here *la nena*. No! Here (*la*), and here *come* (*come*).
And here? (*caramelo*)	*Caramelo* (candy). *La nena está comiendo caramelo* (the girl is eating candy) (points to *un caramelo*).
Say it slowly and show me.	*La nena* (the girl) (*la*) *está co-* (is ea-) (*nena*) *miendo* (ting) (*come*) *caramelo* (candy) (*un caramelo*).
Roxana (4 yrs., LC)	*la nena come un caramelo*

(She begins by placing *nena* in the first segment and *caramelo* in the third but does not know what the rest corresponds to. She is asked to give a continuous reading.)

	La nena (points to *la*, hesitates) . . . *come caramelo* (eats candy) (*come*).

Again.

La nena come caramelo (the girl eats candy). (With a continuous gesture from left to right, but without reaching the end of the text by the time she finishes saying the sentence. So she repeats, with a faster gesture, this time reaching the end of each simultaneously.)

Where does it say *caramelo?*   (*la*)

Where does it say *nena?*   (*nena*)

Does it say *come?*   *Come caramelo* (eats candy).

Where does it say that?   Up to here (points to end of text).

To understand this data one must have in mind:

- Changes in attributions corresponding to changes in directionality (beginning from right to left and then shifting left to right, as Javier does) relate to a different difficulty and should not interfere with interpreting the data we are concerned with here.
- The problem seems to consist of determining how to break up the oral sentence so that it corresponds to the observable breaks in the text. These children believe that both nouns are represented in writing, but they have a very hard time conceiving that the verb is represented separately from the object. (In some cases they also have difficulty conceiving of the verb as separate from the whole sentence.) To have a deeper understanding of the reasons behind this response, we must review other kinds of responses.
- There is a distinction between continuous reading, during which all the words appear and even seem to be located precisely in the text, and answers to questions that require attention to separate parts of the text. What seems to be written in the first case does not seem to be written in the second. We will return to this distinction between what is written and what is said about or relating to what is written.
- With this type of response the attributions are less stable. They may change from one moment to the next, and children may say apparently contradictory things about the same written segment. However, this instability or lack of consistency looks like stability and consistency in comparison to the responses we consider next.

Response Type D   Impossibility of Separating the Utterance into Parts That Can Be Matched to Parts of the Text

We use several indicators to place a response in this category. When the researcher asks where a certain word is written, the

child points in a vague, erratic, and contradictory manner (referring as much to the whole sentence as to various parts, or to pieces
of one part). Also, the child points inconsistently in answering reiterated questions about the same word. Javier (4 yrs., LC), for
example, for PAPÁ PATEA LA PELOTA matches the whole utterance to any part of the text (except *papá*, which he locates separately by pointing to LA; this does not prevent him from locating
it in all the other parts, since the whole sentence is in each of
them). He can also attribute any of the words of the sentence to
any part of the text. And, for Javier, it is all compatible with a
continuous reading similar to that of other children:
"*papá / patea / lape- / lota,*" while pointing, from left to right, to the
four segments of the text.

Another indicator of this type of response consists of completing verbally each of the researcher's questions, an action equivalent to negating that isolated words are written. Examples of this
are abundant:

Gustavo (4 yrs., LC), when asked if *patea* (kicks) is written, responds: "*papá
patea* (Dad kicks); here is *la patea* (kicks it), here it says *patea la pelota* (kicks
the ball)," pointing to the last two letters of PAPÁ.

Atilio (5 yrs., LC)	ELOSOCOMEMIEL (THEBEAREATSHONEY)
Does it say *miel* somewhere?	No.
Does it say *oso* somewhere?	(Points to whole text.)
Does it say *come*?	No.
Does it say *come miel*?	No.
What does it say?	*Oso come miel* (bear eats honey) (ges-tures from right to left over the whole text).

The last indicator, complementary to the previous ones, is that
when the researcher points to one segment and asks what it says,
the child's verbal response is more than one word. The significance of this response type is multiple. In a certain sense, it constitutes what might be called "level zero" for this task. Our questions, which tend to require breaking apart sentences into words,
appear way beyond the capacity of children at this level. The sentence they hear constitutes a unit in several regards: an intonational unit, a syntactic unit, and a unit of meaning. The text, however, contains spaces which permit the distinction of parts. These
children still have no facility for dealing with this particular text
property (segmentation). Because of this, they attempt alternately
to place the entire utterance in just one part or to locate any of
the words in any of the parts, and they deny that a single word
can be written (even a noun). In addition, there is nothing that

leads them to assume that the order of the written parts can be matched to some other order. Because of this they fluctuate between attributed meanings.

Let us consider the positive side of this problem. Concluding that a certain behavior represents a failure serves no purpose unless we attempt to discover the causes of the difficulty. Why is this task so difficult? From listening to these children we are able to pose a new question. The fact that our questions demand a special form of identity had not occurred to us. For adults, it seems obvious that if we start with the sentence "dad kicks the ball," when we ask if "dad" is written there, we are referring necessarily to the same dad of "dad kicks the ball." When we start with the sentence "the girl eats a candy" and we ask if "girl" or "candy" are written there, it is clear to us that we mean the same girl and the same candy that we spoke of before. But is this obvious at all levels of development? The children at this level suggest that for them it is not. "The girl eats a candy" is written but "candy" is not. One is not deduced from the other, because when we isolate an element from the oral message and present it out of context, we change its meaning in some way. "Candy" by itself is probably a label, while "candy" in "the girl eats a candy" is a particular candy in a particular relationship with the girl in question. Basically, when we ask if "candy" is written, we refer to a certain form of writing—our own—which maintains constant the written representation of the word regardless of its relational (and, in turn, meaningful) context. Once again, children have no reason to share with us such a strong and general hypothesis.[1]

Response Type E   The Whole Sentence Is Attributed to One Written Segment; in the Rest of the Text are Other Sentences Congruent to the First

This response category and the following one include the most unexpected responses we have obtained. This E category shares with D the inability to achieve a segmentation of the utterance so that parts of the oral sentence can be matched to parts of the text. But type D is characterized by an always frustrated attempt at segmentation and by the attribution of the whole sentence as much to one as to several parts of the text. In type E the situation is much clearer. The hypothesis these subjects seem to utilize is that the whole sentence is contained in just one segment of the text while the other segments must have similar things, and those things

[1] Authors' Note: We believe that the detailed analysis of this special form of identity can contribute to understanding the psychogenesis of the notion of identity in the child, a problem central to Piagetian theory (Piaget, 1971).

are other sentences semantically close to the sentence read to them. For example:

Ximena (4 yrs., MC) for PAPÁ PATEA LA PELOTA (DAD KICKS THE BALL) proposes the following for each of the segments from left to right:

> *Papá patea la pelota.*
> *Papá grave* (Dad sick).
> *Papá escribe la fecha* (Dad writes the date).
> *Papá se va a dormir* (Dad goes to sleep).

She uses a similar procedure for *la nena compró un caramelo* (*the girl bought a candy*).

Where does it say *caramelo?*	(Points to *la.*)
Where does it say *nena?*	(Points to *nena.*)
Where does it say *compró?*	(Points to *compró.*)
And here? (*un*)	That she's going to bed, and here (*caramelo*) that she's going to play in her room.
How does it go, then?	*La nena va a comprar un caramelo* (the girl is going to buy a candy) (*compró*), she's going to bed (*un*) and to play in her room (*caramelo*).
But where does it say *caramelo?*	Here it says caramelo (*caramelo*). The girl is going to play.

Liliana (5 yrs., LC) for *la nena come un caramelo* (*the girl eats a candy*), initially identifies herself with the subject of the sentence. She thinks it says *"comí caramelo"* (I ate candy) in the first two written parts and proposes *"comí chocolate"* (I ate chocolate) for the three remaining ones. Then, she reformulates her proposal in the following way:

> *Comí caramelo* (for *la nena*).
> *Comí chocolate* (for *come un*).
> *Comí galletita y comí un chupetín* (for *caramelo*) (I ate a cookie and I ate a sucker).

One sees in the examples what we understand to be close or similar semantic field. In Ximena's case semantic identity is assured by the identity of the subject of each of the sentences. In Liliana's case, in addition to subject identity there is also verb identity and the variations involve only the objects of the verb, all taken from the same class (sweets).

One also sees in Ximena's examples that "dad is going to sleep" or "the girl is going to bed" serve to mark the end of a sequence of activities, as if this were a story ("and now my tale's told out"). The behavior of the same girl for *la nena compró un caramelo* (*the girl bought a candy*) illustrates well the purpose served by this kind of response and the conditions under which it appears. Ximena begins by accepting the researcher's questions as valid (in the sense that isolated words can be written) but is limited to establishing the order of the written parts by matching the order of the questions to the order of the parts. However, she changes her strategy when she sees a leftover segment.

Examples like this show, once again, that the problem is always the same: there is a leftover part in the text in terms of the child's expectations, and the various observed responses correspond to more or less successful attempts at wiping out this disturbance. On the other hand, the fact that we do not get this type of response for sentences written without spacing between the words shows that the basic hypothesis of these children is that the sentence constitutes a unit which cannot be represented by a fragmented text.

In some cases in this category, children solve the problem by proposing sentences similar to the model, differing only in the verb. These verbs can be organized as a sequence of actions or as synonyms of the same action. David (5 yrs., LC), for example, works with the sequence "the girl eats a candy, she unwraps it," and, not able to find another link for the chain, he repeats the last one until he gets to the end of the text: "the girl / eats it / here she unwraps it / she eats it / and here . . . does she eat it here? . . . she eats it here" (from left to right, for each segment).

In a similar way, Erik (5 yrs., LC), for *la nena compró un caramelo* (*the girl bought a candy*), works initially with the pair "the girl bought a candy, the girl has candy," and later with the pair "the girl bought candy, the girl eats candy" (attributed in this order to the last two text segments going from right to left), and then proposes "the girl bought herself candy," read twice for the two remaining parts (skipping the segment *la*).

The same Erik works with synonyms of the same action for DAD KICKS THE BALL. Attributing one sentence to each segment from right to left, he proposes the following: "Dad kicks the ball / he's playing / he's kicking the ball / he's playing."

David's and Erik's examples are highly significant. In spite of not achieving a segmentation of the original sentence, they attempt to respect at least two things: the number of text parts (since they propose as many sentences as there are written parts) and the underlying unit of the whole text, expressed by a particular thematic (or semantic) unit. This unit is maintained throughout the reading of the text and is carried out through changes in the verb expressing a sequence of actions (which can be conceptualized as a single action with distinct steps, for example, unwrapping and eating a candy), or through verb changes maintaining synonymous options which do not modify the event referred to.

In some way, then, even the responses which seem to be the

most nonsensical reflect an internal logic, a coherent option which has been thoughtfully developed.

Response Type F Only Nouns Are Represented in the Text; Compatible Nouns May Be Placed in the Leftover Portions of the Text

This response category is the last and, by far, the most original (in the sense of being least expected by an adult). It is also the one that most obliges us to revise our ideas about the beginnings of literacy. Unlike type E, this kind of response is extremely frequent. The following examples are grouped by the text they are responding to:

PAPÁ PATEA LA PELOTA (DAD KICKS THE BALL)

Alejandra (5 yrs., MC)

Where does it say *papá*?	(Points to PATEA LA.) Here, because it's longer.
Where does it say *pelota*?	(Points to PELOTA.)
And here? (indicating PAPÁ)	. . . *Mamá.*
How could you tell?	Because it wasn't written.
And it was missing?	Yes.
If *papá* is there . . .	*Mamá* has to be there.
All together, what does it say?	*Papá, pelota, mamá.*

Gladys (6 yrs., LC), after repeating the sentence correctly several times, although vacillating greatly in placing the words in the text, ends up proposing (from left to right): "*papá / pelota / la cancha* (the field)" (this last being for the last two segments).

Leonardo (5 yrs., LC) repeats the sentence as "*papá tira la pelota*" (dad throws the ball).

Is *papá* written there?	No.
Is *pelota* written there?	No.
Is *tira* written there?	No.
What is written there?	*Papá tira la pelota.*

(The researcher continues trying to obtain a reading for isolated parts, and finally Leonardo proposes (from left to right): "*papá / mamá / tío* (uncle) / *pelota.*"

Alejandro (4 yrs., LC) places the whole sentence in PAPÁ and for the rest proposes from left to right: "*la cancha* (the field) / *los árboles* (the trees) / *y la tierra* (and the dirt ground)."

Atilio (5 yrs., LC) repeats the sentence as "*papá juega a la pelota*" (dad plays ball). He places *pelota* in the last segment and *papá* in the first (correctly), and proposes *patea* (kicks) and *juega* (plays) for the two middle parts. But he immediately corrects himself and shifts to (from left to right): "*papá / pelota / fútbol. . . .*" He hesitates and then proposes, also from left to right part by part: *"papá / futbolista* (football player) / *pelotita* (little ball), *pelota / patio."*

la nena compró un caramelo (the girl bought a candy)

Gladys (6 yrs., LC) proposes from right to left: *"nena / caramelo / almacén, kiosco"* (market, candy stand) but is unable to attribute meaning to the two remaining segments. This does not prevent her from going on to say that the whole thing says *"la nena fué a comprar caramelo"* (the girl went to buy candy).

la nena come un caramelo (the girl eats a candy)

Alejandro (4 yrs., LC) proposes segment by segment from right to left: *"la nena* (the girl) / *chupetín* (sucker) / *caramelo* (candy) / *el nene* (the boy)." He then changes the order of the reading, and when he is asked "say it and show it to me all together" he attributes the following to each part from left to right and identifies himself with the subject of the sentence: *"Alejandro está comiendo* (Alejandro is eating) / *un caramelo* (a candy) / *chupetín* (sucker) / *y mi hermana* (and my sister)."

These responses were not obtained by modifying our interview procedure; we interacted in the same way with these children as with all the others. Furthermore, the first time we obtained responses like these we were as surprised as the reader must be, thinking them to be totally peculiar ideas coming from one individual child. But when many children began to respond in this strange way, we were forced to examine it. We became convinced that these responses provide one of the keys to understanding the very beginnings of literacy and the appreciation of the writing system as an object of knowledge.

To avoid any misinterpretation, we must emphasize the frequency of this kind of behavior. The examples we have presented are to a certain degree "pure cases," that is, cases in which this strategy appears exclusively or predominantly. But traces of it can be seen in many other subjects. For example, in category B where we present the children who think that all the words except the articles are written, we cite Alejandro (6 yrs., MC). This child, for PAPÁ PATEA LA PELOTA, correctly locates both nouns and the verb. His whole problem consists of interpreting the fragment LA. He begins by supposing that "it is part of *pelota*," the "pe" part (that is, a syllabic fragment), but he ends up saying "I bet that's part of something, of some name. . . . That's a part that means the goal," and congruent to this interpretation, the one that most satisfies him, he proposes a rearrangement of the written sentence (PAPÁ PATEA PELOTA LA), in order to read *"papá patea la pelota, al arco"* (dad kicks the ball, to the goal).

A very clear example is that of Ximena (4 yrs., MC) working with *elososcomemiel* (*thebeareatshoney*) (in cursive without spacing). She begins by dividing the text into two parts which seem to correspond to subject and predicate: "here *el oso* (the bear), and here *come miel* (eats honey)." But she immediately reformulates this to *"el oso y la miel que se la comía el oso"* (the bear and the honey the bear was eating), suggesting a shift only in the representation of the two nouns. However, when the researcher asks if it is written all right all together, or if it is necessary to leave blanks like the ones before, Ximena proposes dividing it into three parts and tells the researcher where to separate it. The result is *elosoco me miel*. Looking at this result, she appears perplexed. First she reads it, from left to right as *"el oso* (the bear) / *come* (eats) / *miel* (honey)," but something seems incomprehensible to her until finally she exclaims, "Oh, now I know! There are two bears and the honey."

It is useful to point out that the hypothesis that only nouns are represented can be seen in the cases where new nouns are introduced, but a response can belong to this category even if new nouns are not introduced. At the beginning of this chapter, we gave the example of Facundo (6 yrs., MC) who locates only *papá* and *pelota* in the text and denies that the verb is represented. He, too, is an example of this category of responses.

Until now, we have provisionally characterized these responses as being based on the expectation that only the nouns of the sentence are represented. Now it is useful to ask if children expect to match parts of text with enunciated nouns or with objects referred to. The question is not irrelevant. The first case relates to certain privileged parts of the sentence, the second case to the objects referred to. The question, then, could be translated as "do the children expect certain parts of the oral message—as formal elements—to be represented, or do they only expect the content referred to in the message to be represented, but not in the same linguistic form?"

The detailed analysis of these responses leads us to think that, for these children, written language is a particular way of representing objects or, if one prefers, a particular way of drawing. Seen from this point of view, the apparently wild responses become transparent: Alejandra, in attributing *papá* to the longest piece of writing (since dad is big, he must be represented by something bigger than the rest, just as we would draw him); Atilio, in changing "football" (the sport), not representable as such, to "football player," which is representable; and the same Atilio, in thinking that LA should say "little ball" rather than "ball," due to the smallness of the representation; and all of them in introducing designations for new objects absent from the original utterance but compatible with it, not for purposes of paraphrasing (as "dad plays ball" does) but as background scenery or decorations of the action.

If dad kicks the ball, he must do it somewhere, that is, on the field, and this field would normally be a dirt one for children from a *villa miseria*. Or perhaps dad kicks the ball on a *patio* or toward the goal. If the girl bought a candy she must have bought it at a market or candy stand. If the boy is eating a candy, it would be only fair for his sister to have a sucker. Finally, if dad is there, then mom or other members of the family could also be there.

In all of the cases the responses attempt to complete the scenery or put the scenery together in accordance with the number of written parts present. What is important is that the number of parts is seen as representing, in a most abstract and singular way, a number of other objects. Once again the leftover problem confronts the child: only *papá* and *pelota* should be represented, but there are more written parts, so a whole object is matched to each one. Here there is no recourse to syllabic segmentation or to entire sentences but to a homogeneous whole composed exclusively of objects.

How is it possible to read "dad kicks the ball" from "dad" and "ball"? But if we were to draw this, what would we draw if not these two things? Action cannot be drawn. It can be suggested by the whole picture. Drawing represents an instant in time and action is a development in time. If one draws a dad and a ball in the air, the drawing suggests the reconstruction of an earlier state; if one draws a dad whose foot is near a ball, it suggests a later state. Strictly speaking, the action is not representable in itself. But the drawing has the continual resource of the interpretive component, and from this comes the distance between what is actually represented and what the drawing means.

In the case of written texts, this distance would come between what is written and what the text says or what can be read from it. In this way we can read "the girl went to buy a candy" from "girl / candy / market." If we were to draw these three elements in a certain order, would we not be able to say that we have drawn a girl who went to buy a candy? Think about what children do when they draw a house. They may add a tree, a yard, a flower-pot, a dog going down the walk, but even with all these things it does not stop being the drawing of a house. None of it changes either the basic intention or the designation of the total object. We feel that something very similar happens here. One can continue reading the same sentence, even though one thinks that the market or the candy stand are represented. The original utterance does not have to be modified since the added things are implicit in it and form part of the shared assumptions that make communication possible.

Evidence that children at this age consider labels to be properties of objects (Vygotsky, 1962) supports our idea that written lan-

guage appears as a particular way of representing certain properties of objects (their names). Since names are not analyzed as
words but rather as properties of objects, conceiving written language as a representation of names (of objects) does not prevent
other properties of the same objects from appearing in the representation as well (see chapter 6).

The Child's Point of View: Do You or Do You Not Have to Separate?

The "do you or do you not have to separate" is not meant in a
normative sense. It is the product of a survey we did of our subjects to find out whether, in their opinion, spacing is necessary
when writing a sentence. This matter is rather easy to investigate.
The children watch us write a text in which we omit the spaces
conventionally left between words. We read it and agree on its
meaning. Then we compare it to other pieces of writing and discuss whether we should introduce breaks or segmentation or leave
the text as it is.

We work with the same children who provided us with all the
data presented in this chapter. To facilitate comparison, we use a
sentence similar to the others (transitive verb, subject, and direct
object complement composed of one noun with or without an article). We present the sentence either in cursive or print.

We use the sentence ELOSOCOMEMIEL (conventional spacing
should be EL OSO COME MIEL [THE BEAR EATS HONEY])
and we conduct the interview in the same way with two exceptions: first, we do not ask about the article; second, we ask as soon
as possible the questions specific to this task. These questions are:
"Does it look like it's written okay, all together? Do we need to
correct something? Look at how we wrote before. Which is better?" In some cases when the child does not propose any separation, we ask, "That looks okay to you, right? But what if we had
to leave some spaces like before? If we had to do it, where do you
think we would separate it?" Of course, if the child proposes some
separation, we ask what is written in each part.

From our data, we conclude that writing in this way neither
impedes nor favors the appearance of any of the response categories we have distinguished, with one exception. Attributing the
whole sentence to just one segment and similar sentences to remaining segments is automatically eliminated for obvious reasons.
So is syllabic segmentation, not a particular response category in
itself but a general approach to solving the problem of leftover
pieces. In this case there are no leftover pieces since there is just
one piece.

It is significant that the responses we have characterized as exclusively locating nouns (later analyzed as locating the objects referred to or their names) also appear for this task. This is one more indication that this conception is not an ad hoc solution, appearing or disappearing depending on the nature of the stimulus, but is a very important step in psychogenetic development. Since there is no graphic segmentation, one might think this would favor focusing on the utterance as a whole. But this does not happen. Also absent is the introduction of new nouns, not mentioned in the original sentence. The appearance of other nouns (such as mama, field, players) occurs only when there are leftover parts. The hypothesis that only the labels (or the designated objects) are represented becomes evident when new nouns are introduced, but it can also be noted without them, as we can easily see in the next example. Gustavo provides a particularly clear case, fluctuating between locating the objects referred to and analyzing the sentence but unable to achieve a separation into parts.

Gustavo (4 yrs., LC)

(*elosocomemiel*) (*thebeareatshoney*) (Repeats sentence correctly, pointing from left to right.)

Does it say *miel* somewhere? (Nods, affirmatively, and points to last two letters.)

Couldn't it say *miel* here? (first five letters) — No. *El oso* starts here.

Could it say *miel* here? (middle of text) — No. Because it says *el oso come miel* here.

Where does it say *el oso*? (Points to first three letters.)

Where does it say *miel*? (Points to last two letters.)

Where does it say *come*? . . . *la miel* (completing).

So, *miel* is here? (Shows last two letters.) — Yes, because here it takes out the honey.

And *oso*? — Here (pointing along the whole text from left to right). And here it takes out the honey (the last two letters). Here's the head.

(Covers the last two letters, leaving *elosocomemi*.) What does it say now? — *El oso come la miel* (the bear eats the honey). Here, too (pointing along the whole text, this time from right to left).

And where does it say *miel* now? (Points to first two letters.)

(Covers beginning and end of text, leaving *oso*.) And now? — *El oso come miel* (gestures from right to left over visible part).

(This time leaves visible *emie*.) And now? — *Miel. El oso come la miel* (the bear eats the honey).

This example is instructive for many reasons: first, because the figural references are particularly clear—Gustavo speaks as if the text were an image ("from here it takes out the honey; here's the head"); second, because the whole sentence can be in any of the parts (the procedure of covering part of the text and asking for a reading of the rest is useful for verifying this); third, because it cannot be concluded that Gustavo says just anything, since he rejects suggestions which are contrary to his opinion; fourth and last, because we gain a glimpse into a problem we shall approach later—knowing what kinds of responses are compatible with each other. Gustavo's case shows us that responses characterized by difficulty in separating the sentence into parts and those characterized by locating the referents are not mutually exclusive responses nor do they represent different developmental moments. They are probably two alternate ways of responding, at the same level of conceptual development, to the problem posed. One may focus on the utterance as a linguistic form or on the content of the message in terms of the reality referred to.

Most children find nothing inconvenient about writing without spacing and say that it doesn't matter, that it is okay. When the sentence is presented in cursive, there is a further justification for not leaving blanks. Javier (4 yrs., LC) says that you don't have to separate "because the writing is all together." He is indicating that in cursive writing the letters are joined together. Diego (4 yrs., MC) also says you don't have to separate because it's "for signing," and they all go together. Cursive writing is designated by Diego as "writing for signing." Maximo (5 yrs., MC) emphatically states, "with these you don't separate," meaning with this kind of letter.

In comparing this unconventional writing to the sentences written with conventional spacing, we sometimes get surprising results:

Alejandra (5 yrs., MC) compares THEBEAREATSHONEY to DAD KICKS THE BALL. We ask her if she thinks it is okay and she says no. When we ask if something should be corrected, she responds, "Here I have to put other letters," and she begins filling in letters in the blank spaces of the sentence with the conventional separations.

Laura (5 yrs., LC), making the same comparison, but with *thebeareatshoney* in cursive, states: "These (DAD . . .) have to be separated because they're just letters. These (*the bear* . . .) are for reading and you have to put them all together." Congruent to what she says here, Laura objects to the writing of *"the girl eats a candy"* in cursive and demands that all the fragments of this text be joined together.

When we propose a forced task to some children who reject the idea of segmenting the text (if you had to separate, where?), the results are highly varied: some propose cutting off the paper above and below the text, or at the ends, but in no way consider segmenting the text itself; others propose an arbitrary number of

separations which they are not able to interpret later; others propose separating letter by letter; others, finally and fewest, propose
a division into two parts, placing "bear" in one and "honey" in the
other. Of the fifty-six children we interviewed on this task, only
eleven (two LC and nine MC) indicated that some separation had
to be made.

Six of the eleven propose dividing the text in two (interpreted
in three cases as the representation of both nouns, in one case as
the direct complement separated from the whole sentence, and in
the two remaining cases as subject-predicate). One suggests a division in three parts, locating respectively in each the subject, the
verb, and the object. Another divides it into four parts, but then
is unable to interpret them because he really expects a subject-
predicate correspondence. Another says it must be separated but
does not know where. Only one proposes dividing it into four
parts in the conventional sense (one of three children who already
know how to read, but the only one of these three who demands
this division). The other two, even though they can read, think it
makes no difference if one writes "together or separate": "They're
both the same," says Miguel.

Ximena (4 yrs., MC) whom we referred to in category F is, without a doubt, the most interesting case. As we related previously,
she tells the researcher how to rewrite the sentence in three parts
but then becomes perplexed in trying to interpret the resulting
elosoco me miel. She reads it to herself without understanding: *"el
oso come miel . . . el oso, el oso come miel. . . .* Oh, now I know!
There are two bears and the honey." This response helps us understand the difficulties in moving from dividing a text into two
parts to dividing it into three.

The Reading of a Sentence after Producing a Transformation

In examining the issue of locating the parts of the sentence in the
text, one question we have posed is when are children able to
deduce the result of interchanging two terms in the sentence? To
explore this question, we use a sentence that allows the interchange of the two nouns without causing a marked semantic ab-
normality. We work with the sentence EL PERRO CORRIÓ AL
GATO (THE DOG CHASED THE CAT) in the same way as with
the other sentences (asking for a location of the parts). Then we
shift to writing EL GATO CORRIÓ AL PERRO (THE CAT
CHASED THE DOG). This time, instead of reading the sentence
to the children, we ask them for an "anticipated reading" of the
text. As we transform the written sentence we carefully describe
the changes we are making as well as what we are leaving in its

original place. (Writing beneath the model we say: "I'll leave this here; I'll put this one over here.") After writing the new sentence we ask, "What do you think it says?"

To deduce the possible meaning of the new text, children must use the information given when the first sentence is read to them along with the information given through the transformation. The similarities to the word transformation task we analyze in chapter 6 are striking, but there are also marked differences. When we produce transformations on one written word it is necessary—from a certain level of development—to work through breaking up the word into smaller nonmeaningful units (in general, syllables); but here it is possible to work at the word level, in terms of their linear position within the sentence.

After reviewing the multiple difficulties children face in attributing meaning to segments of a written sentence and finding that only late in development do they assume that the linear order of the text corresponds to the temporal order of the utterance, one might suspect that anticipating the result of this kind of transformation is not an easy task. It would not be surprising to discover that none of our subjects could do this correctly, since, according to any conventional definition, they do not yet know how to read (with few exceptions). However, some subjects are able to reach the correct solution in spite of not knowing how to read.

If we attempt a developmental ordering of the responses (twenty LC and thirty-four MC) we come up with the following categories:

- It says the same thing; the change has nothing to do with the meaning (seven LC responses and four MC). These children take note of the transformation, but, since the original written parts are all still present, they find no reason to suppose that the meaning has changed. "It still says the dog chased the cat," Favio (5 yrs., LC) maintains. The relationship between these responses and those we observe with respect to transformations of the child's own name (chapter 6) is evident. If the letters of the name are there, it says the same thing, even though the order may have changed. In the same way, since the letters of the original sentence are still there, the rest is irrelevant. The observed change does not yet constitute a disturbance to the child's hypotheses.

- It says the same thing, but the reading order must be changed (three LC responses and three MC). The possibility of responding this way is obviously linked to flexibility in the directionality of reading. If the child feels that one can read from right to left as well as from left to right, a possible interpretation of the transformation consists of retaining the meaning (since the letters are the same) but changing the order of reading (since what was at the right was moved to the left, and vice versa). Fernando (4 yrs., MC) says, "If it's turned around, this must turn around," and he repeats the initial sentence, inverting the direction in which he reads.

- It says the same thing and it doesn't (three LC responses and two MC). These children feel that something has changed, but they do not know what. They remain indecisive between the observed similarities (the letters are the same, and so, the meaning must be the same) and the differences they have also observed (the order is not the same and therefore something about the meaning must have changed). Two MC children are able, with some difficulty, to explain themselves:

Maximo (5 yrs.): "It's wrong. It's all turned around. It says the dog chased the cat but it's wrong."

Ximena (4 yrs.): "It says the same, but different things. The same, but with different things."

- It says something else (three LC responses and one MC). In this case, the perception of the differences wins out over the similarities. Roxana (5 yrs., LC) responds: "I don't know. It says something else." She rejects the researcher's suggestion, "Could it say the cat chased the dog?" Two children manage to reconcile, to a minimal degree, change and permanence by keeping the subject of the original sentence. In this way, Jorge (4 yrs., MC) maintains that now it says "the dog ran (*el perro corrió*) and that's all," and Leonardo (5 yrs., LC) thinks that now it says "the dog is in the doghouse."
- Refusal to predict (two LC responses and five MC). In this group we include both the cautious and those who answer "I don't know," because they cannot strike upon a hypothesis to deal with a problem that is beyond them. This is a mixed category that does not represent a developmental progression. However, we present it because, in some cases, the answer "I don't know" precedes the sudden discovery of the correct response in the next category.
- Discovery of the correct response after responding "I don't know" or "it says the same thing" (one LC response and eight MC). In these cases the children begin by refusing to predict or by minimizing the transformation, supposing that it still says the same thing, but later—and generally quite suddenly, as if it were a surprising discovery—they come up with the exact meaning of the inverted sentence. This does not eliminate uncertainty in at least three cases, but in other cases the deductive component appears quite clearly. Marina (5 yrs., MC) makes the discovery in the following way: "I know . . . it says . . . the dog chased the cat and the cat . . . (chased) the dog."

- Immediate deduction (one LC response and eleven MC). The immediate deduction of the result of the transformation appears only in five- and six-year-old children. Their own justification of this deduction is based on the interchange, conceived as writing the same thing but "turned around" (*al revés*):

Martín (6 yrs., MC): "Turned around. It says the cat chased the dog."

María (6 yrs., MC): "Because it's turned around."

Alejandro (6 yrs., MC): "Because here it says the opposite. It has to be the same but turned around."

The time these children need to think about the change is minimal. Some respond before the researcher has finished writing the sentence, and Vanina (6 yrs., MC) responds as soon as the researcher announces what she is going to do, before she has had time to begin writing.

The use of deduction in these cases seems sufficiently evident. None of these children attempt to decipher the text. They do not need to since, as Alejandro says, "it has to be the same but turned around."

Which children are capable of making such admirable immediate deductions? Looking at the kinds of responses they give to the other sentences, we note that they are all at least at the level of assuming that the verb can be represented as an independent element, and that most of them are at the level of assuming that the article can be represented independently as well.

In other words, the ability to deduce the result of the operation carried out on the text seems to reflect the child's level of development in conceptualizing written language. The concept of written text as representing emitted words and of its spatial order—fixed and not fluctuating—as corresponding to the order of the emission are indispensable prerequisites for solving this transformation task. In a parallel sense, the children who think that the new text says the same thing in spite of the transformation are at the most elementary levels of conceptualization when dealing with the other sentences.

Distribution of Responses

By Age Group

Table 4.1 shows the distribution of responses by age group.[1] In quantitative terms, the type A responses—those that suppose that

---

[1] Authors' Note: By response we mean the set of responses given by each child to all of the questions regarding the same sentence. The total number of responses (or sets of responses) analyzed is 228.

Table 4.1. *Distribution of responses by age.*

	A	B	C	D	E	DF	F
4a (Σ = 69)	1 (1.45%)	15 (21.74%)	21 (30.43%)	9 (13.04%)	3 (4.35%)	3 (4.35%)	17 (24.64%)
5a (Σ = 83)	7 (8.43%)	29 (34.94%)	22 (26.51%)	4 (4.82%)	4 (4.82%)	4 (4.82%)	13 (15.66%)
6a (Σ = 76)	10 (13.16%)	23 (30.26%)	12 (15.79%)	16 (21.05%)	——	1 (1.32%)	14 (18.42%)

$D\ E\ F$

4a = 32 (46.38%)
5a = 25 (30.12%)
6a = 31 (40.79%)

the article is written along with the other words of the sentence—are practically nonexistent among the four year olds and, although they increase with age, constitute only 13 percent of the six year olds' responses. This indicates that the vast majority of children who begin school learning at the age of six are not able to accept, immediately, that these elements of language (and probably prepositions and conjunctions as well) have a written representation.

The type A and type B responses together represent the total number of responses that suppose that the verb can be written independently. These go from 23 percent of the four year olds to 43 percent of the five and six year olds. The type C responses diminish with age, obviously, in the sense that they go on to join the ranks of types A and B. Type E—the attribution of the whole sentence to just one segment and of other congruent sentences to the remaining segments—is a relatively rare response, found only among four and five year olds, as are the responses designated DF, that is, those in which the children fluctuate indecisively between F, attributing a noun to each text fragment (with the resulting problem of leftovers), and type D, an attempt at working on a segmentation of the whole sentence (but with neither congruence nor stability in the attributions). The D and F responses go through a curious evolution, which we will attempt to understand through an analysis considering both age and socioeconomic background.

By Socioeconomic Group

Comparing the distribution of responses in the two socioeconomic groups, disregarding the age variable, we note (table 4.2) that the more advanced responses occur more frequently in the MC children: the A and B responses represent almost half of the MC responses (47.71 percent). Inversely, the least advanced responses (types D, E, and F) occur more frequently among LC children, accounting for almost half of the total LC responses (49 percent). The type C responses—characterized by analyzing the sentence without conceiving of the verb as being written independently—appear about as frequently in each group.

Disregarding age in a study concerned with development yields little useful information. Reintroducing the age variable while maintaining the distinction between the social groups leads to several different interpretations. In table 4.2 it is possible to observe the advanced development of the MC children in relation to the LC children. But it is also possible to note marked differences between four and five year olds, reflecting evidence of progress in both groups. There are mixed indications between the five- and

Table 4.2.   *Distribution of responses by age and socioeconomic group.*

	A	B	C	D	E	DF	F
Middle class							
4a ($\Sigma = 38$)	1	11	9	6	3	—	8
	(2.6%)	(28.9%)	(23.7%)	(15.8%)	(7.9%)		(21.1%)
5a ($\Sigma = 41$)	4	17	13	1	—	—	6
	(9.8%)	(41.5%)	(31.7%)	(2.4%)			(14.6%)
6a ($\Sigma = 51$)	8	21	6	9	—	—	7
	(15.7%)	(41.2%)	(11.8%)	(17.6%)			(13.7%)
Total ($\Sigma = 130$)	13	49	28	16	3	—	21
	(10 %)	(37.7%)	(21.5%)	(12.3%)	(2.3%)		(16.1%)

62
(47.7%)

40
(30.8%)

	A	B	C	D	E	DF	F
Lower class							
4a (Σ = 31)	—	4	12	3	—	3	9
		(12.9%)	(38.7%)	(9.7%)		(9.7%)	(29 %)
5a (Σ = 42)	3	12	9	3	4	4	7
	(7.1%)	(28.6%)	(21.4%)	(7.1%)	(9.5%)	(9.5%)	(16.7%)
6a (Σ = 25)	2	2	6	7	—	1	7
	(8 %)	(8 %)	(24 %)	(28 %)		(4 %)	(28 %)
Total (Σ = 98)	5	18	27	13	4	8	23
	(5.1%)	(18.4%)	(27.5%)	(13.3%)	(4.1%)	(8.2%)	(23.5%)

23
(23.5%)

48
(49 %)

23
(23.5%)

six-year-old groups, however, showing progress in some cases and regression in others. For example, although there is an increase, almost double, in type A responses among the MC group, there is also a marked increase in type D responses, while type F remains constant. Between the LC five and six year olds we note very little evidence of progress and a considerable increase in type D and F responses.

One reason for these differences might be the differences in background of the four- and five-year-old groups and the six-year-old group. The four- and five-year-old MC population attended private kindergarten/preschools, while the six year olds attended a public school. Even though all MC subjects were children of independent professionals, at the time we were carrying out this research there was a tendency among parents of this professional category to send their children to private schools. One could suppose, then, that although they belong to the same social group, there might be different expectations or demands of school achievement among these families.

In the LC group, the differences are undoubtedly greater. Given the limited access this population has to kindergarten/preschools, children who are able to attend them comprise a special group. It is evident that there must be differences between first graders who have previously attended kindergarten/preschool and those who have not had this opportunity.

However, it is not our intent to establish quantitative differences between the two chosen reference groups. Nor do we hope to guarantee that our data is representative of the population of Buenos Aires. Our fundamental objective in contrasting the two groups of children is to find out if the same responses appear in both groups or if there are responses specific to each group. In this sense, the data is conclusive: no response type is exclusive to a social group. All the responses are represented in both groups, although with varied frequencies. Even the responses that are, without a doubt, the most primitive (such as type F, the supposition that only the names of objects or personages referred to are represented in writing) are far from being exclusive to the LC group. From four to six years old, they appear in both groups.[1] At the other extreme, the type A responses (which are closest to adult conceptualizations) are not exclusive of the MC group but appear at the same ages, although less frequently, in the LC group (see figure 4.1).

---

[1] Authors' Note: The responses we have designated DF do not constitute a new response type, but rather the subjects' vacillation between the two response types, where neither manner of considering the text prevails.

Figure 4.1. *Distribution of responses according to levels of concep-*
tualization.*

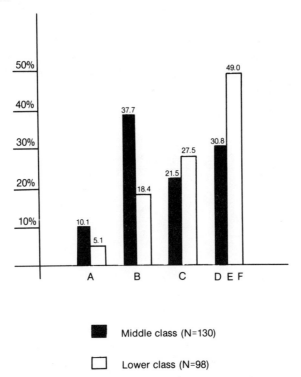

*Author's Note: Response types D, E, and F belong to the same level of con-
ceptualization.

By Subject

Tables 4.1 and 4.2 represent the total responses by age, regardless
of whether they are from the same or from different subjects, but
we must also establish the distribution of responses for each child
in the study. If one subject can present responses ranging from
what we have considered to be the more advanced levels to the
least advanced, our very classification system would be challenged.
If, to the contrary, we find that the responses of each subject are
within limited variability, our idea of levels of conceptualization
would be supported.

We have presented a series of response categories in a certain
order, from those closest to adult conceptions (A) to those furthest

away (D, E, and F). Do the intermediate categories (B and C) constitute, from a psychogenetic point of view, the links that join the two extremes; in other words, must one go through these earlier response types to arrive at type A? Since our study is not longitudinal, that is, we have not followed the same subjects over a period of time, the only thing we can observe is whether for each subject the response range is limited to categories described in our initial classification as being contiguous.

Table 4.3. *Total number of subjects presenting response types D, E, and F exclusively.*

	D	E	F	D/E	D/F	E/F	D/E/F
Middle class							
4a	2				1	1	
5a							
6a	1				3		
Lower class							
4a			1		1		
5a			1			1	1
6a	1		1		3		

Table 4.3 shows the distribution of responses D, E, and F by subject. A total of eighteen children give these three kinds of responses exclusively. The subjects presenting more than one response type are concentrated in the D/F column. These are subjects who give, for example, two type D responses for two different sentences and type F for the other sentences (or, inversely, who begin with type F and shift later to D). Type E is not a stable response type. Not only is it infrequent, but it seems to constitute a highly unstable solution, in the sense that the subjects who give it (three in all) also give type F responses. But there are subjects who maintain type D or type F responses exclusively from one sentence to another.

D and F seem to constitute stable response types; the coexistence of D and F occurs more frequently than the presence of either of these response types alone; D and F responses can coexist in the analysis of the same sentence, which has led us to record separately DF responses. The DF responses indicate that the text analysis form pertaining to type D and the one pertaining to type F are both being used, without creating a new synthesis but with neither having primacy over the other.

These facts suggest the following interpretation: D, E, and F responses are not ordered psychogenetically, but rather they constitute alternatives belonging to the same level of conceptualization about written language. In the conclusions below we indicate what their affinity might be.

If we believe that response types D, E, and F reflect the same level of conceptualization, what happens with the other response types? Figure 4.2 and tables 4.4 and 4.5 show the distribution of the data. The most important result we can abstract from this new data is that only seven subjects, of a total of sixty-eight, give responses that do not conform to the psychogenetic progression hypothesized in our initial classification. In other words, 90 percent

Figure 4.2. *Number of subjects presenting at least three responses from the same category (by percentage).*

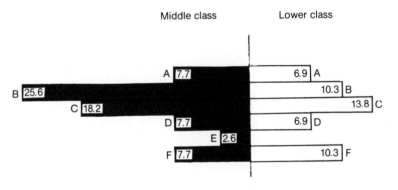

of the subjects give exclusively responses of just one category or of contiguous categories. A subject who gives type B responses may also give type A or type C, but no other kind; in the same way, if a subject gives type C responses, then type A responses are excluded.

This result is extremely important because it strongly supports our basic hypothesis that our initial classification is not simply a way of distinguishing responses without establishing the relational ties between them. It establishes a psychogenetic order which determines the successive levels of conceptualization of written language.

An analysis of the exceptions is useful, because it allows us to reduce the number of exceptions from seven to five. Two MC children (one four and one five year old) present a greater response range, not during the same session but from one session

Table 4.4. *Number of subjects presenting exclusively responses of one type or of contiguous types.*

	A	A/B	B	B/C	C	C and D/F	D/E/F	Others
MC								
4a (Σ=11)	—	1	1	1	1	1	4	2
5a (Σ=12)	—	2	3	4	—	2	—	1
6a (Σ=16)	2	2	4	2	—	1	4	1
LC								
4a (Σ= 9)	—	—	1	—	—	6	2	—
5a (Σ=11)	—	1	—	3	—	2	3	2
6a (Σ= 9)	—	—	—	1	—	2	5	1

Table 4.5. *Number of subjects presenting only responses of one category or of contiguous categories (by percentage).*

	A	A+B	B	B+C	C	C+D/F	D/E/F	Others
Middle class (Σ = 39)	5.1	12.8	20.5	17.9	2.6	10.2	20.5	10.2
Lower class (Σ = 29)	—	3.4	3.4	13.8	—	34.5	34.5	10.3

Total (Σ = 68) —one category = 26.5
          —contiguous
             categories   = 63.2
          —others   = 10.3

to the next. One gives type F responses exclusively in the first session and gives one type B response in the second, with no record of having produced any type C response. The other gives one type D and two type C responses in the first session and one of type B in the second. There is no reason why these children could not have advanced in their conceptualizations in a seven to ten-day period, especially if we have in mind that, although our interview would not have favored one form of analysis over another, some learning might have taken place through having been confronted by conflictive situations.

The true exceptions to our developmental hypothesis probably constitute examples of rapid learning in subjects who are already disposed toward a change in conceptualization. Some of the LC cases especially seem to suggest that it is possible to induce a rapid change in response in certain children simply by confronting them with potentially conflictive situations. So, for example, David (5 yrs.) gives a type E response, a DF, and, finally, two type B responses. Evangelina (6 yrs.) moves from a type C to two type A responses, as if initially she were looking for the satisfactory way to segment the utterance, taking into account the properties of the written text, and was rapidly able to find a solution in accordance with adult conceptualizations.

(Subsequent research studies are permitting us to verify in general the results presented here. Furthermore, the same response categories appear in the analysis of other kinds of sentences.)

General Interpretation

The developmental line emerging from the data presented in this chapter is the following:

- Throughout this evolution—and up to the level closest to adult conceptions—written language is not considered to be a replica of the oral emission, a mirror image of the oral act. To the contrary, a written text provides indications for constructing an oral utterance in accordance with the rules of one's internal grammar. But the text is not considered to reproduce this utterance to the last detail. In short, reading appears to be an act of actual construction.
- At an initial level children expect only the objects and personages referred to (or their names) to be represented. In other words, they expect only the referential content to be represented but not the message itself as a linguistic form. This conception encounters obstacles when applied to the object of knowledge—that is, to the written text in its concrete reality—since the text contains a greater number of parts than person-

ages mentioned. One way to resolve this conflict consists of introducing the names of other objects to match the leftover parts. These new objects form a background scene for the event expressed in the utterance.[1]
- Alternately, and at the same level of development, children may focus on the linguistic form itself but have difficulty conceiving that the oral sentence—syntactic, semantic, and intonational unit—can be broken up to fit the realities of the graphic notation. In fact, they are not able to segment the sentence in any way that can be matched to the actual text segments, and they find no contradiction between locating the whole sentence or just one of its words in any part of the text.
- Forming a bridge between the focus on the referential content of the message and the focus on the linguistic form, we encounter responses, still at the same level of development, that place the entire sentence in one written part and opt for reading other sentences congruent to the first in the remaining parts. We call this a bridge between the previously summarized D and F responses because the sentence appears once more as a unit that cannot be represented in fragmented form, and upon introducing new sentences as part of reading the text, new referents are introduced.
- An important step occurs when children suppose that the verb can also be represented in writing (or, more accurately, that not only the objects but also the relationship between them can be represented). In the sense that the relationship is not representable independently of its terms, the child is not able to conceive that the verb can be represented as an independent element. Out of this come very surprising responses consisting of placing both nouns in distinct parts of the written text and the whole sentence or the whole predicate in the remaining parts. This implies supposing that the nouns are represented twice (once by themselves and again accompanying the verb). However, we do not believe this to be the child's thought at this level. Our hypothesis (highly speculative for the moment but supported by some highly suggestive indications, which future research will confirm or refute) is that the child expects to find neither a phonological nor a semantic-referential representation of the

[1] Authors' Note: We have since corroborated the accuracy of this interpretation in a research study done in French. We use the sentence *maman prepare trois gateaux* (mom makes three cakes), as a nonconflictive sentence, since it has as many written parts as objects referred to. Many children who have difficulty utilizing text segments when the number of segments does not match the number of objects referred to have no trouble handling the segments in this sentence. When asked if *gateau* is written, they respond, for example, *'oui, un, deux, trois gateaux,'* (yes, one, two, three cakes) pointing to three written segments.

utterance, but rather a representation of its logical structure. In other words, after going through a level in which writing is considered to be some form of drawing (differing from drawing only in that what is drawn are the names of the referents and not their figural characteristics) and before coming to suppose that writing represents, although imperfectly, distinctive speech sounds, children go through a level in which the basic assumption is that what is indicated in the text is the particular value of object-variables and of the relationship that links them. Since children know no formal language, they necessarily express the relationship as well as its terms with lexical elements, attributing to the text both the utterance and the implied logical relationships.

- The above level may be a pivotal point between viewing the written text as a representation of referents and viewing it as a representation of the words of an utterance. Or it may be an actual passage through logical relationships, a bridge between the referential and the phonological approaches. It does open the door to a new conception characterized by the following assumption: what we write are the words we pronounce in the order of their emission. However, this assumption does not resolve all problems; it overcomes some only to have new ones appear. The major problem it solves is the written representation of the verb as an independent segment. The new problems that arise relate to the written representation of elements of language that do not, to the thinking of children at this level, constitute words. This is true for articles, and we suppose that it must also be true for conjunctions and perhaps for some prepositions. The notion of word that five- and six-year-old children have is far from the adult notion. Written language continues to be a representation of some of the elements of oral language from which it is possible to reconstruct an oral translation. Only in the oral domain do the specific restrictions of the language system function, and only there do we find articles, which do not need to be represented in writing since the gender of the nouns is indexed under the corresponding lexical entry. (In other words, we do not need a written representation of the article because we already know that a certain noun is masculine and another feminine.)

- Finally, children, still not able to decipher written texts (and, a teacher would surely say, not knowing how to read), manage to locate all the written words correctly, guided by a double assumption: that even elements of language without a specific content (function words) are represented in writing, and that the order of writing has a one-to-one correspondence to the order of emission.

· Throughout this evolution there is a persistent problem which adopts different forms at different levels: how to establish a one-to-one correspondence between the observable parts of the written text and the various segmentations of the utterance. This problem of establishing correspondence between elements considered to·be units is not exclusive to print but is not alien to it either. One-to-one correspondence engenders some of the basic logical structures. Educational psychology in mathematics has come to realize that it has a great deal to do with the psychogenesis of the notion of number. Assuming that it has much bearing on the system of written language seems to require some justification.[1] Our response to this is simple. Comprehending the writing system is a process of knowledge. The individual has a logical structure that serves both as the framework and as the instrument for defining the characteristics of the process. The individual's logic cannot be absent in any learning which takes the form of an appropriation of knowledge.

---

[1] Authors' Note: One must not confuse the kind of correspondence we are discussing here with phoneme-grapheme correspondence, which is only conceived as a particular associational technique that allows an automatic translation and which, in its theoretical base as much as its practical applications, appears totally alien to the complexities of the logical construction of the equivalence between sets.

V READING ACTS

Each day adults perform a series of reading acts in front of children, without explicitly transmitting the meaning of these acts. Adults look for information in print, not only when they read the newspaper or a book but also when they read street signs, the instructions on a medicine bottle, the menu in a restaurant, the TV guide, and so on.

It would be difficult to list all the reading acts children witness from very early ages. Reading directed specifically toward children is included among these everyday acts. What cues do children use for deciding whether someone is reading? Do our research subjects—not yet readers in the traditional sense—need to hear someone read a text out loud to know that they are reading? Is the presence of the voice the only indication of a reading act? Obviously not. Posture, the direction in which the eyes are focused, and the movement of the eyes are also indications of reading. What cues help children know whether an adult, interacting with printed material, is reading?[1]

Adults do not need a specific setting in order to read. They read the paper while seated comfortably in a chair, medical instructions while standing up, street signs while traveling in a vehicle. They read from many different support materials: sales tickets, books, magazines, signs, newspapers, and print on various objects. And they read different kinds of graphics: cursive letters and printed ones of various sizes and colors. They read transmitting or commenting on the information they have obtained and they read silently or even involuntarily. All these forms of reading are different, but, whatever the printed material or the setting, they are all reading acts.

What happens with children? How do they interpret this series of acts, of implicit messages? Children tend to imitate the models of their world even when their function or purpose has not been explicitly transmitted to them. For example, two and three year olds imitate the act of talking on the telephone, using gestures clearly resembling the imitated model. In the same way, children make believe they are reading, reproducing gestures they observe in adults. They look intently at the pictures, hold the book in a certain way, and even relate what they see, using markers (intonational or lexical) clearly indicating the intent of differentiating

---

[1] Authors' Note: We use the terms "printed material" or "support material" for any object which carries print, including books, medicine bottles, food labels, newspapers, billboards, and so on.

this act from other verbal acts. These imitations implicitly take into account a great number of cues and specific actions—including those of holding, looking, and speaking—relevant to the reading act. Also, these acts are not carried out with just any object, only with those that lend themselves to reading activity (such as books with pictures). Children imitate, and in doing so they learn and understand many things because spontaneous imitation is not passive copying but, rather, an attempt to understand the imitated model. Of course, the presence of the model is essential, but for children adults are indirect models since many of their reading acts are not explicit. There is a difference between adults' voluntary acts, when they express the written content to the child (for example, declaring "here, it says . . .") or when they give instructions ("to read you have to learn the letters"), and reading acts that do not have the purpose of teaching but are daily models for children.

Our objective is to understand how children interpret the model, what they recognize to be cues of reading activity, and what objects (printed material) they evaluate as being readable. To define printed material as something one can read one must have discovered its specific function. These objects may have other, nonspecific functions. A newspaper may be used for wrapping, a book for pressing or supporting. When children discover the attribute specific to printed materials they are differentiating in terms of function.

Once we have established a difference between behavioral cues that indicate reading and those that do not, we explore the relationship between written content and different kinds of support material. A journalistic style differs, for example, from a biblical style and from the style of a scientific text. These differences are reflected in the specific characteristics of both content and style.

Written language differs from oral language, both in structure and in value and function. Adults are so used to putting content in its context that before beginning to read they can predict the characteristics of a particular text from external aspects of the print. Is this true for children? Do they establish some relation between the carrier of the print and the written content? Are they capable of predicting the content as they identify the kind of support material? Which cues do they consider in deciding whether an utterance pertains to oral or to written language? In short, to interpret an act of silent reading and predict the written content from its support material, one must have attached some meaning to the gestures readers make. One must also have heard and evaluated texts, relating them to specific kinds of printed material by stylistic cues or content specific to certain print settings.

This is a complex problem, affected by both psychological and social factors. The population for this research consists of middle and lower class children living in an urban setting. Obviously the importance attached to reading activity differs from one social group to another. The amount of written material and number of readers available to children also differs. But even children from the most disadvantaged sectors live in a literate culture (although their parents may be illiterate). A walk down the street will confirm the pervasive presence of print in the environment. Its social value is such that one could not imagine being without it. Because of this we start from the hypothesis that even for children from the poorest urban setting print is a potential object of attention and intellectual reflection. Recognizing that this is one of the most difficult areas to explore and that our experimental situation does not exhaust all aspects of this problem, we believe the presentation of the data we have gathered and our interpretations serve a significant purpose.

The experimental task we use consists of two parts. First, we perform an act of silent reading: holding a newspaper, we read silently, accentuating gestures, position, length of time of focusing on and exploring the text, things which are required in any reading act. The instructions we give are: "Look carefully and tell me what I'm doing." We also ask the children to justify their responses. Next, we leaf through the paper and ask again: "What am I doing now?" Third, we proceed to read out loud with all the formal characteristics of a reading act but with an element of conflict: we use one type of support material while reading the content of another. First, we read the text of a children's story while holding a newspaper. Then, we read a news clipping while holding a book of children's stories. And, finally, while holding the newspaper we read a typically oral dialogue in conversational style. (These three reading examples were not actual reading but they shared all of the formal characteristics of a true reading act.)

The three texts we use are the following:

Story: "Once upon a time, in a faraway land, there lived a very good little girl in a very poor little cottage." (*Había una vez, en un país muy lejano, una niña muy bondadosa, que vivía en una casita muy humilde.*) (Read while holding the newspaper.) This selection uses a stylistic form typical of children's stories.

News clipping: "A violent collision between a public transport vehicle and a passenger car occurred in the vicinity of Station Eleven while numerous passersby looked on in amazement." (*"Prodújose una violenta colisión, en las inmediaciones de la Estación Once, entre un vehículo de transporte colectivo y un automóvil particular, ante el estupor de numerosos transeúntes que circulaban por la zona.*) (Read while holding a book of children's stories.)

The vocabulary and style used in this selection is typical of journalistic writing. (*Prodújose* is a form used frequently to begin newspaper articles in Buenos Aires.)

Oral dialogue: "You know? When I was on my way here, I saw a fire in the factory around the corner over here. It looked like a real mess." (*"Viste, cuando venía para acá, vi un incendio en la fábrica de acá a la vuelta. Se armo un lío bárbaro.*) (Read while holding the newspaper.) ("You know" is a common dialogue marker in English; *viste* is a dialogue marker typical of the Argentinean capital.)

The function children attribute to print is quite relevant to what we are exploring here, but it is an overly vast and complex issue. Because of this, we limit ourselves to children's identification of the reading act and to the relationship they establish between the written content of texts and the support material where they appear. Of course, implicit in this identification and in drawing this relationship is the function of print in general and of the different media (books, newspapers, magazines, and signs, in particular).[1]

Interpretation of Silent Reading

First we will analyze which acts children consider to be reading. The responses can be classified as follows:

Level 1   Reading Cannot Be Conceived as Voiceless
Children at this level judge both silent reading and leafing through the paper as a search that takes place prior to actual reading. In order to read, the action must be accompanied by the voice. Note the following examples:

Javier (4 yrs., LC)
(Silent reading)

What am I doing?	Looking at the newspaper.
And I'm not reading?	You're looking at the letters to see the newspaper and read it.
And in order to read it?	You have to talk.
(Leafs through the paper)	Looking at the letters.
Like before?	Yes.
What was I doing?	You were doing like this (gesture of silent reading) and you couldn't tell what you were saying.
And to read?	You have to talk or say.

[1] Authors' Note: We are currently exploring this problem further in a longitudinal study in Mexico.

Ximena (4 yrs., MC)
(Silent reading)   You're looking at the letters.
Am I reading?   Yes, and looking at the letters and
                                           seeing the pictures.
Was I reading?   No, you have to say something.
(Leafing) And now?   Looking.
And am I reading?   No.
Why?   Because you have to say something.

Erik (5 yrs., LC)
(Silent reading)   Looking.
Looking at what?   The newspaper.
What for?   To read.
And am I reading?   No, you're looking.
And to read?   You have to read.
How could you tell?   Because you're not reading, you're
                                           not saying what happens.
(Leafing) And now?   You're looking.

Alejandra (5 yrs., MC)
(Silent reading)   You're looking.
And am I reading?   No.
Why not?   Because if you read it, you have to
                                           read it out loud.
You can't do it like this?   No.

These examples of LC and MC four and five year olds show that although the cultural factor has some influence, it is not the only determining factor. This does not mean that the frequency of this kind of response does not vary according to age and social class.

Tautological definitions such as "to read . . . you have to read" (Erik) are explained by the inability to conceive of voiceless reading. Silent reading is interpreted as "looking" while there must be "talking or saying" to view an act as reading. Evidently, the activities of talking and looking must go together. But what defines reading for these children? The presence of the newspaper and the gestures of the researcher are necessary but not sufficient cues. The newspaper is printed material viewed as something that can be read, but the act of looking at the text must be accompanied by the voice. The requirement of hearing what is being read together with interpreting silent reading as looking shows that linguistic cues must be present to define the reading act. In addition, leafing through the paper is also interpreted as looking. It is fitting to ask, then, what looking means to four and five year olds. In the examples cited, looking goes with looking at something. "Looking at the newspaper, looking at the letters," declares Javier. "Looking at the letters," Ximena says too. These responses indicate a beginning differentiation between looking (equivalent to looking at something attentively) and glancing casually. Looking attentively is an activity implicit in the reading act, although the action is not considered complete without talking at the same time. This interpretation of the observed act is still a relevant interpretation. The activity of silent reading is not confused with any other activity.

Level 2   Reading Is Done Independently of the Voice; It Is Differentiated from Leafing

Children at this level are able to conceive of an act of silent reading. To read one must look, but looking alone is no longer sufficient. The following examples illustrate this category:

Marisela (4 yrs., MC)
(Silent reading)	You're reading.
How can you tell?	Because you're looking.
And that means?	You're reading.
(Leafing) And now?	You're looking for something.
How could you tell?	Because you were looking.
But, was I reading?	No.

Leonardo (5 yrs., LC)
(Silent reading)	Reading.
How do you know?	Because I saw the letters.
Without talking?	Yes.
And how do you know?	And because you're looking at the pages.
(Leafing)	Looking.
And was I reading?	No, because you're looking somewhere else.

María Eugenia (4 yrs., MC)
(Silent reading)	Reading.
How can you tell?	Because I saw.
What did you see?	That you were reading.
(Leafing)	Turning the pages.
And am I reading?	No.
What do you have to do to read?	Look.

Gerardo (6 yrs., MC)
(Silent reading)	You're reading.
How do you know?	Because you're looking at the newspaper.
(Leafing) And now?	You're looking at the pages to see if you like something.

The children in these four examples accept silent reading and reject leafing as being acts of reading. However, their justifications are not very explicit. Both activities can be interpreted as looking, as in the previous level. The novelty in this second level is that what is evaluated as insufficient is stated as being essential: to read you have to look, as María Eugenia tells us. Once again, the meaning of looking is at issue. The subjects in level 1 accept a certain manner of directing the eyes which includes both reading and leafing. For those in level 2, looking is differentiated between looking with something extra which can only be defined as reading itself and just looking. There exists, then, a progressive differentiation between looking attentively as opposed to glancing casually and looking attentively as opposed to looking to read, although reading is not defined. For these children voiceless reading is possible and different from both talking and leafing. The children cited above may seem to contradict themselves as they explain their interpretations of whether the researcher is reading or not. But there is no confusion in the interpretations of the acts themselves since they appropriately differentiate reading from leafing.

We have pointed out the necessity of people reading in children's presence to provide opportunities for them to observe (and imitate) reading behaviors. The mere presence of models, however, does not explain the knowledge and the hypotheses children develop. Note, for example, the responses of identical twins attending the same first grade class: Carlos asserts, "You're not reading because your mouth is closed," while Rafael says, "Reading . . . because you're reading . . . because my dad reads that way." "How?" the researcher asks. "Without talking," Rafael responds. This is a case of genetic identity and social homogeneity, yet it does not guarantee identical conceptualizations. Middle class children have access to numerous examples of adult readers, but children can refer to this observational experience in justifying their judgments only when they have understood the activity of reading. In level 2 children use personal experience to justify assertions regarding the possibility of reading without talking. The following are examples:

David (5 yrs., LC)
(Silent reading)   You're reading.
How do you know?   Because my dad reads that way, sometimes.

Without talking?   Yes.
(Leafing)   Now you're looking to see where you can read.

Anabela (5 yrs., LC)
(Silent reading)   You're reading.
How can you tell?   Because my mom does like that.
But I wasn't saying anything!   . . .
Is that possible?   Yes.

| (Leafing) And now? | You're turning the pages. |
| Am I reading? | No. |

Marina (5 yrs., MC)

(Silent reading)	Reading.
Why?	Because.
(Leafing)	You're not reading.
What am I doing?	You're turning the pages to find what pages you could read.
(Silent reading)	Reading.
But I'm not saying anything!	I know! But you're reading.
How do you know?	Because my dad's reading and I don't hear anything.

The example of adult readers appears as a justification when children have understood the nature of the act. In summary, this second level is characterized by comprehending silent reading as a form of reading.

Once this understanding has been established, reading acts become more easily definable in themselves, based on specific reasons and techniques such as the necessary amount of time and type of visual exploration. This constitutes a third response level, in which previous interpretations continue but with much more highly elaborated justifications.

Level 3   Silent Reading Acts Are Definable in Themselves

Gestures, the way the eyes are focused, and time and type of visual exploration are cues which delineate silent reading activity. The following is the most eloquent example we have obtained from a six year old.

Vanina (6 yrs., MC)

| (Silent reading) | You're reading. |
| How do you know? | Because you move your eyes, if not you'd be in one place like this (fixed stare). And besides, you look a long time. If you move your eyes fast, you're just looking at the pictures. |

Vanina's justification refers to length of time of eye focus and to a certain kind of visual exploration. She still refers to the activity of looking, but this is much more clearly defined for her: "you look a long time." But her example is not unique. There are others who show a clear understanding of silent reading activity and reject leafing as reading, by reason of the rapidity of the act ("you're going too fast").

In summary, differentiating reading from speaking is an extremely important development in children who are not yet readers in a traditional sense. None of these children 'knows how' to read, but most of them 'know' a great number of specific things about reading activity and what it means.

Interpretation of Oral Reading

This experimental task consists of reading out loud ("pretend" reading) the content of one type of text from the support material of another. We read a children's story from a newspaper, a news clipping from a storybook, and an oral dialogue from a newspaper. The objective of this task is to discover at what point and under what circumstances children can discriminate between oral and written discourse as well as how they differentiate contents that might appear in two types of printed material (storybooks and newspapers). The reading act, in this case, assumes an oral expression of the text. The interview focuses the child's attention on two aspects: the oral or written nature of the discourse and the plausibility of its belonging to a certain type of support material.

The subjects have no reason to question a priori the legitimacy of the reading act. But if their expectations are contradicted, they might come to question what they see by reflecting on what they hear. In this way, they might discover the pretense of the observed act. Our task demands one more step: determining the oral or written nature of the discourse in addition to judging the legitimacy of the observed reading.

The first group of examples introduces us to our detailed analysis of each of the response types.

José Luis (4 yrs., MC)
(Holding the newspaper)
"Once upon a time . . ."   Yes, reading.
Where was I reading?   (Indicates newspaper.)
How could you tell?   Because I saw your face.
What you heard is reading?   Yes.
(Holding storybook) "A violent col-   Reading.
lision . . ."
Where?   (Indicates book.)
Is it written in the book?   Yes.
(Holding newspaper) "You know,   Yes.
when I was coming . . ." Am I
reading?
Here? (newspaper)   Yes.

Roxana (5 yrs., LC)
(Newspaper) "Once upon a   You're reading.
time . . ."
What am I reading?   The letters.

Where was that from, what you heard?	. . .
(Repeats text.) Am I reading?	Yes.
From the newspaper?	Yes.
(Storybook) "A violent collision . . .	You're reading.
What am I reading?	The pictures.
Which pictures?	(Points to pictures in book.)
When you listened to me, what did it make you think?	. . .
What was I doing?	Reading.
Where?	(Indicates book.)
(Newspaper) "You know, when I was coming. . ."	Reading.
What am I reading?	The newspaper.

Andrea (6 yrs., MC)

(Newspaper) "Once upon a time . . ."	Reading.
What?	About a little cottage.
What was I reading?	From the newspaper.
(Storybook) "A violent collision . . ."	Reading.
What am I reading?	The book.
(Repeats text.) Was it from the book?	Yes.
(Newspaper) "You know, when I was coming . . ."	You're reading.
What?	Things from the newspaper.

The form of presenting the reading leads all these children to recognize the true value of this act ("you're reading") and not to express any judgment about the content of the text read to them. The reading acts are interpreted as possible occurrences; their legitimacy is not questioned. Nor do these children make any statements regarding the type of printed material. Any such material is accepted as a prototype text for reading. The reading act seems to be considered so generic that it does not relate to any specific content. This is exemplified when we ask Roxana "what am I reading?" and she answers "the letters." These subjects believe that the given circumstances (presence of printed material, researcher's gestures, intonation) indicate that reading acts are taking place. The potentially conflictive element (the discrepancy between the support material and the content read) is not a conflict for these children. They know they are dealing with a newspaper or a book, but since they do not anticipate the content, the conflict does not appear. For this reason there is no discrepancy between the two judgments we ask for: the legitimacy of the specific support material and the nature of the text read.

To do this task without entering into contradiction, children must differentiate between the judgments to be made: one is the legitimacy of the observed act and the other is the nature of the discourse heard. Denying that a reading act is taking place while confirming the written nature of the discourse presupposes a previous hypothetical action, a reading act previous to the present one. There are two possible paths to this differentiation: one must either predict the content by identifying the possibilities of the support material or discover linguistic cues which facilitate determining the nature of the discourse. In the first case, the disagreement between the prediction and the message heard would cause the reading act to be rejected; this rejection may or may not lead to determining the nature of the message. In the second, the nature of the message is judged first, and as a result the support material is rejected. Only in this way can one accept the written nature of the discourse while rejecting the observed action. This double differentiation is far beyond these children. The observable data is sufficient for them to confirm the reading act.

A first level of response can be characterized in the following way: any act of oral reading is accepted as such, without questioning the nature of the text heard.

Level 1   Impossibility of Predicting the Content of a Message by Identifying the Support Material

Level 1a   Focus on the Formal Properties of the Reading Act
The examples from José Luis, Roxana, and Andrea are obviously at this level. However, we must also relate these responses to those obtained in the silent reading task. It is not surprising that these subjects are also at level 1 in silent reading. This is because the absence of the voice is interpreted as a missing element; without it, reading cannot take place. Inversely, the presence of the voice—given certain circumstances—is taken as a sufficient indication of the reading act. When the condition demanded for the silent reading task—talking or saying something—appears, the action is accepted as reading. At this level the activity of reading is linked to speaking and does not necessarily relate to any specific content. In the examples presented there is one constant: the matter-of-fact acceptance of the reading act.

It is useful to examine the questions we use and to evaluate the identifications we ask children to make. When we ask "am I reading?" we are asking for a response to the act being performed. The affirmative answers at this level respond to the contrast between the oral reading we have produced and the previous silent reading. We also ask "what was that from?" or "where was that from, what you heard?" These questions, in adult thinking, constitute queries regarding the nature or origin of the discourse heard. Do children understand these questions in the same way? Apparently not. To do so they must be able to differentiate between "you're not reading, but it is something to read." Only when they have made this distinction can they answer the question "is it reading?" This questioning rests on the possibility of differentiating support material and written content; it requires a reflection on the relationship between the discourse heard and the object carrying the text. The responses we have presented thus far indicate that our questions are beyond these children's understanding. For them, the presence of the voice, the letters, and the reader's gestures are sufficient evidence to justify their answers.

There are also children, capable of differentiating reading from speech (level 2 of silent reading), who cannot predict the content of a message on identifying the support material. Differentiating reading from speaking is one thing; predicting the content of varying support materials is another. To be able to make such a prediction one must have prior knowledge of what is anticipated, one must be familiar with these different kinds of reading material. This knowledge permits children to move from evaluating the conditions of the situation to considering the content of the conveyed message. If one does not know about the relationship between the graphic material and the written content, any discourse goes with the support material in view. Such objects are considered one of the formal properties of the reading act and not necessarily connected to the content of the discourse.

Level 1b   Beginning Focus on the Thematic Content of the
           Discourse
The initial focus on content relates to the topic being mentioned, regardless of the formal properties of the text. In this level we analyze two kinds of responses, different in appearance but similar in the children's implicit reasoning.

Some children verify what they hear without questioning either the reading act or the support material; they demand the presence of a picture to prove whether what they heard corresponds to the support material in view. The topic of the message transcribed in the text must appear in the picture. The correspondence between text and pictures allows these children to judge the appropriateness of the message they have heard. Their responses characteristically define the content read as being a story while they label the observed act as reading. These children have a prototype reading material: the picture book, which they call "story." The following are examples:

Diego (4 yrs., MC)

(Newspaper) "Once upon a time . . ."	You're telling (*contando*).
What am I telling?	About a little girl.
Was I reading?	I don't know.
Or telling?	Telling.
Where did I get it from?	From the newspaper.
From the newspaper?	No, it's from a story.
How could you tell?	Because there aren't any pictures.
(Storybook) "A violent collision . . ."	Telling.
What am I telling?	About cars.
Where does it come from?	From something from the newspapers.
And does it come from here?	. . . From there.
How is that?	There aren't any cars . . . there are pictures and people are in them (picture).
And was I reading?	You were reading.
Where?	(Indicates book.)
Am I telling you a story?	You're telling this (picture).
Am I telling or reading?	Reading.
Are telling and reading the same?	Reading it is more different from . . . it's more different.
(Repeats text.)	You're reading.
(Newspaper) "You know, when I was coming . . ."	Reading.
What?	The newspaper.

Carolina (5 yrs., MC)

(Newspaper) "Once upon a time . . ."	You're reading a story.
How could you tell?	Because I know how to read stories.
What made you think it was a story?	Because you were reading a story and the pictures from the story.
The pictures, from here?	They're not there.
(Storybook) "A violent collision . . ."	Reading.
Where?	There.
How could you tell?	Because this is a story that has letters.
(Newspaper) "You know, when I was coming . . ."	You're telling a story.
From where?	It's not from there, it's from here (looks for comics).
How do you know?	Because you were looking at the picture.

The possibility of having read from certain printed material is justified a posteriori by a correspondence between the thematic element of the discourse and the picture in the printed text. The judgment is not based on the relationship between the content and the support material. Proof of this is that for the child the news clipping can be read from the book provided a picture supports the thematic content. Diego and Carolina, who fluctuate between "you're telling" and "you're reading," both demand the presence of pictures.

What is curious about this kind of response is that the children pick out, from the discourse they have heard, the thematic content rather than its formal aspects. This thematic content is reduced to the referential content of the message. Diego states that the first text is about "a little girl" and the second is "about cars." This initial form of focusing on the discourse is further evidence of children's criterion regarding what print represents (see "Sentence Reading Task" in chapter 3 and "The Separation of Words in Writing" in chapter 4).

Why is it that these children demand letters and pictures? (They require pictures in the case of the newspaper—or as Carolina does, they look for the comics—and letters in the case of the storybook.) We believe that the fluctuations between "reading" and "telling" can be explained by this requirement. Material containing a written text and pictures can be read, but it can also be told in the sense of relating what appears in the pictures. How do children determine which of the two actions is taking place? Does one imply the other or are they unrelated? The following examples may help clarify this issue.

Machi (5 yrs., MC)

(Newspaper) "Once upon a time . . ."	Reading.
What?	A story.
I have a newspaper	But there are stories here.
In the newspaper?	But you made it up.
I made it up, but was it something to read?	Yes.
What made you think it was from a story?	Because I saw it was about a little girl.
(Storybook) "A violent collision . . ."	Telling a story.
And was I reading?	Yes.
A story?	I don't know.
Was it from a story?	Yes.
(Repeats text.)	Yes.
Am I reading?	Yes.
From where?	From a story.
(Newspaper) "You know, when I was coming . . ."	Yes, you're reading.

What?	A story.
A story!	From here (looks for the pages).

Carolina (5 yrs., MC)

(Newspaper) "Once upon a time . . ."	Reading.
What?	A story.
How could you tell?	Because you're reading.
(Shows her the newspaper.)	(Confused) I don't know.
What am I doing?	Looking . . . reading.
Looking or reading?	Reading . . . both.
(Storybook) "A violent collision . . ."	Reading!
How could you tell?	I could tell.
What?	The story.
(Newspaper) "You know, when I was coming . . ."	You're reading.

At first one is tempted to claim that these children have understood the discourse, but this is not so as they define everything as "story." What does story mean to them? It is not defined by the support material, since there can be stories in newspapers as well as in books, or by the content of the message.

To illustrate the difficulty of defining "story" (*cuento*), we will review the various meanings found in daily language. Story can mean "what is in books," but telling a story can also be synonymous with relating events, or more specifically with imaginative narration. In addition, story is used to label any piece of false information related as if it were true (in the sense of "they told me a sob story" as being synonymous with "they put one over on me"). Perhaps for these children story is a generic term for texts that are read, or more specifically, for texts that adopt a narrative form, and is not linked to any specific support material or content.

The action of "telling" (*contar*) may or may not be interpreted as being synonymous with reading, depending on the context. One can tell a real event as well as tell about a piece of written information. A story (specifically, a children's story) can be told through reading or without reading. The action of telling presupposes that the teller's attention is directed toward a particular topic. In spite of having such broad meanings, telling is not confused with talking since it assumes an intent different from just talking. In any case, we wish to emphasize the ambiguity of the terms story (*cuento*) and telling (*contar*).

Returning to our examples, story seems to be synonymous with narrative, a generic label not referring to any specific content (as "reading" is used in the previous set of examples). The story may be printed in the newspaper or in books and may assume different linguistic forms. It may also have an oral origin. It remains, then, to question whether for these children telling is compatible with reading or is opposed to it. Our hypothesis is that they are compatible but distinct. This distinction can be seen in the children's thinking that the support material must contain letters and pictures. Reading and telling are two actions carried out on these two elements respectively: one reads from the letters and tells about the picture. Diego is quite explicit in this sense when he states that "reading it is more different from" telling. Carolina maintains that a piece of discourse can be read because "it's a story that has letters." Whenever the content presupposes a printed text with letters and pictures, the responses fluctuate between reading and telling: two actions carried out on different parts of the printed material. It is essential to remember that the fluctuations may be due to judgments regarding the observed act. But the observed act is considered legitimate if it meets certain conditions, in this case, that it be carried out on material containing a written text and pictures.

These children's reasoning consists of proposing the presence of pictures and letters as the premise for the action. If one looks at the pictures one is telling, but when there are letters one is reading. We include these responses in level 1b because the story is a prototype for texts read out loud for the majority of the children at this level. In terms of the content, however, only the fundamental thematic element is retained from the discourse. In this sense, any topic may be material for a story. There may be stories about little girls, faraway lands, little cottages, cars, public transport, and even about a fire.

The second response type in this level is characterized by accepting the reading act carried out on the support material in view, without requiring the presence of pictures, focusing primarily on the topic being mentioned. In this sense, they are similar to the ones analyzed previously. The following are examples:

Leonardo (5 yrs., LC)
(Newspaper) "Once upon a time . . ."
What was I doing?
From where?
What was I reading?
From where?
Is it something from the newspaper?
(Storybook) "A violent collision . . ."
From a story?
For children?

There was a little girl . . . who lived in a very poor little cottage.
Reading.
From here (newspaper).
About the house and the little girl.
From here (newspaper).
Yes.

From . . .

Yes.
Yes.

(Repeats text.) What was I doing?   Reading.
What was I reading?   About the stop . . . about the bus.
And that comes from here?   Yes.
(Newspaper) "You know, when I   Uh . . . you know, around the cor-
was coming . . ."   ner over here there was a factory,
                                           there was a real mess.

What was I doing?   Reading.
From where?   From here (newspaper).
That comes from here?   Yes.

José (4 yrs., LC)
(Newspaper) "Once upon a   Reading.
time . . ."
And what was I reading?   From here (newspaper).
(Repeats text.)   About a little girl.
And you can read about that in the   Yes.
newspaper?
(Storybook) "A violent colli-   Reading.
sion . . ."
What was I reading?   About cars.
From here? (book)   Yes.
(Newspaper) "You know, when I   . . .
was coming . . ."
What was I doing?   . . .
Was I reading?   Yes.
What was I reading?   About the factory.
Where?   There (newspaper).

The questions "what was I reading?" and "what was that from?" are understood as "what topic did you hear about?" The answers to these questions, consequently, are "about a girl," "about a car," "about the factory." The reading act is not questioned, and the differences between the varying kinds of discourse are not discovered. These responses are like the previous ones in retaining the topic of the message, but they differ in not requiring a picture relating to the topic or using the generic term "story."

These two kinds of responses correspond generally to the two different social groups. The MC children look for pictures while the LC children respond to the topic itself, not attempting to confirm their judgments with reference to pictures. What does this mean? The most plausible interpretation is that middle class children are more often read to and have more direct contact with books (basically, storybooks). But lower class children do not often have reading acts directed toward them. If they do witness them, it is as passive spectators of what adults read. In addition, lower class people tend to read the newspaper more than anything else. What do lower class children hear relative to print? They hear the commentary made after the reading has taken place, commentaries referring to the topic of what has been read.

In any case, neither of the two groups express reservations regarding the reading situation, and they accept the nature of the varying selections of discourse. These aspects are closely linked together. Specifying the nature of the discourse implies questioning the situation and vice versa.

Level 2   Possibility of Predicting the Content According to a
          Classification of the Support Material

The classification of printed material influences predictions of its content. In fact, we can practically confirm that it determines the interpretation of the discourse. Classifying the type of content each printed material transmits leads the children at this level to identify the discourse they hear according to the established classification. If they expect the newspaper to transmit certain kinds of information, they will judge the message they hear in accordance with their expectations. The children at this level do not pose reservations regarding the reading situation, since their attention is directed toward interpreting the text according to its support material. The value of the reading act is not placed in judgment; the conditions of the situation are accepted.

The predictions rest on previous experience with the different kinds of printed texts. This familiarity allows the message to be anticipated. Familiarity with the kind of support material not only determines the content but also the action to be carried out. The action relating to the newspaper may be defined as reading, while telling may be the action relating to the storybook. Children who use this classification give answers of reading when the newspaper is the support material and answers of telling in reference to a book. These answers are given with no regard for the discourse heard. The actions are judged by a classification of printed texts. The judgments seem to relate to definitions based on function, according to children's criteria. In most cases, the classification at this level relates to the plausible content corresponding to each text carrier. In the newspaper, according to children, one reads "things that happen" or "important things" or "things that are true," while things "that don't happen" or "that are lies" appear in storybooks. Another classification variant is based on whom the support material is directed to. The newspaper is "for grown-ups" and the story "for kids," or "it has pictures."

We will analyze the responses that judge the support material according to plausible written content. The most important fact is that the different support materials are no longer defined simply as "for reading" or "they have letters." At this level, each kind of material imposes restrictions on the content. Here are some examples:

Martín (5 yrs., MC)

(Newspaper) "Once upon a time . . ."	Reading.
What?	A story . . . but you were reading a story in the newspaper . . .
Can that be?	Not really . . . but it might be. Maybe you got it from there (book).
How could you tell?	The words . . . those words are from a story.
What words?	Because newspapers have information but that didn't have information. Because I could tell that wasn't for real . . . so it was from a story.
(Storybook) "A violent collision . . ."	You're reading.
What?	A story.
How could you tell?	It has pictures, and stories don't have true information.
(Repeats text.)	Of course, because if not this would be from a newspaper. If not from a story, what is it from?
What was it about?	About some cars.
And could it be from the newspaper?	It can't be from the newspaper. It's not information about anything, like that the navy is going to war tomorrow.
(Newspaper) "You know, when I was coming . . ."	That's a lie . . . from a story.
Was I reading?	Yes, but from a story. Maybe it's reading from a story.

Carlos (6 yrs., MC)

(Newspaper) "Once upon a time . . ."	You're reading.
Where?	I don't know.
From the newspaper?	No . . . because those things, they never say them in the newspaper.
What things are in the newspaper?	Important things, about sports, soccer, everything.

These responses illustrate the possibility of classifying two kinds of printed texts: newspapers and storybooks. Each form of support material is linked to clearly defined contents. For Martín, the newspaper presents "true information," while the story contains "what is not true." This dichotomy obliges him to polarize the contents without recognizing the truth value of a piece of information (in spite of an initial doubt: "it's not going to be from the newspaper"). For Carlos, on the other hand, the newspaper presents "important things." The most significant aspect of these responses is the prediction of the content based on identifying the text carrier and the resulting deductions: the newspaper has true information, what I heard is not true information, therefore it is not from the newspaper (both Martín and Carlos use this reasoning).

Other children define the content of the newspaper as "everything that happens." In these cases, the orally transmitted discourse is evaluated on criteria of reality. The reasoning, similar to that used in the previous cases, can be described like this: "What I heard happens, therefore you can read it in the newspaper since everything that happens is in the newspaper." Before presenting the examples, we must pose two issues. First, content is predicted more easily for newspapers than it is for books. Perhaps the content of newspapers is more clearly defined (real events, political information, sports), while the content of a book is more difficult to predict. A book can include the same topics as the newspaper, as well as others. This would explain the more advanced responses obtained for the first selection, even in cases where children have less experience with newspapers than they have with storybooks. The second issue refers to the possibility of differentiating oral language from written language in the discourse selections presented. In the examples from levels 1 and 2, none of the responses offer any indication of such differentiation. In our experimental situation this task is extremely difficult because the oral dialogue matches the support material in terms of topic.

Anabela (5 yrs., LC)

(Newspaper) "Once upon a time . . ."	Yes, you're reading.
What?	The newspaper.
What you heard is from the newspaper?	. . .
(Repeats text.)	Um . . . the little girl was very poor.
And that's from the newspaper?	Just that I see it, that there are many little children who are poor.
And can you read about that in the newspaper?	Yes, sometimes you can. Because my mom told me that last night a lady was going along with a little boy and the soldiers shot, aiming at the man and they killed the lady.[1]

[1] Authors' Note: The information Anabela offers, reaffirming the information she heard, refers to a real incident. Offering it as a real incident implies that newspapers transmit real incidents, because we, as well as Anabela and her mother, learned of the incident through the newspapers.

And that comes out in the newspapers?

Yes.

(Storybook) "A violent collision . . ."

Yes, you're reading.

What am I reading?

A story.

Is that from a story?

No.

What is it from?

What I just said, the other one from the newspaper and the other one from TV.

(Repeats text.) And this one?

. . .

(Newspaper) "You know, when I was coming . . ."

Yes, you're reading.

What?

About a mess.

Is it something you can read about in the newspaper?

(Yes.)

Yes, what?

Yes, you can read about it in the newspapers. Everything that happens is in the newspapers.

And so . . .

That's why there's newspapers; if there wasn't people wouldn't know anything.

Laura (5 yrs., LC)

(Newspaper) "Once upon a time . . ."

You were reading.

What was I reading?

A girl lived in a house.

Where did I read it from?

(Indicates newspaper.)

And what is this?

A newspaper.

And you can read about that in the newspapers?

No, it happens and they put it there.

And so?

. . .

Can you read about that in the newspaper?

Yes.

(Storybook) "A violent collision . . ."

You were reading.

What?

I don't remember (tries to remember the text).

What?

About car transport.

What was it from?

. . .

Does someone read stories to you?

No.

(Newspaper) "You know, when I was coming . . ."

Reading.

What?

You know what happened here? There was a fire.

Where did I read it from?

From the newspaper.

These two girls represent examples of a certain type of conceptualization. Both define the newspaper as presenting what happens and both attach to the discourse they hear a status of reality which justifies its inclusion in the newspaper. Although the reasoning is similar to that of Martín and Carlos, Anabela and Laura start from different premises. For Martín it is clear that something is transformed into a news item if it is true. But Anabela uses the criterion of material possibility: if it is a real occurrence, you can read about it in the newspaper. When a topic is interpreted as fact, the legitimacy of its inclusion in the newspaper is accepted as valid. In all of the cases analyzed, the first step is predicting the type of things that go in a particular text. Then, based on these predictions, the reader decides whether to accept or reject a particular type of discourse in that context. Although the conceptualization varies—"important things," "information," "what happens"—the common factor is using criteria to classify the text carriers. In general, there is no reference to stylistic cues, with the exception of Martín's assertion "those words are from a story" referring to "once upon a time," a stereotypic cue, the ritual formula for beginning children's stories.

What is the reason for the differences in valuing manifested by children of different social backgrounds? We will analyze Anabela's and Martín's responses regarding their hypotheses about what newspapers transmit. Anabela (LC) asserts that "everything that happens" is in the newspaper, "that's why there's newspapers, if there wasn't people wouldn't know anything." Because she thinks that what is printed in a newspaper transmits information about a real situation, confirmable through one's own familiarity with the same situation ("I see it, that there are many little children who are poor"), the first text she hears as coming from a newspaper is immediately related to a real situation and becomes material fact. According to Martín (MC), information appearing in a newspaper is "for real" and what appears in a story is not "for real." He judges each text according to these values. What is novel in Martín's response is not only the classification he uses but also the notion that things that are not true can appear in writing. He is beginning to conceive of fiction as a written form.

It is possible that the prototype text carrier for lower class children is the newspaper, to which they make frequent references, while for middle class children it is probably the storybook. Common to all the examples presented to this point is the impossibility of responding to all of the distinctions we ask for. To do this children must differentiate their judgments to evaluate the situation they observe, the content they hear, and the oral or written nature of the discourse. The difficulty of this task is evident. One either thinks in terms of content or in terms of the observed situation, but what is most difficult is evaluating the nature of the discourse, distinguishing it from the experimental situation. The examples we analyze subsequently clarify this point.

Just as the children at this level are able to classify the different kinds of support material, they are also able to classify the action carried out on these different texts. Classifying the action depends on categorizing the support materials and the conditions for using corresponding contents. The more advanced responses at this level find diverse labels for a wide range of actions, resulting in specific, differentiating labels for each of the conflictive reading acts. From this point on, there is conflict due to the discrepancy between the support material and the text read.

Mariano (5 yrs., MC)
(Newspaper) "Once upon a time . . ." — No, you're not reading.
Why? — Because it can't say that in the newspaper.
(Storybook) "A violent collision . . ." — You're reading.
How could you tell? — Because I know.
(Newspaper) "You know, when I was coming . . ." — No, you're not reading.
Why? — Because you're not.
How could you tell? — . . .

María Paula (4 yrs., MC)
(Newspaper) "Once upon a time . . ." — No, that's a story.
Am I reading? — No, because it doesn't say that here.
How is that? — You told a story in the newspaper.
There aren't any stories in the newspaper? — No.
(Storybook) "A violent collision . . ." — Reading.
Where am I reading? — (Indicates book.)
Was I reading from here? — Yes.
What you heard is a story? — Yes.
How could you tell? — Because I saw the cover.
(Repeats text.) What was that about? — I don't remember.
(Newspaper) "You know, when I was coming . . ." — You're reading.
Am I reading? — Yes.
From here? (newspaper) — No . . . you made it up.
And was I reading? — No.

María Isabel (6 yrs., MC)
(Newspaper) "Once upon a time . . ." — Yes, you're reading.
What am I reading? — A story.
From here? '(newspaper) — I don't know because a story couldn't be in the newspaper.
But was I reading? — I don't know what you were doing of the two.

What two?	Telling a story or reading.
(Storybook) "A violent colli-	You're reading.
sion . . ."	
What am I reading?	Stories.
(Repeats text.)	I don't know.
What story was I reading?	A story about traffic.
(Newspaper) "You know, when I	You're reading.
was coming . . ."	
I'm reading?	Yes, but not in the newspaper.
What am I reading?	You're talking to yourself.

Mariano asserts "you're not reading" when the content he hears does not correspond to what he predicts from the support material (in both cases, the newspaper). However, he is still unable to question the action carried out on the storybook. As we have pointed out, it is more difficult to predict the content of a book. In the examples that follow Mariano's, the possibility of differentiating the action is clear. María Paula and María Isabel distinguish between "telling a story," "reading," and "talking to yourself" or "you made it up." The vacillations in the responses ("telling/reading", "reading/you made it up") indicate judgments of how appropriately the text matches the support material. These judgments are expressed through attempts at labeling each of the conflictive reading acts. This response type introduces the next level.

Level 3 Beginning Differentiation between Oral Language and Written Language

Relating kinds of expressions to kinds of support materials or styles of language implies making judgments about specific forms of written language. Describing discourse in terms of its stylistic characteristics constitutes formal description. In this third level, we find children who clearly focus on the discourse while they evaluate the reading acts. In addition, there are indications of overcoming the conflict involved in this situation. Note this example:

Vanina (6 yrs., MC)	
(Newspaper) "Once upon a	A story, that's not the newspaper!
time . . ."	
How is that?	There could be a story in the newspaper.
Where? (Shows newspaper.)	(Looks) . . . No, there aren't any stories.
No? Am I reading?	Yes, you're reading, but you're not reading what it says here (newspaper).

Is it a story?	Yes, a story from a book.
How do you know?	Because grown-ups aren't going to talk about a very good little girl!
(Storybook) "A violent collision . . ."	That's from a newspaper!
How do you know?	Because in a children's story it's not going to say news!
What word made you think it was news?	Because something about a crash is news . . . about Station Eleven and about a vehicle.
(Newspaper) "You know, when I was coming . . ."	That's something people tell each other, it's news, like, I tell you.
Am I reading?	Yes, you could be reading, but you wouldn't say "you know" (*viste*—familiar expression) because that's not your friend (the newspaper).

Overcoming this conflict can lead to reasoned responses (like Vanina's) but also to laughter or astonishment due to finding the situation absurd. Miguel (6 yrs., MC), for example, hearing a story-type discourse from a newspaper, laughs and then exclaims, "No! That's impossible!" He requests empirical evidence: "Let's see, show me the page you read." The responses of both Vanina and Miguel reflect a thorough analysis of the situation. The possibility of making explanatory statements on the content and the style of the discourse is exemplified by Vanina. She shows how it is possible to differentiate between "you're reading" and "you're not reading what it says here." At the same time she determines the nature of each of the texts: written for the story and the news, and oral for the dialogue between people, what they "tell each other." Vanina is not the only one who is able to do this. Six subjects—all MC six year olds—reach this level. The ability to differentiate oral and written language in children who do not know how to read evidences learning through a nonsystematic social experience. It is not surprising, then, that this small group of children have middle class backgrounds. To evaluate the distance between this level and the most elementary responses, we counterpose Erik (level 1) to Vanina (level 3).

Erik (5 yrs., MC)

(Newspaper) "You know, when I was coming . . ."	Yes.
Yes, what?	I saw it.
You saw what?	Nothing.
Is it reading or talking?	From the newspaper or from a story?
What do you think?	. . .
(Repeats text.)	A lady already told me about it.

And how did she find out?   Because she went.
Where?   There, to the fire.

Erik interprets the selection as part of a dialogue (which the researcher initiates and he responds to, having identified himself as the person the dialogue is directed toward) and not as an object one might wonder about. He thinks the dialogue is actually taking place and considers the linguistic elements to be references that cue the concrete situation.

Psycholinguists have studied the processes of both linguistic knowledge and language use (making a distinction between use and knowledge). Within the area of linguistic knowledge there has been special interest surrounding knowledge of written language style. This is an area open to new research. The ability to distinguish written language from oral language is extremely important in beginning reading and writing. In fact, while beginning to learn to read and write, children are faced with expressions exclusive to written language (so exclusive that no one speaks in such a way). Children who arrive at school already prepared for and capable of making this distinction expect to find certain kinds of linguistic structures in printed texts. These, evidently, are the children who are successful at learning to read from the typical reading primers.

VI   THE EVOLUTION OF WRITING

In previous chapters we have analyzed children's conceptions of reading throughout their development, examining how they interpret printed and handwritten texts. Children also produce their own texts. Middle class children, accustomed to using pencils and paper, show definite attempts at writing, differentiated from drawing, beginning with their first "tadpole men" or sometimes earlier (two and a half to three years old).

Initial attempts at writing take two forms: continuous wavy lines (like a string of cursive *m*'s) or a series of small circles or vertical lines. This is the way two and a half or three years olds start writing, and although it reflects only a global similarity to adult writing, the two basic types of writing appear clearly: continuous wavy lines with the continuity of cursive writing; and discontinuous circles and vertical lines with the discontinuity of print.

However, imitating the act of writing is one thing; interpreting the written product is another. When do children begin interpreting their own writing? When does it stop being lines on paper and become a substitute object, a symbolic representation? This can be answered only through detailed longitudinal studies, starting with two or three year olds, a project we are currently undertaking. Although we cannot yet give the results of this research, one point has emerged clearly: the child's own name is tremendously important, at least among middle class children. (Obviously, comparative studies are needed to delineate the impact of environmental influences as opposed to children's conceptualizations.)

When children begin to interpret their own writing, they may include signs representing their own names in their drawings. If they are working with the print model (separate graphic characters), they may use several similar characters that individually as well as together say their name. The hypothesis that what is written are names becomes progressively generalized to later include the names of objects. Liliana Lurçat (1974) relates some examples of her daughter's writing:

At three years, four months, Helene draws two rectangles of different sizes, one representing a large bed and the other, a small bed. Helene makes a sign by each pictured object, commenting: "I marked a big bed, I marked a small bed." The sign is a semicircle proportional to the size of the bed: a large one for the large bed and a small one for the small bed. The sign is poorly distinguished from the object, similar to an ideogram, and indicates a confusion between what is meant by the sign and by the signifier itself. Another example of the dependence of signs on drawing is the following: Helene draws a series of circles representing bonbons; each is accompanied by a sign in the form of a semicircle and the commentary, 'j'ai marqué." The one-to-one correspondence between the object and the sign also illustrates the initial syncretism of drawing and writing (p. 84).

(In French, children prefer the expressions *j'ai marqué* or *j'ai fait des marques* over *écrire*. *Marquer* is both broader and more vague that *écrire*, because it includes the making of other marks, such as numbers, as well as writing.

Lurçat's example introduces our own data, since many of the children we interviewed are at a similar level at the age of four.

How Children Write Before Receiving Aid in School

We explore children's writing in the following ways: (*a*) asking them to write their own name; (*b*) asking them to write the name of a friend or member of their family; (*c*) contrasting drawing situations and writing situations; (*d*) asking them to write words that are traditionally used to begin school learning (*mamá, papá, nene* [boy], *oso* [bear]); (*e*) asking them to try writing other words that they surely would not have been taught (*sapo* [toad], *mapa* [map], *pato* [duck]); (*f*) asking them to write the sentence *mi nena toma sol* (my little girl sits in the sun).[1]

We did not administer these tasks in an established order, but during our exploration with each child we looked for the most appropriate moment to propose each one. Very few children refused to write and, for the most part, their refusals are interpretable within the developmental framework. Several children told us that they did not know how to write. We accepted this but encouraged them to do it "however you think." In this way they would produce a written response. We always had the children read their written texts (immediately after writing them and, when possible, a few minutes later).

The results we obtained from our research population allow us to define five successive levels.[2]

We will refer briefly to the writing of the child's own name within the context of all the writing produced by each child, but we will focus on this issue later, since it requires separate analysis.

---

[1] Translator's Note: *Mi nena toma sol* translates more directly as "my little girl is taking in the sunshine," but "my little girl sits in the sun" is more typical of an English primer.

[2] Authors' Note: The framework is subject to amendments and complements which will be provided by our current research in this area. Our results here surpassed all our expectations, but our research methodology was not adequately devised to get at much of the potentially obtainable information.

Level 1

At this level writing consists of reproducing the typical features of what the child identifies as the basic writing form. When the basic form is print, children create separate graphic characters composed of curved and/or straight lines. When the basic form is cursive, children make graphic characters—closed or open curves—linked together by a wavy line.

The subjective intent of the writer counts more than objective differences in the result for children at this level. All the written strings look very much alike, and yet children consider them as being different, since their intent in producing them was different (they wanted to write one word in one case and another word in another). For these children writing does not function as a vehicle for transmitting information: we can interpret our own writing but not that of others. As Gustavo (4 yrs., LC) explains when we ask him to interpret something we have written, "I don't know, because people know what they write and I knew what I was writing." If we do not know what we have written, we can hardly ask someone else; writing is not interpretable unless we know the writer's intent (see illustrations 1, 2, and 3).

However, we also see attempts at a figurative correspondence between the writing and the object referred to. The same Gustavo gives an example of this. He works with the cursive model; all his written strings are wavy lines which look very much alike. Gustavo has just finished writing *pato* (duck).

Can you write *oso* (bear)?
Will it be longer or shorter? Bigger.
Why? (Gustavo begins to make a similar written string which turns out to be longer than the other, while syllabicating.) *O-so.* See how it comes out bigger?
Yes, but why? Because it's a name that's bigger than a duck.

Clearly "a name that's bigger than a duck" means "the name of an animal bigger than a duck." Another example of this kind of response is from David (5 yrs., LC). Also working with the cursive model, he produces a written string for "my brother goes to school." We then ask him to write *papá.* He tells us, "It's harder because it's longer."

These children expect the written strings for people's names to be proportional to the size (or age) of the person rather than to the length of the name. We can cite several examples of this. The same David thinks that the written representation for *papá* is longer

Illustration 1

Alejandra (5 yrs., MC)

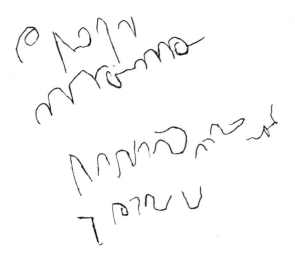

Ximena (4 yrs., MC)

Examples of writing pertaining to level 1

Illustration 2

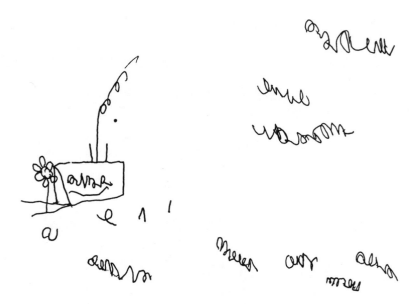

David (5 yrs., LC)

Illustration 3

Débora (4 yrs., LC)

Diego (4 yrs., MC)

Examples of writing pertaining to level 1

than the one for David Bernardo Mendez (his own complete name).[1]

In a totally different context, a girl who has just turned five and is in psychotherapy for a minor affective problem, and who asks her therapist each session to write her name for her, says this time: "Write my name. But you have to make it longer because yesterday was my birthday." In another situation a five-year-old Mexican girl named Veronica writes her nickname Vero, but thinks that when she grows up she will write it with *la be grande* (the big *b*) (that is, Bero). (In Mexico, *v* is called *be chica* [small *b*] and *b* is called *be grande* [big *b*] to distinguish between these two letters which have no phonemic distinction.) Jorge (4 yrs., MC) knows his initials although he does not know how to write his name. He tells us, "the letters of my name is so long . . . longer than my father's name. My father's name has to be longer because he's bigger, and mine is longer" (the intonation indicates that "and mine" means "but mine").

This and other data from diverse situations show a tendency in children to try to reflect in their writing some of the represented object's characteristics. (Lurçat's examples also fall within this category.) Writing represents names, but the carriers of these names have other properties that can be reflected in writing, since the written representation of the name is not yet the representation of a specific sound pattern.

We have found no exceptions to the following rule: the correspondence is established between quantifiable aspects of the object and quantifiable aspects of the written string, not between figural aspects of each. That is, children do not look for letters with certain kinds of angles to write "house," or round letters to write "ball." They do use greater numbers of graphic characters, larger characters, or longer graphic strings if the object is bigger, longer, older, or if a greater number of objects are referred to.

This temporary and nonsystematic search for correspondence between the object referred to and the written representation often occurs with a certain degree of nondistinction between drawing and writing. The following example is from Silvana (4 yrs., LC):

Do you know how to write?	No. I know how to draw: a house, a girl, a sun, a cloud.
(Draws a picture.) Is this drawing or writing?	Drawing.
Write a house.	(Draws a house.)

---

[1] Authors' Note: Throughout the book we keep the children's first names to give an accurate presentation of the data on the writing of children's own names but transform the last names to others with the same number of syllables to maintain anonymity.

What did you write?	A house.
Did you draw or did you write house?	I wrote.
And if you want to draw?	(Points to her picture.)
Is writing the same as drawing?	No.
What did you do on the paper?	I drew.
(Writes something.) Am I writing or drawing?	Writing.
Draw a sun.	(Draws a sun.)
Write sun.	. . . I don't know.
Did you draw or did you write?	I drew it.
Did you write it too?	No.

It appears that difficulty in differentiating writing activities from drawing activities is a momentary, passing thing. Silvana proposes drawing as an alternative to writing. This turns out to be overly problematic for her, but she has no problem identifying the drawing-writing distinction in the adult acts. This is the same issue we deal with in chapter 2 regarding the picture-text distinction in a book. Temporary difficulties in distinguishing where one reads from in a book correspond to temporary difficulties in moving back and forth between writing and drawing. Both produce interpretable graphic characters, but children refer to objects of drawing differently than they refer to objects of writing (even at this level).

Another interesting example of this comes from Edith (4 yrs., LC). She has written various words, working from the cursive model when we ask her to write a sentence:

Can you write "my little girl sits in the sun" (*mi nena toma sol*)?	My little girl sits in the sun? Should I put the sun?
(Repeats instructions.)	A little girl? (Draws a sun.)
What does it say?	It says sun . . . then I'm going to make a little girl.
It says sun or it is the sun?	The sun.
I asked you to write "my little girl sits in the sun."	Like this? (Points to one of the strings she wrote earlier.)
However you think.	(Makes a written string very similar to the others, resembling *mamá* in cursive.)
What does it say?	My little girl sits in the sun.
And what's this? (the sun she drew earlier)	Sun.
Does it say sun?	No, just a sun.

One last example shows even more clearly the difficulty in finding the precise difference between writing and drawing. This comes from Roxana (4 yrs., LC), one of our youngest subjects:

Do you know how to write?	Yes, a little toy (draws a tadpole man figure).
It says little toy or it is a little toy?	It is a little toy.
Write so it says little toy.	(Adds a cursivelike written string beneath picture.)
Now write boy (*nene*)	(Draws a tadpole man as before.) It's a boy.
Now write boy.	(Beneath picture adds a cursivelike string in which curves alternate with wavy lines and which looks like *enene* [not a word].)
Write "my little girl sits in the sun" (*mi nena toma sol*).	(Draws a sun.)
(Repeats instructions.)	(Draws another sun.)
Does that say "my little girl sits in the sun"?	No.
I want you to write so it says "my little girl sits in the sun."	(Above one of the suns adds a cursivelike string composed of curved lines similar to *e*'s and *a*'s.)
Can you write "the little boy eats a lemon drop" (*el nene come un alfajór*)?	(Makes a spiral line that closes over itself.)
What is that?	A lemon drop.
What does it say?	(Adds a cursivelike text that looks like a series of *e*'s.) My little boy eats a lemon drop.
Can you write "stick" (*palo*)?	(Draws five vertical lines.)
What did you write?	Sticks.
And to make it say stick?	(Adds a cursivelike string with lines that look like *e*'s and *n*'s.)

Edith and Roxana both have a way of writing that is quite different from drawing. The question is whether they use drawing as an escape from the difficult task of writing or whether drawing serves a certain function in relation to writing. The data lead us to favor the second interpretation. We saw in chapter 2 that the picture is not totally excluded from what can be read and often functions as a complement to the text. Also, children at initial levels reading texts accompanied by pictures can move back and forth between picture and print with ease (see chapter 3). In a similar way, here drawing supports writing, in terms of ensuring its meaning. The fact that children provide an iconic representation of the object when asked to write seems significant since we do not suggest that they do so. (Our interventions to see whether the children distinguish between drawing and writing tend to encourage writing rather than drawing.) For Roxana, especially, drawing, which always precedes writing, seems to guarantee the meaning of the latter, as if writing alone could not say any specific thing but coupled with a picture can serve to say the picture's name. This coupling leads some children to try to insert the writing into the picture, as David (5 yrs., LC) does:

Do you want to write?	Do I draw?
Is it the same thing?	No. I don't know how to draw pictures.
Then write.	I know how to make a house (draws a house with a tree; adds smoke coming out of the chimney).
What does it say?	Here? Smoke.
It says it or is it drawn there?	It's drawn there.
Do you know how to write "house"?	Let's see if it comes out right . . . here inside . . . (Makes a cursive-like written string inside the house [see illustration 2]. There is a marked similarity between this graphic string and the one which corresponds to the symbolic representation of the smoke.)

One limitation of our interview procedure—which may be partially responsible for the appearance of drawings—is that in asking children to write isolated nouns and then a sentence, we assumed that such things can be written, without previously investigating the child's opinion on this matter. After what we have seen in chapter 4 regarding the possibilities for representing different kinds of words, this appears to be a valid criticism. In current studies we are exploring this issue in depth.

In the examples we have analyzed so far, the writing model is cursive. A total of six children in our sample write this way (three LC four year olds, one LC five year old, one MC five year old, and one MC six year old).

Print can also be the writing model. In this case children produce graphic characters that approximate numbers or letters. Liliana (5 yrs., LC) and Diego (4 yrs., MC) present mixed characters of numbers and letters (including numerous reversals). Simplification and modification of the left-right orientation of characters are the rule. Lurçat also points this out (when Helene's age is four years, one month): "The first letters, although highly modified, are distinct from the hybrids utilized earlier in the imitation of writing. . . . Schematizations are frequent: letters are reduced to their basic elements, stick and circle, stick and two circles, angles, rectangles and triangles appear instead of letters. When the letters are identifiable, reversals in left-right orientation appear."

The reasons for the simultaneous appearance of letters and

numbers have been given in chapter 2. Here and at subsequent levels modifying the spatial orientation of characters cannot be taken as a pathological indication (precursor of dyslexia or dysgraphia) but must be seen as a normal occurrence. In some cases these reversals are voluntary and testimony to children's desire to actively explore difficult-to-assimilate forms. Cynthia (5 yrs., MC), for example, writes all the numbers she knows, once with the conventional orientation and again reversing the right-left or up-down relationships. These are voluntary reversals, some with no apparent cause, others motivated in specific ways. When she reverses the number 2, she tells us that in this way she can make a duck; when she turns a 9 upside down, she explains that in the new position it is a 6.

Whether children write from a cursive or a print model, the linear order of our writing system almost always appears. (Only Diego [4 yrs., MC], in the first interview, utilizes the space on the page in a freer way, without lining up the characters on an imaginary straight line [see illustration 3].)

But only when print is the chosen model do we see evidence of two basic hypotheses children use: the graphic characters are varied and their number is constant. Children at this level seem to work from the hypothesis that a certain number of characters— and always the same number—are needed to write something. Whether this something is one word or an entire sentence matters little. Gustavo and José always write with three graphic characters and Alejandro always with four (all are 4 yrs., LC). A variation in the number of characters does not appear for the word-sentence opposition, but rather for the name-of-a-small-object–name-of-a-big-object opposition.

These three or four graphic characters vary among themselves (at most two similar characters appear in the same string), although when the child is tired, the variation tends to disappear. Diego (4 yrs., MC), for example, uses four or five characters for each string he writes, mixing numbers and letters with several reversals but making sure they are sufficiently varied. At the end of the session, obviously tired, he retains the number but loses the variation: bear (*oso*) is written with a series of five circles, and duck (*pato*), with four backwards 4's.

Finally, at this level the reading of the written strings is always global. The whole-part relationship is far from being analyzable. Each letter stands for the whole.

Level 2
The central hypothesis of this level is that to read different things (that is, attribute different meanings), there must be objective dif-

ferences in the written texts. The most evident graphic progress is that the graphic form of the characters is more defined, more similar to conventional letter forms. The most interesting conceptual occurrence is that children continue working with the hypotheses of a fixed minimum number and a variety of characters necessary for writing something. Some children have a very limited stock of graphic forms and the only way they can comply with the rules is to vary the position of the characters in their linear order. They express differences in meaning through variations in linear order. This is a noteworthy cognitive achievement: they have discovered, in the preoperational stage, the antecedents of a combinatorial system.[1]

Three MC four year olds give impressive examples of this resource (see illustrations 4 and 5). (In presenting this data, we have transcribed the written strings using the conventional characters closest to those produced by the children, without considering reversals.) The following series of written representations, with their corresponding interpretations, is from Marisela:

A	1	I	3	= Marisela
A	3	I	3	= Romero (her last name)
A	3	1		= Silvia (her sister)
A	3	1	I	= Carolina (her mother)
A	1	3	I	= *papá*
A	1	1	C	= bear (*oso*)
A	1	1	3	= dog (*perro*)

Marisela does not exhaust the combinatorial system for two reasons: first, she always starts with the same letter (the *A* is not subject to variations in order and perhaps functions as a symbolic cue for the beginning of a written string); second, she has no method for comparing written strings that are not near each other and so has no way of knowing which of the possible combinations have already been used. There is no question about her intent to use changes in the linear order to express differences in meaning, while she maintains a constant number of characters in a variety of sequences.

Valeria does something similar:

A	r	o	n	= toad (*sapo*)
A	o	r	n	= duck (*pato*)
I	A	o	n	= house (*casa*)
r	A	o	1	= Mom leaves the house (*Mamá sale de casa*).

---

[1] Translator's Note: For discussion of the importance of combinatorial operations in cognitive development, see Piaget and Inhelder, 1969.

Illustration 4

A ^ I{

A{ ^ I
A ^ {|
A{ ^ I
A{ ^ |
A ^ I{   A ^ {I
A I ^ {

Marisela (4 yrs., MC)

Writing sample from level 2

Illustration 5

Romina (4 yrs., MC)

Writing sample from level 2

Finally, Romina may be the one who explores most exhaustively the possibilities for rearranging the linear order with an extremely limited stock of graphic characters. Although she refuses to interpret them afterwards, she proposes the following written strings as being different from each other:

```
R I   O   A
O A   I   R
A R   O   I
O I   R   A
```

Cases like these may indicate a contribution of written language development to the cognitive process. In attempting to solve the problems that writing presents, children face general problems involving classification and serial ordering. Discovering that two different orders of the same elements can produce two different totalities has a tremendous effect on cognitive development in a great variety of cognitive domains.

In the course of this development children may acquire certain stable writing models, certain fixed forms that they are able to reproduce in the absence of the model. One of the most (if not the most) important of these fixed forms is the child's own name. We call them fixed forms, or stable strings, because children at this level tend to reject other writings of their names using the same letters in another order. However, the correspondence between the written representation and the name is still global and nonanalyzable: one whole (the name) is matched to the other whole (the written representation), but the written parts do not yet correspond to parts of the spoken name. Each letter counts as part of the whole but has no worth in itself. (We will see this more clearly when we analyze the responses regarding children's own names.)

The acquisition of these fixed forms is subject to cultural and personal influences: cultural, because MC families tend to offer more frequent opportunities for the learning of these forms (even if all they do is put children's names on their pictures to identify them); and personal, because sometimes an older sibling who has begun school can be a support factor in the absence of other cultural support factors related to writing.

This acquisition (the possibility of reproducing a certain number of stable graphic strings) leads to two opposite kinds of reactions: (*a*) blockage, or (*b*) using the acquired models to generate other written representations.

Blockage seems to respond to the following reasoning: one learns to write by copying the writing of others; writing is not possible in the absence of a model. Eugenia (4 yrs., MC), for example, knows only the initial of her first name ("one that has all the little lines the same," she describes as she makes an *E* with six horizontal parallel lines). But, she tells us, "I know how to write *papá* and Laurita (diminutive for Laura)," and she does so in upper-case printed letters: PAPÁ, LAURA. She refuses to write anything else, with the following argument: "I don't know. Anything my mom doesn't teach me I don't know." (In the second interview Eugenia tells us she knows how to write Ana. She begins writing AM, then she stops and says, "it needs another letter, *A*,[1] to make Ana." She adds one: AAM, but is still not satisfied. Saying "an *R* first," she adds another *M* to get as her final result: MAAM, obviously an attempt at reproducing MAMÁ. (Ana is Eugenia's mother's name. Eugenia, like many other children, believes that both the proper name and the generic name of one's mother can be read from the same written representation.)

Roxana (5 yrs., LC) can write *mamá* in cursive and *papá* in upper-case print but refuses to write anything else with the following justification: "My mom did it like this to learn the things; first she did it all for me and she gave me a paper and I did it all myself," obviously alluding to a situation of copying written models.

Marina (5 yrs., MC) can write her name in upper-case print and *papá* in cursive, but she will not attempt to write other names, although she is quite willing to copy what we write. (She spontaneously copies, backwards from right to left, CAT [GATO] and DOG [PERRO].)

This blockage may be deep rooted (manifesting a strong dependency on the adult and a concurrent insecurity in one's own abilities), or it may be temporary (in a specific situation or for a specific amount of time). Laura (5 yrs., LC) gives us an example of this more temporary blockage. When we ask her what she knows how to write, she answers, "*mamá, papá,* bear (*oso*), Laura. My mom taught me Laura, and *papá,* bear and *mamá* I learned from a little book for starting to read." The different origin of this knowledge is reflected in the difference in letter type: she writes Laura in upper-case print and the rest in cursive (correctly, except that *papá* is written as *popo*). She refuses to write the other words we propose because "that's not in my book." It is interesting to note that Laura, in the task of reading words with pictures (chapter 3), affirms that the text *toy* (*juguete*) in cursive, paired with the picture of a teddy bear, says "bear" (*oso*). When asked if she knows how to write bear, she answers "I know how to write it a different way," and writes it correctly in cursive. In the second writing interview, we manage to break through Laura's blockage. Utilizing

---

[1] Translator's Note: The capital letter indicates that the child is using the letter name.

letters she knows to generate a new written string, she writes *atoao* in cursive to represent "my little girl sits in the sun" (*mi nena toma sol*) (see illustration 6).

Using known models to generate new written representations shares the basic characteristics of the preceding level: fixed quantity and variety of graphic characters. It differs from the preceding level only in that the letters are easily identifiable (with rare exceptions) and the stock of graphic characters is greater. For example:

Mario (5 yrs., MC) can write correctly his name, *papá*, and *mamá* in uppercase print. He maintains a constant number of four graphic characters for his written representations:

OMOP = bear (*oso*)
MOPB = boy (*nene*)
OMPB = toad (*sapo*)
OPBI = my little girl sits in the sun (*mi nena toma sol*)

Rafael (6 yrs., MC) can write his name correctly in upper-case print, but he also knows other letters, and proposes:
SAIFAR = *papá*
MRAFRS = boy (*nene*)
He maintains a constant number of six letters, the number of letters in his name.

Martín (5 yrs., MC; see illustration 7) knows how to write in upper-case print his name, *papá* (written from right to left), and *mamá* (written as MIMÍ, due to typical confusions between vowels, seen as mutually substitutable in forming a whole, and due also to the different ways in which this name can be written, for example, MAMÁ, MAMÍ). From these models Martín produces the following, conserving a fixed number of four or five characters:
MINMA = toad (*sapo*)
MIMIT = duck (*pato*)
OTIM = bear (*oso*)
O TMN = rabbit (*conejo*)
MILTE = my little girl sits in the sun (*mi nena toma sol*)

Gustavo (5 yrs., MC) can write his name in upper-case print, *papá*, also in upper-case print but in altered order (APAP), and *mamá* with a mixture of cursive and print. Using the print model, he produces:
GAELF = toad (*sapo*) (read as "*sa-po*" but without correspondence between parts)
GEVAO = duck (*pato*) (read "*pa-to*" as above)
MNEO = cat (*gato*) (read "*ga-to*" as above)
RLEO = bear (*oso*) (He first writes RLE, looks at the result and objects, "with three letters it doesn't say anything," and adds O; read "*o-so*" as above.)
AOVE = my little girl sits in the sun (*mi nena toma sol*) (He first writes AOV and then adds the *E* as above. In the *A* it says *mi nena*

Illustration 7

Martin (5 yrs., MC)

Level 2

and in the *E* it says *sol,* with no correspondence for the middle letters.)

This last example leads us to an imposing interpretation. Until now we have seen that in writing, children try to comply with two requirements they consider essential: a minimum number of graphic characters (never less than three) and variation of these characters. These are the same basic requirements children have for deciding whether something that has been written can or cannot be read (see "Formal Characteristics a Text Must Possess for Reading to Occur" in chapter 2). There, too, they require a minimum of three graphic characters and variation among them. Reencountering these demands in children's own writing reinforces their significance. (Gustavo tells us, "with three letters it doesn't say anything," a statement repeated many times in the card classification task presented in chapter 2.) Finding this requirement in very diverse contexts is an extremely important indication of its strength, since it is strictly internal, that is, an outcome of children's ideas about writing (no adult taught them that words such as in/on/of/a/an/is [Spanish equivalents: *en/de/el/la/a/y/es*] are not readable).

Acquiring certain stable strings that can serve as models for other written representations appears more frequently in MC than in LC children because of cultural influences and cultural patterns children incorporate in the preschool period. Also, in general there is a marked dominance of upper-case print over cursive in children's writing at this level. This dominance occurs in two senses: first, because stable strings in upper-case print largely precede cursive strings, clearly indicating the extrascholastic origin of this knowledge (we remind the reader that cursive is used from the beginning in school instruction in Argentina); and second, because the quality of writing on the whole is superior in print (in terms of similarity to the produced model). Lurçat also observes this in her daughter and indicates that at four and a half she can correctly copy several words in print, but the same words copied in cursive "are rapidly deteriorated." Lurçat concludes: "the primacy of the print model appears clear" (p. 90).

Level 3
This level is characterized by an attempt at assigning a sound value to each of the letters that compose a piece of writing. In this attempt, children go through a period of great developmental significance: each letter stands for one syllable. We call this the syllabic hypothesis. With this hypothesis children take a qualitative leap forward in relation to the preceding levels.

The qualitative change consists of (*a*) overcoming the global correspondence between the written string and the oral expression and progressing to a correspondence between parts of the text (individual letters) and parts of the utterance (syllables), and (b) working clearly for the first time with the hypothesis that writing represents sound segments of speech.

The syllabic hypothesis can appear with graphic characters that do not resemble conventional letter forms as well as with well-differentiated characters. In the latter case, the letters may or may not be assigned stable sound values.

It is surprising that the syllabic hypothesis can appear without sufficiently differentiated graphic characters, but we found at least one true case. Erik (5 yrs., LC) uses only circular forms, closed or open, to which he occasionally adds a vertical line (producing something like a *p*). Working with these separate forms, he writes two characters for *sapo* (read syllabically as *"sa-po,"* while he points, clearly matching one syllable to each letter). He also writes two characters for *oso* (read *"o-so"* matching syllables to letters as before). But he writes three characters for *patito* (read *"pa-ti-to,"* with the same method of correspondence). (See illustration 8.)

An example of using the syllabic hypothesis with differentiated graphic characters but without stable sound values comes from Javier (4 yrs., LC): AO is *"sa-po"* and PA is *"o-so."* (See illustration 9.) The writing of *sapo* as AO could suggest a syllabic writing based on a stable vowel correspondence, but looking at Javier's written texts on the whole, we find no other traces of this. (The *A* appears frequently and assumes a wide range of sound values.)

To the contrary, there are other cases (all from MC six year olds) where the same written string (AO for *sapo*) takes on other meanings, due to stabilization of sound values for some letters, particularly the vowels. Facundo, who can correctly write his own name, writes *palo* as AO. He writes another *A* to begin *mapa* but is unable to finish due to the insurmountable conflict he faces: he cannot add another *A* because the result would be AA which he must reject due to the criterion of variation of characters. He cannot use a *P* for the second syllable "pa" because it is *la pe* (the name of the letter in Spanish) and he needs *la pa*.

Juan proposes AO for *palo* and later writes AO again for *sapo*. The identical representations do not disturb him since the *A* in the first case is "pa" and in the second it is "sa"; the *O* in the first case is "lo" and in the second it is "po." He uses this same syllabic analysis to write the sentence *mi nena toma sol,* resulting in IEMAD. (For Juan, *M* is *n* and functions here as the representation of the syllable "na." The only syllable not represented is "to.")

Mariano also writes *sapo* as AO, but writes *palo* as PO. He does a complete syllabic analysis of the sentence *mi nena toma sol* and writes IEAOAO (see illustration 10).

In these examples the vowels have stable and conventional written representations. However, the representations can stand for any syllable in which these vowels appear. Our data are insufficient to answer the equivalent question for consonants.

These four six-year-old MC children use the syllabic hypothesis to write the words we propose to them, in spite of the fact that they know how to write their own name and other words (like *mamá* and *papá*). One may ask how such a thing can occur. This truly appears to be a case of potential conflict between distinct notions that lead to contradictory results: on one hand, the fixed strings, provided by the environment and learned with a global correspondence between the name and the written string; on the other, a hypothesis constructed by children themselves in their attempt to move from global correspondence to one-to-one correspondence, which leads them to assign a syllabic value to each letter. As we will see with the writing of children's own names, the coexistence of fixed forms along with the syllabic hypothesis is a source of multiple conflicts. These conflicts are of the greatest importance in the subsequent developmental process.

When children begin to work with the syllabic hypothesis, two important characteristics of earlier writing may disappear temporarily: the demands for variation and minimum quantity of characters. It is possible to see identical characters appear (when there is not yet a stable sound value for each one) when children are too busy trying to produce a syllabification of the word and are unable to attend simultaneously to both requirements. Once the syllabic hypothesis has been well established, however, the variation requirement reappears. (Consider, for example, Erik's writing, and the case in which Facundo avoids writing AA as the representation of *mapa*.)

The problem of the conflict between minimum quantity of characters and the syllabic hypothesis is even more interesting in view of its consequences. Working with the syllabic hypothesis, children are obliged to write two-syllable words with only two characters (which is often fewer than the minimum amount they deem necessary). The problem is even more difficult with one-syllable nouns (infrequent in Spanish, although *sol* [sun] and *sal* [salt] are examples of words used commonly in initial instruction).

The clearest example of this conflict we have encountered comes from a five-year-old boy interviewed in Mexico. He draws a car and we ask him to write car (*carro*). The boy writes four letters: AEIO. We ask him to read what he has written and he says "*ca-rro*," pointing only to AE. We ask him about the remaining part; he hesitates and then says "*mo-tor*" pointing to IO. (In his picture the car's motor is transparently visible and most of his attention was dedicated to that part while drawing.) This illustrates a cognitive conflict: by virtue of the demand for a minimum number of characters (four for this child), he produces a certain result; by virtue of the syllabic hypothesis he uses when reading, he encounters a surplus which must be interpreted since it cannot be eliminated (there would be only two letters left and "you can't read" with two letters). In attempting to interpret the leftover part, this child uses a behavior we characterize in chapter 4 as a type F response: when children at this level find a leftover in the text, they work with the hypothesis that the leftover contains the names of other objects congruent to the total meaning. We have seen, for the sentence "dad kicks the ball," interpretations including things like "field," "players," "goal." Here we see "motor," an inherent part of the object, something that goes with the car, something we allude to implicitly when we use the name "car."

When children begin to use letters with a fixed sound value, the conflict between the syllabic hypothesis and minimum quantity takes on new characteristics. Isabel (6 yrs., MC) resolves it in a most original way, sticking in the letter *U* as a sort of dummy element, without giving it any sound value:

AUO = *pato*

IEAOAUO = *mi nena toma sol* (She carries out an exact syllabic correspondence with the vowels; when she gets to *sol*, instead of writing just *O*, she writes *UO*.)

TUE = *mate* (She accompanies this writing with the verbalizations: "I don't know how to make the *T*. Oh, yeah! [writes *T*]. My mom puts this letter to make *tia* [aunt] for the telephone [directory]. Now you have to put *U* (writes *U*). Now it's missing the *E* (writes *E*.)"

Before moving on to the next level we must stress three important points:

- In recognizing individual letters (see chapter 2), one of the first stable ways of identifying consonants is to assign them a syllabic value in accordance with the name they belong to (for example, *G* is "gu" for Gustavo, *F* is "fe" for Felisa). This can obviously occur with vowels as well, but we cannot test the syllabic hypothesis here since vowel names constitute syllables in themselves. In this chapter, to the contrary, we have seen that *A* can represent "pa," "ma," or "sa," in accordance with the name one wishes to write.
- The syllabic hypothesis is an original construction of children and cannot be attributed to adult transmission. Not only can it coexist with stable strings learned globally (Isabel, for example, can write MARÍA, PAULO, MAMÁ, and PAPÁ, but utilizes the syllabic hypothesis for all other writing), but also it can appear

in children who are not yet writing letters in the conventional sense (as with Erik).

• In moving from writing nouns to writing sentences, children may continue to use the syllabic hypothesis (as in the cases of Isabel, Mariano, and Juan), or they may move to another kind of analysis, but still look for the smaller units that make up the whole they wish to represent in writing. In other words, the linguistic analysis of the utterance depends on the initial categorization: analyzing a word, they work with its immediate constituents (syllables); analyzing a sentence they work with its immediate constitutents (subject/predicate or subject/verb/complement).

Erik (5 yrs., LC; see illustration 8), who systematically produces as many circular characters as syllables for names, writes something like OOC for *mi nena / toma / sol*.

Atilio (5 yrs., LC) writes ooo for *mi nena toma sol* and something like P65 (with the 5 rotated 90 degrees to the right) for *el sapo* (the toad) / *mira* (looks at) / *la flor* (the flower).

Javier (4 yrs., LC; see illustration 9) consistently uses two letters for two-syllable names and he also uses two for sentences, because he breaks them down into subject/predicate. He writes OA for *mi nena / tomando sol* (my little girl / sitting in the sun) and OW (the *W* is really an inverted 3) for *los nenes juegan con la pelota* (the boys play with the ball). He reads this last sentence in the following way: "the boys (*O*) / play (does not point to anything) / with the ball (*W*)."

Level 4

This level marks the passage from the syllabic to the alphabetic hypothesis. In this fundamental evolutionary moment, the child abandons the syllabic hypothesis and discovers the need for an analysis that goes beyond the syllable, a result of the conflict between the syllabic hypothesis and the minimum quantity of graphic characters (strictly internal demands, in the sense of being original hypotheses of the child) and the conflict between graphic strings provided by the environment and the reading of these strings according to the syllabic hypothesis (a conflict between an internal requirement and a reality external to the child).

The conflict between the syllabic hypothesis and fixed strings received from the environment can be seen more clearly in the case of children's own names. It is necessary to present here some of the data from our discussion in the following section ("The Child's Own Name") to demonstrate the importance of this conflict. María Paula (4 yrs., MC) provides us an excellent example. Trying to compose her name with movable letters she produces the following sequence, with just one intervention from the researcher:

She places an *M* and a *P,* well apart from each other, and says "*P,*[1] goes in Ma-rí-a- Pa, Paula." Referring to the *M* she adds, "María, *I,* I need an *I.*"

She places *A* and *I* next to the *M* to get: MAI P. The researcher shows her an *R* and asks her if it goes in her name. "*R?* Yes. Ma-rí-a-Pa-u-la. I don't know . . . it doesn't go. Don't you see? María Paula."

She looks for an *L* and adds it: MAI PL. She reads each of the letters in the following way: "Ma (M) rí (A) I (I), Paula (P), *l*[2] (L)."

She continues reflecting to herself, "pau . . .*A,* pau . . .*U* . . . María Paula. . . ." She adds a *U* and moves the *L:* MAI LPU.

She reflects upon this last configuration, moves the *L* again and introduces another *A:* MAIL PAU.

She reflects again and says, syllabicating in correspondence with each letter: "Ma (M) rí (A) a (I), this *L* doesn't go here."

She moves the *L* and the second *A* and reads:

MA I A P U L "ma/rí/a pa/u/la . . .*A,* it needs an *A.*"

But instead of putting in another *A,* she removes one from the first name and reads:

M I A "ma/rí/a . . . No!" She corrects:
M A I A "*m*/a/rí/a."

She hesitates for some time, vacillating between a syllabic or a phonetic interpretation of the first two letters. She removes and replaces the *A* immediately following the *M* several times. When three letters are there, she has as many letters as syllables, but the visual image of the name is not accounted for, since she knows that MA are the first two letters. When she puts the *A* back in she has two alternatives for reading the result, both unsatisfactory to her: either she must use two letters for the first syllable and only one for the remaining syllables or produce a reading which starts out phonetic and ends up syllabic—"*m*/a/rí/a."

She finds a compromise solution:

M M A I A P U L "ma/*m*/a/rí/a Pa/u/*l* . . . *l*-a."

This does not turn out to be a satisfactory solution either, and she goes back to MAIA PUL, feeling that María is written correctly but Paula is missing something.

The following is the sequence of written strings María Paula produces in writing her name:

M	P	"*P,* goes in Ma/rí/a/pa, Paula"
		"María, *I,* I need an *I*
MAI	P	
MAI	PL	"Ma/rí/I; Paula, *l*

[1] Translator's Note: It will be useful to remember here that a capital letter in the child's dialogue indicates use of the letter name.

[2] Translator's Note: The letter in lower-case italics in the child's dialogue indicates that the child is sounding it rather than saying its name.

MAI	LPU	
MAIL	PAU	"Ma/rí/a; this *L* doesn't go here
MAIA	PUL	"Ma/rí/a/Pa/u/la . . . *A*, it needs an *A*
MIA	PUL	"Ma/rí/a . . . No!"
MAIA	PUL	"*m*/a/rí/a"
MMAIA	PUL	"Ma/*m*/a/rí/a Pa/u/*l* . . . *l*-a"
MAIA	PUL	

We have presented in detail, although summarized, the long sequence of this child's attempts at writing her name because it illustrates quite comprehensively the number of notions she laboriously tries to coordinate: there is an underlying syllabic hypothesis that demands as many letters as syllables (because of this "María" moves with such difficulty from three to four letters; "Paula" never surpasses three letters, and only reaches three due to separation of the two vowels in the first syllable). The syllabic hypothesis conflicts with the sound value attributed to the letters when MAI is the written representation for "María," since the syllable "ri" is read for *A* and the syllable "a" is read for *I*. This contradiction is resolved with the written string MIA. But MAI is closer to the visual image of the name than MIA, due to the stronger weight of the first two letters. The long period of doubting between MAIA and MIA has a brief moment of resolution when she tries MMAIA, which has the advantage of separating the two potential values of *M* ("ma" and "mm"), but the disadvantage of moving away from the visual image of the name which does not include two initial *M*'s. (We point out in passing that for María Paula, *M* is also "eme," just as *P* is "pe" and *L* is "ele," but her knowledge of the names of these letters does not conflict with her using them syllabically or alphabetically.)

The conflict between the syllabic hypothesis and the demand for minimum quantity of characters becomes more evident when children attempt to write names for which they have no stable visual image:

Pablo (6 yrs., MC), who works basically with the syllabic hypothesis, manages to write *mesa* (table) as EZA.

Gerardo (6 yrs., MC), in transition between the syllabic hypothesis and alphabetic writing produces:
MCA = *mesa* (table)
MAP = *mapa* (map)
PAL = *palo* (stick)

Carlos (6 yrs., MC), at the same transitional point as Gerardo, writes:
PAO = *palo*
SANA = *Susana*—rewritten later as SUANA
SAB = *sábado* (Saturday)—rewritten later as SABDO

When we shift from writing names to writing sentences, the alteration of the syllabic or phonetic value of different letters becomes evident:

Carlos writes *pato* (duck) the same way he writes *palo*:
   PAO   OMSO = *el pato / toma sol* (the duck sits in the sun)

Gerardo also utilizes space to separate the sentence into subject and predicate:
   MINENA TOMCSO = *mi nena / toma sol* (TO was provided by the researcher, in response to Gerardo's question, "which one is 'to' (*la to*)?" meaning, "how do you make the letter 'to.' "[1]

Martín (6 yrs., MC) writes *pato* as PO, but realizes that something is missing. His written representation of the sentence *mi nena toma sol* and his subsequent reading of it are as follows:
   NI N A P O MA S "mi/ne/na/to/ma/s . . . I don't remember (meaning, 'I don't know what goes next')."

Miguel (6 yrs., MC) is faced with the same problems, and some others, as he tries to write the same sentence: MINAT is read as "mi/ne/na/t . . . it's with *O*" and he adds OL to get MINAT OL, leaving a space for something he knows is missing from the middle. He reflects, then changes his hypothesis as if it occurs to him that all he really has to write is *nena* (little girl) and *sol* (sun), and he ends up with: MINATENAOL, in which the ENA stuck in the middle means *nena* and the final OL means *sol*.

We have presented various examples to fully illustrate the extraordinary richness of this passage in children as well as how difficult it is for them to coordinate the multiple hypotheses they have elaborated with information provided by the environment. By this level children have developed two very important ideas which they resist leaving behind (with reason): that a certain number of letters are necessary for something to be readable (reinforced by the new notion that writing something means representing progressively the sound segments of the name), and that each letter represents one of the syllables that compose the name. The environment has provided a stock of letters, a series of sound equivalents for some of them (assimilated easily for vowels, which constitute syllables in themselves, but necessarily modified for consonants), and a series of stable strings, the most important of which is undoubtedly the child's own name.

When the environment does not provide this information, one of the occasions for conflict is missing. This is why the LC chil-

---

[1] Translator's Note: As explained previously, the feminine article precedes letter names in Spanish. In this case, as in many others presented, the child uses the syllable in which the phoneme appears as the name of the corresponding letter. The conventional letter name for *T* in Spanish is "te."

dren in our sample reach the level of syllabic hypothesis but no further.

However, the environment itself cannot create knowledge. Many MC children, in spite of environmental stimulation, learn something different from what their social medium would expect. Alejandro (6 yrs., MC) is an eloquent example: he can write his name in upper-case print and *mamá* and *papá* in cursive. But when he sees "pi" written on a card in cursive (from the card classification task, chapter 2), he initiates the following dialogue:

	It's part of *papá*, the first part, the "pa" part.
And what's missing?	Another one, another little hump and another *I*.
(Compares the "pi" card to Alejandro's writing of *papá*.)	Oh! I forgot the *I*. If you want, I'll do it over. (Writes *pipi* in cursive.) That says papá.
(Proposes *pepe* in cursive.)	That's *papá*, too, a different way.
(Proposes *pupu* in cursive.)	Also, a different way.
What does it say here? (his writing of *papá*)	That's *papá* but a . . . funny way.
And here? (*pipi*)	This is the one we all know; it's the easiest. This one (*pepe*) is a little hard, and this one (*pupu*) is the hardest of all.
What's this? (*mimi* in cursive)	*Mamá*. I was already forgetting. I thought and I remembered.
And this? (*mama* in cursive)	*Mamá*, another way. That's the easiest. (Adds accent marks over both *a*'s.)
And this? (*meme* in cursive)	*Mamá*. I know that one too.
And this? (*mumu* in cursive)	It says *mamá*. All the ones that have *a*, you have to put this (accent mark). If it doesn't, you don't.

Obviously, neither Alejandro's parents nor his teacher have taught him this. But what he believes is not totally removed from the teachings of his social medium, either. It is simply that he has retained what he is able to retain, not what he is supposed to retain. *Papá* and *mamá* are composed of a series of alternating characters, and while this alternating pattern is maintained, it still says "*mamá*" or "*papá*." But, one thing is sure, as Alejandro lets us know: if we write *mamá* with *a*, we must put an accent mark on it! (We should point out that this occurs in a child who recognizes several letters by name and can recite orally in sequence the vowels and the first ten letters of the alphabet [*abecedario*]—or, as he says, the "dictionary" [*diccionario*].)

Finally, some refusals to write can be attributed to the difficulties involved in this transitional level. Gustavo (6 yrs., MC) provides an example of blockage due to an acute consciousness of difficulties which cannot be overcome:

	(Knows how to write *GUSTAVO* and *MAMÁ*, but refuses to write *papá* and *oso*.)
Can you write *sapo* (toad)?	No.
What does it start with?	With *s*. But I don't know how to write it.
(Offers him letter cards so that he can look for it.)	It's this one (*Z*).
What else is in it?	I don't know. At the end it says *o*.
Can you write *mapa* (map)?	It starts with "ma" (*la ma*).[1]
	MA A
	Here (blank space) it needs other letters.
One or a lot?	A lot.
Can you write *gato* (cat)?	It starts with *a*, then *m*; it's the opposite of *mamá*.
	AM
	Here it says "ga"; the *O* comes at the end.
	AM O
	(Doesn't know what goes in the middle, thinks it might be another *M*.)

It is in this period, in our judgment, that the long and often unfruitful phonic analyses of words occur, as well as repeated requests for reassurance and multiple questions referring sometimes to a syllable and sometimes to an isolated phoneme (the same child may ask "how do you make 'to'? and a little later "how do you make *t*?").

Level 5

Alphabetic writing is the final step of this evolution. In reaching this level children have broken the code; they understand that each written character corresponds to a sound value smaller than a syllable, and they systematically analyze the phonemes of the words they are writing. This does not mean that they have overcome all problems: from this point on children face the difficulties specific to orthography, but they do not have writing problems in the strict sense. This distinction is most important, since

[1] Translator's Note: This is another case where the child uses the syllable in which the phoneme appears as the name of the corresponding letter. The conventional letter name for *m* in Spanish is "eme."

spelling problems are often confused with difficulties in understanding the writing system. Vanina (6 yrs., MC) provides an excellent example for understanding the scope of this distinction:

Can you write *mesa* (table)?	(Writes MESA.) I think it's with S.
And if it's not S?	With Z.[1]
What does *zapatero* (shoemaker) start with?	I think with Z. I don't know for sure.
And if I write it with S?	It's okay.
Can you write *palo* (stick)?	(Writes PALO.) I'm sure it goes like this because there's no other way, no other P, no other A, no other L, no other O, unless it's in cursive.
Write *yo me llamo Vanina* (my name is Vanina).	(Writes LLO ME LLAMO VANINA, syllabicating as she writes.) I'm not sure if it goes with LL or with Y (in reference to LLO). With both it means the same thing, only different . . .
Try writing *lluvia* (rain).	(Writes LLUBIA, hesitates.) I don't know which one goes there (reflects on LL and B). LL is like *ye* (regional pronunciation, see discussion in chapter 7).
What letter is this? (H)	H.
What's it for?[2]	For example, you spell *huevos* (eggs) with an H in front of the U.
Why?	Because that's how you spell it.
And how do you read it?	When I read it in *huevos* you always say *huevos* but when I read it in . . . in *chapa* (doorlock) it turns into *ch*.
Write *huevos*.	(Writes HUEVOS.) If it has a C in front it says *chuevos* (invented word).
And like this? (Covers H leaving UEVOS visible.)	*Huevos* too. The H is for writing *huevos*, but if you don't know it has H and you don't put it, it still says *huevos*.
What does it say here? (CIELO) (sky)	*Cielo*.
Is there another way to write it?	(Writes SIELO.) I don't know if it starts with Z or with S.
Can you write *cubierto* (cover)?	(Writes CUBIERTO.) Or with K. Not with S because it would say *subierto*. (invented word).

[1] Translator's Note: In Argentinean Spanish, as in most continental American Spanish, *s* and *z* do not represent distinct phonemes.

[2] Translator's Note: In Spanish, the *h* is a silent letter unless it follows the *c*, in which case it forms the *ch* sound /č/.

Could you write it some other way?	(QUUBIERTO.) The *U* is to make it (the *Q*) say *K*; without the *U* it doesn't say anything. It's a balloon without the *U*.
How do you think you could write *examen* (exam)?	(ESAMEN). But it could also be like this (ECSAMEN) or like this (EK-ZAMEN) or this (EQUXAMEN).

When we ask Vanina how she could find out how to spell a word (conventionally), she tells us, "I'd ask my mom"; she knows "because she asked her mom when she was little, if they didn't teach it to her in school."

Vanina has no difficulty with the alphabetic laws of composition. All her difficulties center around letters which correspond to more than one sound value (in Spanish this is a relatively small group of letters: *c, g, h, x, y*), or inversely, sets of letters which correspond to the same sound value. (In most continental American Spanish these sets tend to be: *b/v; c/s/z; c/qu/k; g/j; gu/hu; h/ø ll/y* [*j* also occasionally represents this sound in borrowed names and words]). When Vanina writes *palo* and explains to us that all her doubts disappear "because there's no other way, no other *P*, no other *A*, no other *L*, no other *O*, unless they're in cursive," and when she shows us the different possible spellings for *cielo, cubierto,* and *examen,* she is explaining with great clarity the difference between understanding the internal mechanisms of the alphabetic code and orthographic convention.

Vanina is not afraid of making mistakes in spelling (a fear close to terror in many children beginning elementary school). As she herself says, if you spell something another way—unconventionally—"it's okay," or dealing with the letter *h,* "if you don't know it's spelled with *H* and you don't put it, it still says *huevos.*" In other words, for purposes of communication, different spellings of the same word can function because they "mean the same thing." However, Vanina knows that there is a customary way of spelling each word, and she surely will not have difficulty with spelling in the future.

A total of four MC children (two five and two six year olds) are at this level. All of them (except Vanina) write sentences without spacing between the words (for example: MINENATOMASOL) and indicate that it might be segmented (as an option, not a necessity) only when we ask them to do so. The only segmentation they propose consists of separating the subject from the predicate (MINENA TOMASOL, see illustration 10).

They all face spelling problems similar to Vanina's. Mariano writes KESO (cheese—the conventional spelling is *queso*) and CAMIÓN (truck—conventional spelling), but also accepts KA-

MIÓN (unconventional spelling of the same word); Rafael writes CUEJO for *cuello* (neck).

All four children write in upper-case print. This reflects the extrascholastic nature of this learning. ("I don't know cursive writing too well; I know printing," one says. "I don't know it in excursive," says another.)

The Child's Own Name

The child's own name as a model of writing, as the first stable written string and as the prototype of all subsequent writing often fulfills a very special function in the psychogenesis we are studying. The writing of proper names appears to have played a very important role in the development of writing systems throughout history. Gelb (1952), studying the beginnings of Sumerian writing (around 3100 B.C.), makes the following comments:

The signs used in the earliest Uruk writing are clearly word signs limited to the expression of numerals, objects, and personal names. This is the stage of writing which we call logography or word writing and which should be sharply distinguished from the so-called ideography. . . .
In the most primitive phases of logography it is easy to express concrete words, such as a sheep by a picture of a sheep, or the sun by a picture of the sun, but soon a method must be evolved whereby pictures can express not only the objects they originally depict but also words with which they can be secondarily associated. Thus, a picture of the sun can stand secondarily for the words "bright, white," later also "day"; similarly, a picture of a woman and a mountain can stand for "slave girl"—a combination derived from the fact that slave girls were normally brought to Babylonia from the surrounding mountains.
Logography of this kind has, of course, its drawbacks in its inability to express many parts of speech and grammatical forms; this is not very serious, however, since the intended meaning can frequently be understood through the "context of situation," to use a term introduced by Malinowski in his study of the meaning in primitive languages. Much more serious are the limitations of the system in respect to the writing of proper names. The primitive device of the American Indians for expressing personal names may have been sufficient for tribal conditions but it certainly could not satisfy the requirements of large urban centers like those in Sumer. In an Indian tribe, where everybody knows everybody else, it is normal for every individual to have an exclusive name. In large cities, in spite of the proximity of living conditions, people do not know each other and many different persons bear the same names. Therefore, in documents, persons with the same name have to be further identified by their paternity and place of origin. Furthermore, names of the Indian type, such as "White-Buffalo" or "Big-Bear," which can be expressed in writing with relative ease . . . were relatively rare among the Sumerians, while common Sumerian names of the type "Enlil-Has-Given-Life" were difficult to express by the Indian device (pp. 65–66).

These observations lead Gelb to the following conclusion: "The need for adequate representation of proper names finally led to the development of phonetization. This is confirmed by the Aztec and Maya writings, which employ the phonetic principle only rarely and then almost exclusively in expressing proper names. . . . Phonetization, therefore, arose from the need to express words and sounds which could not be adequately indicated by pictures or combinations of pictures" (pp. 66–67).

We have cited Gelb extensively because of the clarity of his argument. When Gelb speaks of the shift to phonetization he is not referring to utilizing conventional characters with stable sound values (like our letters), but to utilizing sound identity or similarity between words to represent new words, as in using a drawing of knees combined with one of the sun to express "Neilson," or the drawing of a disk together with a cord to express "discord" (examples from Gelb, p. 67). In these cases the written representation does not refer directly to the meaning connected to the object but to the sound of the corresponding name. For this reason it differs sharply from ideography. Gelb indicates that once introduced, this principle of phonetization develops quite rapidly and progressively comes to require standardization of utilized forms, stable correspondence between signs and syllabic values, adoption of conventions relating to the spatial orientation and directionality of writing, and the need for establishing an order of the signs corresponding to the order of oral emission.

Finally, Gelb rejects the hypothesis that the need to represent grammatical elements (as difficult to draw as abstract ideas) leads to the development of phonetization. "That the need for indicating grammatical elements was of no great importance in the origin of phonetization can be deduced from the fact that even after the full development of phonetization writing failed for a long time to indicate grammatical elements adequately" (pp. 66–67). This point is extremely important because it relates to what we have seen in individual development. Children do not expect strictly grammatical elements to be represented in writing until they have reached a rather advanced level of development (see chapter 4).

In many cases the child's own name functions as the first stable form endowed with meaning. We suspect, although we have no precise data in this respect, that a typical middle class cultural pattern is to provide children early opportunities for learning to write their name. Perhaps parents put name and date on their children's drawings or paintings, or maybe they label the children's clothes. In Argentina, where the use of the school smock is the general rule, parents are asked to label the smock with the child's name to avoid confusion.

At the time of our interviews, many children knew how to write their names correctly, always in upper-case print. But the social differences are clear, as the following table shows:

	Correct writing	Approximate writing (some letters)	Don't know
4 yrs., MC	1	4	7
5 yrs., MC	13		2
6 yrs., MC	19	1	
4 yrs., LC	1	1	7
5 yrs., LC	5	1	5
6 yrs., LC			9

Although both four-year-old groups look alike, since most of the children at this age do not yet know how to write their names regardless of social origin, we see marked differences among the five year olds. At six the differences are striking: all of the MC six year olds know how to write their name (except for one who only knows some of the letters), while none of the LC six year olds do. The difference between the LC five and six year olds may be related to the fact that almost none of the six year olds interviewed had attended preschool/kindergarten. Without any specific type of scholastic stimulation and lacking an encouraging cultural pattern, they arrive at first grade unable to write their own name and without other stable graphic strings.

When children were not able to write the graphic characters themselves, we offered them movable letters from which they could compose their names. If they could neither write nor compose their name with these letters, we tried to see if they could recognize it when we wrote it.

We were also interested in how children read their name, once written, assigning values to the distinct parts. To find this out, we do the following: (*a*) We hide part of the name with a card and ask if "it still says x" (x = child's name) in the visible part; if the answer is "no," we ask "then, what does it say?" (*b*) We perform diverse transformations on the name, changing the order of the letters; we produce these new written strings beneath the original, indicating the new position of each letter ("I'll put this one here, this one over here."); we also ask if "it still says x" and "what does it say?" if the answer is negative, emphasizing that all of the original letters are written there ("All the ones from your name are there. Why doesn't it say x anymore?").

Following are the results relating to the writing and reading of the child's own name (the reading includes reading of the parts as well as of the whole), and the reactions to the transformations of the name. We will present these results so they are comparable to the writing levels in the previous section.

Level 1

The children at this level cannot write their own name, or they write it as they write other written strings, with an indefinite or variable number of graphic characters. The name can be read as much from the child's writing as from the one proposed by the adult. The fact that the graphics are perceptively different does not matter. Furthermore, one can read from the same written string both the first name alone and the first and last name together, globally, with no search for correspondence between parts. When only part of the name is visible, the name can still be read. There is no differentiation between the value of the whole and that of the parts. The only apparent restriction is that if only one letter remains visible, it can no longer be read because the minimum-quantity-of-characters hypothesis intervenes. Transformations of the name are, of course, irrelevant. Sometimes there is an alternative attempt at reading either the transformations or parts of the name: the names of other members of the family result from transformations of the child's name.

Some examples will help to understand this better:

Guillermo (6 yrs., LC) knows how to write, in cursive only, the vowels, which he names correctly. We write his name, also in cursive, but he does not recognize it. When only the last part of his name remains visible, it "says *mamá*." When the middle part is visible, it "says *papá*." The first transformation of his name (GULLIERMO instead of GUILLERMO) "says grandmother (*abuela*)." With the subsequent transformations he tries to continue with other members of the family but is unable to think of who they might be.

Sylvia (6 yrs., LC) does not know how to write her name either. We print it for her and she does not identify it:

Here, it says Silvia.	Silvia Pereyra.
No. Just Silvia.	Just Silvia? Sil-via (without pointing).
Does it still say Silvia? (SILV//)[1]	Silvia; just a little because it's covered.
And like this? (////IA)	Silvia Pereyra.
And like this? (SILV//)	. . . Silvia.
And like this? (////IA)	Silvia.

[1] Translator's Note: Slashes indicate letters covered by the researcher.

Alejandra (6 yrs., LC) does not know how to write or recognize her name. When we show it to her in written form, in any part of two or more letters, no matter which letters, it says her name. But if only one letter is visible, "it doesn't say Alejandra."

Favio (5 yrs., LC) always uses the same number of characters, but not the same ones, to write his name. In the first interview he composes his name with movable characters and ends up with 3VE (with the 3 backwards). In the second interview he writes his name 500 (with the 5 backwards). On both occasions he reads globally "Favio."

Javier (4 yrs., LC) composes his name with movable letters but without anticipating the necessary number. He ends up with: NEMBPKUA (with two inverted letters and not knowing whether he must continue). When we ask him where it says Javier, he points to each letter one by one: in each letter it says Javier, and the whole thing also says Javier. We show him the label on his smock, where his last name—Baldomiro—is embroidered, and we ask him what it says. He answers that it says "Javier."

Diego (4 yrs., MC) composes his name with movable letters: ZDAZD. When we cover up parts of the name it says "nothing," but when we ask him about transformations of the name (with all letters visible) it says "another name, I don't know which one it says."

These examples do not represent perfect homogeneity but a variety of responses sharing certain common parameters. None of these children know how to write their names or recognize them when they see them written. When they write or compose it with movable letters they use a certain number of characters, not derived from an analysis of the length of the oral name but from ideas they have about the number of characters necessary for something to be readable (since they use the same number for any other written string they produce). A lack of differentiation between the properties of the whole and its parts (the name can be read in all the letters, in each one, or in groups of more than one) alternates with the idea that transformations of the name can give way to other names close to the original one (for example, names of other members of the family). Finally, where the first name alone is written one can also read the complete first and last name.

This first level is represented in very similar proportions by four and five year olds of both MC and LC backgrounds. No MC six year old falls into this category, while all LC six year olds (with one exception) are in this group.

Level 2
Before characterizing this level we give this intermediate example between levels 1 and 2.

Débora (4 yrs., LC) writes from the cursive model, using variations of her fixed form *mama,* the only one she knows. She writes her name, also in cursive, and produces something like *nsana*, which she reads globally as "Débora." When the position of the page is inverted, she reads "Elena," her middle name, from the same written string and she ends up reading "Débora Elena" from any angle.

A little later, in the same interview, we ask her to compose her name with movable letters. She uses only two letters (CZ), one for each name. But two seem very few to her so she adds two more (EMCZ), with the resulting problem when she proceeds to read: she reads "Débora" for *E* and "Eleeena" for the rest, elongating the vowel to make the emission coincide with her pointing gesture.

We make transformations on this composition, modifying the order of the letters or hiding some. When only two letters (//CZ) remain visible she maintains that it says "just Débora." With three visible letters it says "Débora Elena" and with four it says "Débora Eleeena." She suddenly decides that she has one too many letters, and from the three remaining ones she reads "Débora Elené Gomez." From this final configuration (CZE) she is systematic: if any two letters are visible, she reads her first and middle names; if all three are visible, she reads first, middle, and last name.

Débora's case illustrates the reasons leading to level 2: attempting to find a rational limit—compatible with the minimum-quantity hypothesis—for the number of letters in their name, children discover the possibility of a one-to-one correspondence between each letter and a part of their full name. The correspondence is established between letters and word-parts, not syllable-parts (which characterize the next level).

Level 2 shares with level 1 the idea that the written representation of the first name can also represent the full name (first, middle, and last), but it differs from level 1 in that the children begin to move away from global reading and attempt a correspondence between parts. This level has the following inherent limitation: the search for correspondence is with complete parts of the full name, not between the constituent parts (syllables) of first, middle, or last name.

Level 2 is the only one represented by all ages in both social groups. This means that even six-year-old MC children who know how to write their names are faced with serious problems when they must interpret this writing. This occurs, evidently, because the written name is received initially as a global form, not easily analyzable. In the difficult task of finding a value for the parts compatible with the value of the whole, nothing is either obvious or immediate.

Note the following examples:

David (5 yrs., LC) does not know how to write his name and chooses movable letters to compose it. He initially picks seven letters, but he uses only three, composing VSl (with the *V* rotated 180 degrees). He gives the following justification: "David Bernardo Mendez . . . and that's all because it's short, so there would be three." (The order of the three characters is totally irrelevant to him.)

Silvia (6 yrs., LC), trying to compose her name with movable letters, settles on TRS, which says "Silvia Beatriz Landeros," one name for each letter. (She remains consistent with this interpretation when parts of this written string are hidden.)

José (4 yrs., MC) writes his name JLF which is actually the writing of his initials (José Luis Fernandez). On writing *J* he says "the jo (*la jo*) for José, the *J* (*la jota*)," but on reading the complete written string he says "Jo/sé/Luis." (With movable letters he produces the same composition and reads it the same way.) Transforming the order of the letters does not disturb him in the least, because he modifies the order of reading to conserve the correspondence: *J* = jo; *L* = sé; *F* = luis. So, for FJL he also says "Jo/sé/Luis," while pointing to the letters in 2–3–1 order; he does the same for LJF, pointing to the letters in 2–1–3 order. It becomes clear that José's hypothesis belongs to level 2 and not level 3 when we cover up parts of the writing: in (/LF) it says "Jorge and Luis"; in (JL/) it says "Luis and Jorge"; in (/L/) it says "nothing, because there's just one letter"; and when the three letters are all visible again and we ask where it says José, he simply points to the whole thing saying: "now the one for Fernandez; we need the one for Fernandez."

This level appears much more purely in the LC children who do not know the conventional manner of writing their own name. The MC children who have precociously received and assimilated the written form of their name treat this fixed string as a whole composed of ordered parts, but without understanding the reasons behind this order. This stable graphic string plays a very important role beginning with level 3, but in level 2 it appears to block any possibility for analysis, since the number of written letters surpasses any attempt at matching letters and names. Mariano's case illustrates this clearly:

Mariano (6 yrs., MC) can write his name, but he reconstructs it in an arbitrary order, not knowing the laws of composition. For example, after writing MA he hesitates and says: "I think the *R* goes here . . . or the *A* goes like that next to the *M* . . . I think I have it written back here (on his smock)." He finally reconstructs it, depending exclusively on a visual image, with no analysis of the sounds. Consequently, when parts of the name are covered up, the remaining parts "don't say anything," and he rejects the transformations, insisting on the rigid memorized order.

Level 3
This level is characterized by children who systematically utilize the syllabic hypothesis in writing and reading their own name. The reading tends to be limited to the first name. However, the reading of both first and last name may appear in two situations:

when the first name contains only two syllables (since two letters are often too few for something to be readable), or in children capable of writing their name correctly (since they end up with leftover parts when reading syllabically, matching a syllable to each letter).

The difference between this and the previous level does not lie in the greater or lesser correctness with which children write their names, but rather in the extremely important shift from a correspondence between individual letters and names to a correspondence between individual letters and parts of names (syllables).

By virtue of the way children read fragments of their name (when we cover up part of it) we can distinguish two sublevels: a first sublevel, 3a, when children can read syllabically the beginning of the name but fail when attempting to read the end of the name; and a second sublevel, 3b, when children are more systematic with their syllabic segmentation and manage to apply it to various visible parts of the name.

Here are examples of sublevel 3a:

Walter (5 yrs., LC) knows how to write his name in upper-case print. When only the first part of his name is visible (WAL///), he reads "Gual" (he pronounces his name "Gualter"), but when only the last part is visible (///TER) he cannot read it. If we move from (WAL///) to (WA////) and then to leaving only the intial letter visible, he begins to have doubts: with one, two, or three of the beginning letters visible he reads it the same way, since *W* is "gua" to him, or "gual," because he identifies the initial letter with the initial syllable of his name.

Rosario (5 yrs., LC) writes her name correctly, but from right to left: OIRASOR. She reads it also from right to left, "Ro/sa/ri . . . i, o," matching the first three syllables to the first three letters, leaving the next two letters with no oral correspondence, and correctly naming the last two vowels. When we move to reading parts of the name, she reads the first syllable ("Ro") for any visible part (///ASOR, OIR////, /////OR), but then she changes her hypothesis. With the first four letters visible (///ASOR) she reads syllabically "Ro/sa/ri/o," pointing to each letter from right to left. When only the first three are visible (////SOR) she reads "Ro/sa/ri." The conflict shows up when five or more letters are visible. Her way of resolving this is to continue reading syllabically, but skipping over some letters (for example, when the whole name is visible, "Ro/sa/ri . . . o," pointing to the first three letters and the last), or she may alternatively repeat a syllable (for example, "Ro/sa/ri/ri . . . o").

Atilio (5 yrs., LC) is actually at an intermediate level between levels 2 and 3. He shares with level 3 the attempt to find a syllabic correspondence for each letter. He writes his first name correctly and reads from it both first and last name to account for leftover parts. Attempting to find an exact correspondence for ATILIO he goes through several rehearsals and reads successively: "A/ti/li/o . . . A/ti/lio/Riva/sio . . . Atilio/Ri/va/sio . . . Ati/li/o/Riva/sio . . . Ati/lio/Ri/va/sio."

Similar examples come from MC children. Gustavo and Rafael (6 yrs., MC) write their names correctly but can read syllabically only the beginning, not having the slightest idea of how the rest can be read. Marcela (6 yrs., MC) gives the first syllable ("mar") for any visible part of her name which she herself has written correctly. The clearest example of the difficulties inherent in this task, even for a six-year-old MC child, is the following:

Alejandro (6 yrs., MC) writes his name correctly, but his troubles begin when only the first part remains visible:

(ALE//////)	Alejan-e; a-le-ja; alejá.
(ALEJA////)	A-le-já; ja-ooo. No! I'll keep this one (pointing to the final *A*). A-le-ja-já; with ja, jo. A-le-jó. That's what they call me, Alejo.
(////JANDRO)	I don't know.

It is easy to imagine the kinds of responses that characterize sublevel 3b, since the progression comes about by the children's ability to find a syllabic segmentation for the last part of the name. Two examples will suffice to provide an idea of the magnitude of the difficulties encountered and to distinguish these responses from those in level 4:

Emilio (4 yrs., MC) writes the letters of his name in upper-case print in the correct order (with the *M* and the *L* backwards) and he reads the visible parts in the following ways:

(EM/////)	Emi
(///ILIO)	-milio
(////LIO)	Emili, emi-li . . . mili
(EM/////)	Emi (*M* is "mi" by syllabic hypothesis.)

Lorena (5 yrs., MC) writes her name correctly. When we change the order of the letters in her name, leaving the first two in the same place (LOERNA, LONARE), she tells us that "it doesn't say Lorena, but this little piece (LO) says lo-re." She produces the following while reading parts of her name:

(LOR///)	Lo
(///ENA)	-re
(//RE//)	I don't know that one.
(L/////)	Or that one either.
(/////A)	-na

These examples represent the limits of level 3. The syllabic hypothesis, applied to a fixed string received from without, enters into continual conflict. It is precisely this conflict that makes it necessary to go beyond the syllable to find a more satisfactory correspondence. This is what occurs in level 4.

Level 4

We shall present this level and the next briefly since the findings for level 4 and level 5 in the previous section on the writing of other words is applicable here. Typical of readings at this level is the use of the syllabic hypothesis coupled with developing alphabetic principles. This was apparent in our detailed analysis of María Paula writing her name. It also appears when children read parts of their name, as in this case:

Gerardo (6 yrs., MC) knows how to write his name in both print and cursive. (Cursive, for him, is "the way grown-ups write.") The following are readings of his name in printed form:

(GE/////)	Ge
(GERAR//)	Gera
(/////DO)	-deo
(//RARDO)	-ra-deo
(//RAR//)	-rra

Level 5

At this level writing and reading operate on alphabetic principles and the new problems that appear are orthographic in nature. These children have no problem reading parts of their name:

Mariano (5 yrs., MC) reads:

(MAR////)	Mar
(/////NO)	No. It says "no."

He also knows how to write his friend Florencia's name, and reads:

(FLORENCI/)	Florenci
(FLO//////)	Flo
(///RENCIA)	-encia

The orthographic problems are exemplified quite well by Miguel.

Miguel (6 yrs., MC) writes his name correctly. When we begin to change the order of the letters Miguel tries to read the results of the transformations (typical behavior of children at this level but impossible at previous levels):

(MIUGEL)	Miug-e, miug-e, miug-ele (laughs). That doesn't say Miguel!
(MIGULE)	Mi-gue-u-le, mi-gu-el-le. It's like this (takes pencil and writes MIGUEL). Miguel, mi-g-u . . . mi-gu-e-el . . . (seems totally disconcerted by the result of his reading) migu-e-el, migu-e-el . . .
Does it say Miguel or not?	No. The *E* has to go here (next to the *G*).
Put it there!	(Writes MIGEUL). Miguel. Mi-g-e-u. . . . The *L* has to be (next to the

> *E*) . . . then it doesn't have a *U!* My
> mom always writes it with a *U.* She's
> crazy! (Writes MIGEL.) Now it says
> Miguel!

Miguel provides a beautiful example of the appearance of a new problem area. Obviously he has written his name for quite some time without being puzzled by that strange *u,* stuck in between the *g* and the *e.* That *u* has no reason for being there, since Miguel believes the *g* to represent only one sound and not two.[1]

Certain apparent regressions in spelling, like this one, are actually signs of progress. They indicate a shift from a global form, repeated exactly but not analyzed, to a reasoned composition of the same form, during which spelling conventions, for the moment, have no place. (Facing a problem quite similar to Miguel's, another child, who had learned to write QUESO with no mistakes, writes KESO at a moment when the graphic form, inherited but not "owned," gives way to the spontaneous form produced by the child's own construction. Read (1975) has done a series of studies on the spontaneous orthography of English-speaking children, studies that are highly instructive as they show how spontaneous [or invented] spelling reflects children's phonological judgments.)

Our dialogue with Miguel did not end here. In the second interview he reproaches us, blaming us for the orthographic discovery he had made, saying, "You told me that Miguel's not spelled with a *U,* and it is spelled with a *U!*" He writes his name as he had done originally, but refuses to read it in parts. He has again adopted the standard written form of his name, forcing his own comprehension into retreat: the form has its properties and that's the way it is, a physical object that continues to be what it is even though the individual cannot understand it entirely.

Distribution of Writing Levels by Age and Social Background

We present here some quantitative results regarding the frequency and distribution of the different levels we have characterized. For our work, though, qualitative analysis is the primary form of analysis. The quantitative data cannot be taken as representative of these age groups in the total population of Buenos

---

[1] Translator's Note: In written Spanish the *u* following the *g* and immediately preceding the vowels *e* or *i* serves to distinguish the representation of /g/, (sometimes called in English the "hard g sound," as in "good") from /x/ (similar to the sound represented by the *h* in "hat", but harsher), the sound *g* represents when it immediately precedes *e* or *i* and is not followed by *u.* The /x/ in written Spanish is also represented in many words by the letter *j.*

Aires. It does, however, provide an overall view. The tables place each child at one of the different levels. The totals correspond to the total number of subjects, not to the total number of responses (some children produce many written texts while others produce few).

Table 6.1 presents the data relating to the children's writing of their own names. In the three MC age groups, the successive levels correspond to a progression in age: most of the four year olds are at levels 1 and 2 and none of them reaches level 5; the five year olds are distributed among all of the levels concentrating at level 3 (this indicates, among other things, the tremendous differences found among children of the same age and social background); none of the six year olds is at level 1 and several are at levels 4 and 5. This data corresponds in part to the data presented at the beginning of the previous section, "The Child's Own Name." There we indicate how many children are capable of writing their own name; here we consider, in addition, how they interpret transformations of their written name and how they read parts of it.

The data regarding the LC children is completely different. Although the four year olds are very close to the MC four year olds, the differences from five years on are dramatic. No LC child goes past level 3. Furthermore, the six year olds present a regression in comparison to the five year olds. There are two main reasons for this regression: one is that most of the LC six year olds did not attend preschool/kindergarten; the other is that we were unable to have more than one interview with these children, who have a tendency to become totally blocked in any remotely scholastic situation.

Table 6.2 shows the distribution when children write something other than their own name. In the MC group, the four and six year old distribution follows the same pattern as shown in table 6.1 (the four year olds are almost all at the first two levels while the six year olds are mostly at the higher levels). The five year olds, however, are mostly at level 2, which means, comparing with table 6.1, that MC five year olds are markedly more advanced at writing and interpreting their own names than they are at other writing.

We have eliminated the LC six year olds from table 6.2 because the majority of them refuse to write. They hold fast (almost desperately) to the little they are sure they know, not daring to explore other possibilities. *They know that they don't know.* Worse yet, they believe that only by copying will they come to know.

Results for the LC four and five year olds shown in table 6.2 agree, in general, with table 6.1. The comparison of MC and LC groups of the same age provides some noteworthy indications: the

Table 6.1. *Children's writing of their own names.*

Level / Age	1	1–2	2	2–3	3 a	3 b	3–4	4	5
4a MC (Total = 12)	3		5	2		1		1	
5a MC (Total = 15)	2		2		3	2	1	3	2
6a MC (Total = 20)			5	1	4	3		3	4
4a LC (Total = 9)	3	2	3	1					
5a LC (Total = 11)	1	1	2	3	3	1			
6a LC (Total = 9)	8		1						

Table 6.2. Writing of other names.

Level →	1	1	2	2	2	2–3	3	3	4	5
	Cursive model	*Print model* (Produce other words)	*Without stable strings* (Produce other words)	*With stable strings* (Refuse to write other words)	*With stable strings*		*Without conventional letters* (Without stable sound value)	*With conventional letters* (With stable sound value)		
Age										
4a MC (Total = 9)	1	3	3		2					
5a MC (Total = 11)		3		5	3					
6a MC (Total = 20)				3	2	4		4	5	2
4a LC (Total = 7)	3		1	2				1		
5a LC (Total = 11)	1	2			3		1	1	1	2

few LC children who use the syllabic hypothesis do so with writing where letters, in their conventional form, are absent, or they do so using letters but without stable sound values. The MC children employing the syllabic hypothesis utilize well-differentiated letters with sound values.

This point is very important. If we had interviewed only MC children, it would have been easy to conclude that the syllabic hypothesis is no more than a distorted assimilation based on information provided by the environment (for example, *m* would be "ma" simply because the child is familiar with the written words María and *mamá* and their corresponding global readings, and from this would arise the attempt to find a sound value for the letters). However, observing eight LC children who explore the syllabic hypothesis (some with their own name, some with other writing, some occasionally, and some systematically), in spite of not being able to give stable sound values to the letters, suggests another explanation: the syllabic hypothesis develops independently of information provided by the environment and arises from the internal necessity of coordinating the value of the whole to the parts.

The fact that one can arrive at the syllabic hypothesis independently of the environment does not mean that one can continue progressing without new information—this time, dependent on the environment. The way one arrives at the syllabic hypothesis (with or without letters having stable sound values) may be a determining factor in the continuing evolution. To find this out other kinds of research studies are necessary, such as the longitudinal ones we are doing currently.

Transformations of Other Words

In this section we approach a problem halfway between the problems of production and interpretation of texts. We include this because it is one of the tasks for which we have comparative data for preschool/kindergarten children and first graders. The results were not what one might expect.

We follow the same procedure as for the transformation task with children's own names, but with words that are the prototypes of beginning writing instruction: *mamá, papá,* and *oso* (bear). This might be considered a reading task since it involves interpreting a written text produced by transforming another written text, but we do this with the forms that constitute the first writing models. The objective is to find out what, in these elementary written forms, is considered essential for the interpretation to remain the same. Will children think that "if the letters of *mamá* are there," in whatever order, it still "says *mamá*"? Will they take into account the necessary number of similar characters? Will order, number, type, and distribution of characters always be considered equally or will there be a hierarchy? These were the questions we started with. The results have obligated us to pose new ones.

Our procedure is to ask the children to write the words; if they are unable to, we try to see if they recognize them when someone else writes them; once we agree on the interpretation of the written word, we proceed to rewrite it, modifying it in certain ways (from OSO we move to OOS, OS, OSOS, SOS). After each rewriting we ask if it is still the original word; if the response is negative, we ask what it says. We use two methodological precautions: the transformed words are always written beneath the original to facilitate comparison; and the researcher vocalizes while writing, to emphasize that the original word is being used as the departure point, but without naming letters or giving them sound values. (For example, in going from OSO to OSOS we say, "Look, now I'll write it again . . . and I'll put another one of these at the end." In going from OSO to OOS our comments would be "I'll put this one here, this here and this here," pointing out the original position of each letter.)

From Four to Six Years Old, before Receiving Aid in School

Response Type 1
The most primitive level is represented by children (relatively few) for whom all transformations are irrelevant (in all of them "it still says" the original word), or who accept or reject them without conviction. The results parallel what we saw in chapter 2: when we presented children a series of cards to classify in terms of can/cannot be read, we found an initial level where all can be read, or one can and another cannot based on no objective criteria. In this word transformation task, one can read *mamá* from all of the proposed texts if we start with *mamá*, or *papá* if we start with *papá*, and so on. Or, some texts continue to say the same thing at one point, but a few minutes later they say something else. The children here have no objective criteria for deciding either way.

Response Type 2
Much more interesting are the responses which reject some transformations and accept others based on some objective criterion. Here are some examples:

Gustavo (5 yrs., MC) accepts only APAP for *papá* and AMAM for *mamá* since he demands alternating characters of a certain number and does not consider the question of which one to start with.

Andrea (6 yrs., MC) is very similar to Gustavo. She rejects PPAA because "it can't have the two *P*'s and the two *A*'s together." But she accepts AMAM: "It says *mamá,* but the accent mark is missing," and she places it over the final *M!* She says that MA "doesn't say anything because there's two letters."

Alejandro (6 yrs., MC), cited in the first section of this chapter (level 4), thinks that *mimi, meme,* and *mumu* are alternative ways of writing *mamá,* but specifies that the form written with *a* takes an accent mark.

Laura (5 yrs., LC) successively uses several criteria which she does not manage to coordinate: alternation of characters, presence of the accent mark, and quantity of characters:

PAPÁ   = . . . Pa. It doesn't say *papá* because it doesn't have an accent mark.
PAAP   = It doesn't say it. Because there's two *A*'s together and . . . it doesn't have an accent mark.
PAÁP   = Now it says *papá.*
PAPAPA = Paaa, papaaaa. It doesn't say *papá* because here it's longer . . . because there's three *A*'s.

What is typical of these cases is that only some of the properties of the original string are retained as essential, or the children alternate from one to another without coordination. It is not an easy task to retain the order, alternation, and quantity of the characters as well as the position of that special graphic element called the accent mark.

Response Type 3

The most surprising responses consist of supposing that transformations of a certain word correspond to other words, different in sound but close in meaning. Transforming *mamá* or *papá* we get names of other members of the family.

Walter (5 yrs., LC) gives the following series of equivalencies:

mamá   = *mamá*
ámam   = *papá*
papá   = *hijo* (son)
ápap   = *hija* (daughter)
mpapá   = *primo* (male cousin)
What's missing? = *prima* (female cousin)

Alejandra (5 yrs., MC) interprets the following for transformations of *mamá:*

AMAM   = *papá*
MAAM   = *mucama* (maid)
MAMAM = *hermano* (brother)

Martín (5 yrs., MC)

MAMA   = *mamá*
MAAM   = *papá*
MAMAMA = *papá* and *mamá* (Three letters for each name, since he finds it too long to say just one thing.)

Atilio (5 yrs., LC) also accounts for the additional length of the written string when new characters are added, but instead of introducing two names, he adds the last name on to the first. For him, MAMÁ, AMAM, and AMMA are equivalent variants of *mamá,* but MAMAMA says *"mamá Rivasio."*

Leonardo (5 yrs., LC)
    PAPÁ   = *mamá*
    APAP   = *papá*
    APPA   = *tío* (uncle)
    APAP   = *abuelo* (grandfather)
    APAPAP = *abuela* (grandmother)

This response type is not among the most primitive. We do not find it in four year olds, but from five on in both groups. A total of nine children respond systematically in this way, and three others do so occasionally. Occasional residuals of this, followed by self-corrections, are found among MC six year olds.

Carlos (6 yrs., MC), working with transformations of NENE (boy), correctly tells us that NE says "ne," but:
    NENENE   = It says *nene;* but here's another one of these (NE). Oh!
                         It says *nena* (girl) . . . but you have to put an *A.*
    NENENEA = Yes. That way it's *nena.*

The same child gives us the most advanced example of this variant: attempting to read the transformations of *mamá* (mom), he ends up proposing *madre* (mother), that is, a synonym to the original word, rather than one that is semantically close but with a different referent:

    mamam = *mamé, máma, mamame, mamé* . . .
    maam   = *ma-má, mamá* . . . No. What was it? *Ma-ma* . . . *madre* (mother)!

We will interpret this response type later, because it is not exclusive of preschool children but found also among children who have already begun to learn to write in school.

Response Type 4
Several five and six year olds reject the transformations without attempting to read them, basing their responses exclusively on the presence or absence of the required letters and whether they are in the correct position. All these children know how to write the word which serves as the starting point. Knowing how to write the word is a necessary but insufficient condition for rejecting transformations. Some of the children we cited for the preceding response types also know how to write the word, but in their cases

knowing how to produce the graphic representation does not correspond to a conceptual knowing.

This example demonstrates this new level of response:

Laura (5 yrs., MC)

MAMÁ	= *mamá*
MAAM	= *Mamá* again, oh no! I don't know, wait . . . it doesn't say *mamá*. After this one (*A*) comes this one (*M.*)
AMAM	= No, because it has to start with *M*.
MAMAMA	= It's very long. There's one, two, three, four (counts letters of the original model), and here there's one, two, three, four, five, six. It's up to here (first four letters).

Response Type 5

Finally, a few children (MC five and six year olds) reject transformations but attempt to read them. This reading may be correct or approximate, but the argument for rejecting the transformation is always the same: the original string has been modified, and in doing so we have created another written text which is readable and different from the original.

Mariano (5 yrs., MC)

OSO	= *oso*
SOSO	= It says *soso*.
OSOS	= *osos, muchos osos* (many bears)

Diego (6 yrs., MC)

OSO	= *oso*
OOS	= *os-o, so-o*. It doesn't say *oso* because they're turned around.
papá	= *papá*
paap	= *paa-pa*
ppaa	= *pa*
papap	= *paaa*

Six and Seven Year Olds, Receiving Aid in School

We used the task of transforming familiar words with the children we interviewed in our first research study: six- and seven-year-old lower class children who were attending first grade for the first time. We saw these children individually at the beginning, the middle, and the end of the school year. We did this task with them during the middle session. By this time the teachers had presented at least six words (and supposedly taught the children to read and write them), including the traditional *mamá, papá, nene* (boy), *oso* (bear), and *ala* (wing). We proposed to this group of children the same transformations described previously (modification of the order of the letters, addition or omission of letters) and one variant: adding to one familiar word the initial letter of another familiar word (for example, going from *oso* to *moso* or *poso*). In all cases we used cursive writing, the school writing form in Argentina.

We classify the responses we obtained in the following way:

Response Type 1

Utilization of letters as graphic cues indicating the presence of a certain word. For example, *p* is not just one of the letters of *papá;* it is the cue which confers meaning on the whole word.

Estela: oso transformed to *poso* is *papá* and transformed to *moso* is *mamá.*

Griselda: oso transformed to *oos, osos,* and *soso* is still *"oso,* because it has the *s* and the *o."*

Alejandra: papá, amá, malá, mamá, alá are all equivalent to *"mamá,* because there's two *A*'s and the little dot (the accent mark)."

The graphic cues chosen by the children are varied: Estela uses the initial letter; Griselda uses two of the letters in the word; Alejandra uses two identical letters, one with an accent mark. For all of them, though, if the graphic cue is present, the rest matters little since the chosen cue determines the meaning of the whole.

Response Type 2

Consideration of the number of letters of each type necessary to construct the word, but independent of the order in which they appear.

Griselda thinks that *mamá* transformed to *amam* is also *"mamá,* but the accent mark is missing." The accent mark can go anywhere; she is satisfied when we place it over the first *a* (*ámam*). The transformations of *papá* produce the following responses:

    ppáa = *pa-pá*
    ppa = An *A* is missing.
    appá = Now it says *papá.*

Daniel accepts as being equivalent to *oso* all the transformations modifying the order (*soo* and *oos* also "say *oso*") but not the ones which modify the number of letters of each type (*soso* "doesn't say *oso* because it has two *s*'s").

Response Type 3

Consideration of the order, but only in terms of symmetry. Some children think that *oso* and *sos* are two variants of the same word, but they reject the other transformations because they do not have two identical letters with a different one in between.

Response types 1, 2, and 3 can appear in the same child, alternately, in going from one transformation to another. All these children are at the same level of cognitive development: the pre-operational stage (with the notion we tested, they were at the stage of nonconservation of number). After presenting the other responses types, we will comment on the relationship between cognitive level and responses produced by the children (see below, "How Children Write Receiving Aid in School").

Response Type 4
A slight graphic change (adding letters to the word) must correspond to a slight change in meaning.

Daniel thinks that *oso* tranformed to *osos* is *osa* (female bear), and transformed to *soso* is *osito* (little bear).

Sandra also thinks that in going from *oso* to *osos* we shift in meaning from *oso* to *osa*.

Response Type 5
A slight graphic change must correspond to a slight change in sound, not affecting meaning. In the following examples we see various procedures employed: elongating the vowel or the consonant sound, treating the added-on element as separate, and an accidental passage through a type 4 response.

Gladys, trying to interpret the transformation of *oso,* to *osos,* makes the following attempts: "*oso-s, ososss, osa, osooo, oso-sss, ososs, osoo.*"

Miguel reads *sol* (sun) correctly, but moving to *solo* he elongates the vowel reading "*soool,*" which to him means, simply, *sol.*

Rubén reads the transformations of *oso* in the following ways:
   osos = osso, oso, o-sso
   soso = os-osso, the *S* with *oso, oso*

Response Type 6
This level is a mixture of types 4 and 5, giving way at times to beautiful compromise solutions in which a whole sentence may appear in response to a transformation.

Omar recognizes the written word *nene* (boy) and reads the transformation *pnene* as "*nenépa,* which according to him means "boy who is grown up and is a father." But the same letter (*p*) added on to another word results in a different interpretation (and the contrast tells us that it does not function as a graphic cueing letter):
   oso   = oso
   poso = oso-pa
   osos = oso-p, osop

When we ask him what "osop" means, he tells us: "*un oso que toma la sopa*" (a bear that's eating soup).

Walter makes several attempts on the transformation *osos* ("*oso-esa, oso-se, oso-e*") without being satisfied. The next transformation, *soso,* is clear to him: "*oso* (male bear) backwards, *osa* (female bear)." He faces similar problems with the transformations of *sol* (sun):

    sol   = sol
    solo = sol-lo, sol-o, so-os, sol y nube (sun and cloud)
    solos = os, os-ol, sol-os

There is a common denominator among response types 4, 5, and 6: all children who give these responses are at the intermediate level of cognitive development (passage from the preoperational to the operational stage).

We will skip over the few cases of correct responses (given by children at the intermediate or operational stage) to attempt an overall explanation of all of these results.

Four to Seven Year Olds, before Receiving or Receiving Aid in School

Our most surprising finding is obtaining very similar responses from both preschool children and children who are exposed systematically, day by day, to the alphabetic code and its mysteries (presented as if there were no mysteries). We interviewed the group of six- and seven-year-old first graders at the middle of the school year. How many times must their teachers have written, broken down into letters and sounds, combined and recombined these beginning words? Nothing appears more simple: *m-a*, ma; ma-ma, *mamá*. It is a question of analysis and synthesis, in the traditional conception of instruction. But this traditional conceptualization differs from reality: while teachers demonstrate the apparent simplicities of this analysis (of the word and its components) and present the synthesis of these components as obvious and natural, children are learning something else.

Some school-age children, as well as some preschool ones, attend to the number of letters of the same type, ignoring their order, while others attend to the overall order (in terms of alternation or symmetry), forgetting the number of letters of each type. This focus on one or the other aspect of the written word becomes more comprehensible when we observe the nature of the first words (and sentences) that children learn in school, words that can be read the same way going from left to right or from right to left (*ala, oso, ama, ese*) or words with interchangeable syllables (*mamá, papá, nene*). These kinds of words constitute the universe of beginning literacy in school. They have been chosen intentionally as easy words. But easy for whom, from whose point of view, and from whose definition of easy?

The four to six year olds' responses regarding their own names (which rarely meet the prerequisites of being easy) suggest that it is easier to discover the existence of a nonrandom order of letters when the characters are more varied than when the same characters are repeated. Of course, it is one thing to reproduce a graphic string as a succession of characters in a fixed order and something totally different to attach a stable interpretation to the fragments of this series. The great majority of the six- and seven-year-old group, as well as the four to six year olds, are still far from establishing stable sound correspondences.

We obtained a key finding from the six and seven year old sample: all the children who focus on the number of characters to the exclusion of the order, or vice versa, are preoperational. Our interpretation is that instruction forces cognitive activity which is beyond their competence. It is too much for them to work simultaneously with breaking down a whole (the word) into its constituents (syllables and letters), reconstructing the whole from its parts, understanding the composition of subclasses of similar elements, focusing on the number of elements of each subclass (two *m*'s and two *a*'s, two *s*'s and one *o*), and finally, knowing the order of the elements as they form the whole. Preoperational children cannot do all these things at once. They can either take into account the order (in terms of alternations or symmetry), ignoring the number in each subclass of similar elements, or they can take into account the subclasses, disregarding the order of the elements within the whole. For the teacher, it is evident that the two syllables "mama" are abstracted from a whole which can be put back together, since the teacher is able to think of the whole and the parts at the same time. From a cognitive point of view, we have known for a long time that preoperational children are not able to work with wholes and parts simultaneously (Piaget and Szeminska, 1952, chapter 7).

Is it a defect to be preoperational at the age of six? Is it necessary to have reached the threshold of concrete operations—in terms of Piagetian stages—to learn to read and write? To learn according to school dictates it probably is necessary, but to learn in a different way it surely is not, as preschool children suggest. Our results indicate that for children who have little opportunity for extrascholastic learning and who are preoperational, school instruction does not stimulate cognitive activity at their own level, and, hence, does not allow them to approach written language intelligently.

It is evident to the teacher that breaking down the word *mamá* results in the syllables "ma-ma," and breaking down the syllable "ma" gives the phonemes /m/ and /a/, which can be associated with the corresponding letters. It is also evident that combining the phonemes /m/ and /a/ leads to the syllable "ma" and duplicating the syllable results in the word *mamá*. The heart of the matter is that we must learn to mistrust what appears obvious to adults. It is evident to an adult that if we arrive at the same number counting two sets of objects, both sets have the same number of objects. This is not obvious to a preoperational child.

Surprising responses come from children who imagine graphic similarities are associated with similarities in meaning. These responses are not exclusive of LC children. The only difference here between MC and LC is that in interpreting transformations of *mamá* and *papá*, those with MC backgrounds offer the maid as one more member of the family, while those with LC backgrounds are limited to grandparents, aunts, uncles, cousins, brothers, and sisters. What seems unusual is that these responses can come from children who are receiving school instruction concerned with establishing a correspondence between graphic characters and speech sounds. This clearly illustrates the abyss between cognitive activity that children develop and what the teacher believes is taking place. Once again we are dealing with a hypothesis developed by children, an original creation. An adult (teacher or not) would not tell children that words with similar meanings are written in similar ways, regardless of sound differences or similarities between them. It is obviously not a very good hypothesis for approaching an alphabetic writing system since it ignores sound similarities, but it is not a bad hypothesis for writing systems representing meaning in more direct ways. Here, again, is the uncertain demarcation line between writing and drawing. Historically writing represented the objects referred to (in a way that necessitated similar representations for similar objects) before it came to represent linguistic signs as such.

We have limited ourselves in this word transformation task to describing types of responses and not, as we have done for other tasks, establishing successive levels corresponding to levels of development. There are two reasons for this: (*a*) our data varies greatly from one child to another in the preschool group because, although almost all of them have some way of writing or recognizing their own name (and often names of brothers, sisters, and friends), this is not true for the words we use here; and (*b*) the children rarely give one type of response exclusively, and the only analysis compatible with the data would be in terms of alternative response types corresponding to the same level. We can do this with the six- and seven-year-old group. Using an external criterion (operational stage), we can detect the simultaneous utilization of three response types (to the exclusion of other types) in preoperational children and the same in intermediate children (in the transition period immediately preceding the operational stage).

In this sense the alternations that intermediate children present between two contradictory hypotheses is illuminating. These two hypotheses are: (*a*) a slight graphic change must correspond to a slight change in meaning; and (*b*) a slight graphic change must correspond to a slight change in sound which does not alter the basic meaning. When they work with the second of these hypotheses, children elongate vowels or consonants or treat the added-on sign separately (like "oso-se" for *osos*), a treatment consisting of assigning an approximate sound value—usually a syllable—after the emission of the word (even when the added-on sign appears at the beginning). Elongating vowels and consonants in a language like Spanish is introducing affective connotations without modifying the meaning of the message (contrary to languages which make a distinction between long and short vowels.) It also means that in their responses children use their linguistic knowledge. An *s* added to *oso* is correctly perceived as a duplication of one of the original signs and gives way to a prolongation of the oral emission of the word. What the children do not know is whether the consonant or the vowel must be prolonged. It is not yet a good phoneme-grapheme correspondence, but it is still a beginning attempt at varying the sound pattern in relation to the visually perceived variation.

How Children Write Receiving Aid in School

We have referred to the written productions of pre-school/kindergarten children. We now analyze the writing development of the twenty-eight children in our longitudinal study. This is a group of public school children, all from lower class backgrounds, who were receiving systematic instruction under methodologically similar conditions. The teachers of the two first grade groups used the same method and the same reading text. We interviewed this group on three occasions (during a one-year period, at the beginning, the middle, and the end).

With this data we study closely how children's hypotheses evolve as the instructional program advances. At the beginning of this chapter we delineate the development of writing in children who are not yet receiving aid in school, that is, a development independent of any instructional methodology. Here we attempt to discover how writing development takes place when children are exposed to systematic instruction. Comparing these situations may give us new insights into forms of progress, following natural development in the first case and guided by the methodological framework in the other.

The task we use in the first session consists of having the children write, without copying, words taught by their teachers and new words composed of the same letters combined in similar ways. We chose these kinds of words to avoid responses like "I don't know that one" and "we didn't have that yet."

During the second session, we ask the children to write other words, still using familiar letters, and we also ask them to write one sentence. In this session we introduce a new variant: we present pictures and ask the children to write something for each one. They decide what to write (within the limits established by the pictures). We use two kinds of pictures, one representing familiar objects and the other depicting a person involved in some kind of action.

In the third session we do different things depending on the level the child has reached. However, all children are asked to write both individual words and sentences. We ask the more advanced children to do a more complicated task involving the writing of a morpho-syntactic marker, in this case the plural marker. For this, we present a picture in which two girls are jumping rope.

When the children are to write something to go with a picture, we give them time to make predictions and then we ask them to write. For each task we try to pick the most opportune moment to ask the children to write, in accordance with their levels of development. We are careful to state all the words or sentences using intonation patterns of natural speech. These procedures present neither novelties nor extreme difficulties for the children. This situation differs from ones they are accustomed to in school in the absence of corrections on our part and the way we ask questions.

We are interested not only in analyzing the writing produced in each session but also in the development that takes place from one session to the next. We have grouped the responses according to the progress observed from one session to the next. The categorization of the responses is based on the successive levels we proposed earlier in this chapter. During each interview we also test for operational stage using the test of conservation of number.

Having examined the development of these children in terms of the writing levels we have established, we can record their developmental patterns as we do in table 6.3.

Group I (seven children). These children begin the year at response levels 1 and 2. At the middle of the year they all are at level 2. At the end of the year five of them have not gone beyond level 2, while two have advanced toward intermediate responses between levels 2 and 3 (that is, they are moving toward syllabic hypothesis). Five of these children did not advance and two experienced minimal progress.

The fact that this group presents similar responses in all three sessions is quite revealing. To what can we attribute this lack of progress? Certainly not to environmental influences, since they

Table 6.3. *The evolution of writing in first grade children.*

	Session 1	Session 2	Session 3
Level 5		Group IV ——⟩	Group IV
	Group IV ⟋ ⟍		
Level 4	Group IV	Group III ——⟩	Group III
			Group II
Level 3	Group III ——⟩	Group III	Group II
		Group II	Group II
Level 2	Group II		Group I
	Group I ——⟩	Group I ——⟩	Group I
Level 1	Group I		

were attending the same class as the rest of the children and receiving the same instruction. Before answering our question, let us review how we have characterized levels 1 and 2.

In level 1 writing is equated with reproducing the typical features of what the child identifies as the basic form, or model, of writing. For all Group 1 children, the chosen model is the one proposed by the teacher, characterized by a selection of key words like *mamá, papá,* and *oso* written in cursive (see "Traditional Methods of Reading Instruction" in chapter 1). Writing at this level consists of graphic characters similar to those selected by the teaching model: *m* and *p* combined with all the vowels they remember. The graphic reproductions of this group retain only some of the lines that define the characters. For example, the number of humps produced for the *m* varies from one child to another and sometimes even within one child. There are *m*'s with two, three, four, and even five humps. The *p* also presents varied representations: vertical stroke without the curve, looking like an *l;* vertical stroke with a separated curve; and more than one curve for the same vertical line (see illustration 11). In terms of the graphics, we believe interpretations labeling them "dysgraphia" are quite limiting. Recognizing that writing involves a certain development in visual-motor coordination, we formulate the following

Illustration 11

mamá y papá, nene, árbol, mesa

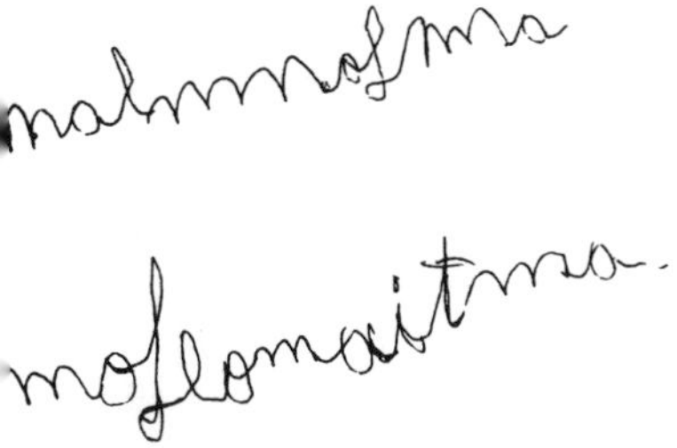

papá, mamá, nene y mesa

mi mamá sala la sopa
ala

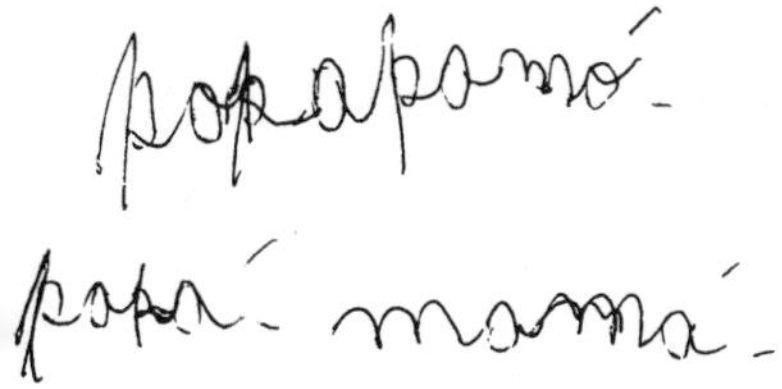

pato, sol y mesa

papá, mamá y nene

Alejandra (6 yrs., beginning schooling)

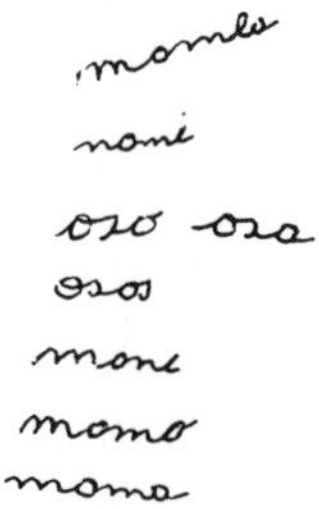

ala, mala, oso, osa, sos,
sol y mi mamá sala la sopa

Estella (6 yrs., beginning schooling)

hypothesis: if writing is the reproduction of the proposed model and the model is reduced to two consonants and five vowels, what possibilities do children have for discovering the distinctive strokes belonging to each of the graphic characters? Working on "one letter at a time," children cannot contrast letters to find their distinctive features. (In order to know that the number of strokes is a fundamental variable, one must know, for example, that *m* is distinct from *n*.)

Another characteristic of this group lies in the value they attach to the written characters. These children always reproduce *m*'s and *p*'s in varying quantities, as if they had some ritual function in writing: "writing is equivalent to making *m*'s" or "*m* means that what follows is writing." (One child uses *m* as the initial letter in nine out of ten cases.)

These children also tend to utilize letters as cues for interpreting words. (If it has an *m* it says *mamá* and if it has a *p* it says *papá*, regardless of the other letters.)

Finally, responses for the word-sentence opposition are identical to those given by preschool children. The differences between written words and written sentences are no greater than the differences between different written words. Children employ two kinds of resources to express differences: either they vary the graphics (in some cases resorting to printed characters) or they modify the quantity, conserving the characteristics of word writing. This is not surprising since for children at this level writing is representing names. They make use of the few resources they have—variation and quantity—to express changes in meaning.

Avoiding a detailed description of the responses, which add nothing to the previously analyzed data from the parallel preschool group, we will compare these responses to the results obtained from the external evaluation of operational stage. This test confirms that all the children in this group remained at the preoperational stage throughout the three interviews. Six children remained at the NC[1] level, while only one advanced to the INT level at the end of the year. In terms of the repeated action of establishing a one-to-one correspondence, none of these children were able to achieve a correct correspondence spontaneously. They arrived at it after many suggestions from the researcher, even though they continued giving NC responses to the evaluation of numerical quantity.

What does this finding mean? We propose a series of tentative hypotheses as possible explanations. It might be useful to think of

---

[1] Authors' Note: We designate as NC/INT/C the levels of nonconserving, intermediate, and conserving, respectively, on the test of conservation of number. For a description of the test see Inhelder, Sinclair, and Bovet, 1974.

the relationship between advances in one domain and advances in the other, involving not direct links but rather procedures fundamental to both domains. One of them, establishing correspondences, is a constituent action in the case of number and an underlying action in the case of writing (clearly expressed in cases of syllabic hypothesis—one syllable corresponds to one letter systematically).

It is also possible that the approach taken toward these two domains is similar in the sense that children are the ones who interpret the object, and they also place limits on what the environment proposes, in accordance with their own operational level. In the case of written language instruction, it is evident that what their teachers intend to teach is not what these children have learned. If the lack of progress in both of these domains cannot be attributed to the social medium, we must look in the domain of writing (as in the domain of logical-mathematical operations) to factors internal to children themselves.

Comparing parallel responses from the preschool group examines the influence of instruction on the children in Group I. In the preschoolers, responses of this type appear among MC and LC four and five year olds and tend to disappear around six years of age in the MC group (see table 6.2). This is in terms of quantitative distribution. Qualitatively, though, there are notable differences between the preschool group and the school-age (first grade) group. The first graders use a much smaller variety of letters, producing written texts which conserve *m*'s and *p*'s from the teaching model. Their stock of graphic patterns is also smaller, since the *mamá* and *papá* models are more limited than models provided by the world outside the school. The progression used in instruction (one letter at a time, beginning with *m, p, s*) can be detected by following the children's written productions. During the first session, at the beginning of the year, two of the seven children write everything they are asked to write according to the formula "*m* + vowel," while the remaining five use the formula "*m* or *p* + vowel." In the second session we note the additional appearance of *s, l, t,* and *n*. Finally, in the third session, some continue using the same set of letters, while others have added *r* and *g,* always in combination with vowels.

How can the difference between these children and the preschoolers be explained? The proposed model is the only possible explanation. If the model is taken from the surrounding world, one finds greater variety in graphic characters and their patterns of combination. If the model is reduced to words with only two graphic characters in repetition, the probability of variation in newly generated written texts is much less. To this we must add cursive writing (as the school writing form), which produces characters with a much smaller degree of differentiation. The difference, then, lies in the external model accessible to the child. Different conceptual mechanisms are not involved, since both groups evidence alternation, a more or less fixed quantity of characters, global, nonanalyzable reading, and so on.

If the results of a long period of systematic learning in these first graders are no different from spontaneous conceptual development in preschoolers, and if progress has been almost nil, what is it that these Group I children have learned.

At the end of the school year these children can write correctly some of the words presented by the teacher (usually *oso, mamá, papá, nene*), but when they agree to write new words their teacher has not taught, they display notable regressions. From a scholastic point of view they have learned to reproduce certain stimuli. From a conceptual point of view, their development has been minimal because learning the correct answer in a given context does not guarantee progress in reasoning. Recognizing and reproducing the elements of the writing code does not imply knowing how the alphabetic system functions. In unfamiliar situations these children follow the patterns of a cognitive approximation of the object, elaborating, according to their own hypotheses, stimuli the scholastic medium has presented.

Group I children persistently refuse to write words they have not been taught. One justifies this, affirming: "I don't know. I have rocks in my head. I'm a dummy!" (*Tengo la cabeza como un burro. Soy un burro!*) Hearing this from the mouth of a six year old after one year of school is distressing. It reveals two of the most serious problems of the instructional system: (*a*) if children do not learn it is their own fault and responsibility, and (*b*) the instructional method has a restraining effect on children's creative possibilities (experimenting and testing new ideas with all of the risks and errors this implies) and establishes a total dependency on the teacher. A significant observation is that resistance to writing increases toward the end of the school year.

Group II (six children). Included in this group are children who begin the year at level 2, reach level 3 (syllabic hypothesis) by the middle of the year, and at the end of the year either continue at level 3 (three children) or advance to a transition between 3 and 4 (three children).

The children in Group I begin at levels 1 and 2 and remain at level 2 throughout the school year. In Group II there are children who start out at the same level as those in Group I but are able to progress further.

The first graders we studied progress through the levels established for the preschool children. This developmental sequence is

more surprising in children exposed to systematic instruction. Obviously, neither of the two teachers taught these children that it is appropriate to write "ao" for *pato*, as the six children in this group do. The following example is quite illustrative (see illustration 12):

Griselda, during the first session, writes *mamá* as *ma*, *papá* as *mp*, *mesa* (table) as *mo*, *palo* (stick) as *mM*, *nene* as *mE*, and *oso* as *mR* (the *R* is an unclear graphic character).

During the second session she writes correctly *oso*, *mamá*, *papá;* and she writes *pato* (duck) as *ao*, *florero* (vase) as *oeo*, *sol* (sun) as *so*, and *sapo* (toad) as *so*.

During the third session she writes *paloma* (dove) as *pama*, *león* (lion) as *leo*, and *nudo* (knot) as *neo*.

Griselda provides a clear example of the progression characteristic of Group II. She starts at level 2 (combinations of the initial *m* plus some distinctive sign which marks the change in meaning), she moves on to level 3 (syllabic writing, one graphic character for each syllable), and she reaches level 4 (almost alphabetic writing with syllabic carry-overs). This progression is surprising because, in spite of the methodological proposals of alphabetic writing presented by the teacher throughout the year, in the middle of the year this girl writes using syllabic criteria and only after this does she arrive at an alphabetic approximation. This demonstrates the internal nature of the syllabic hypothesis, constructed by children and not imposed by the social medium, and it suggests the necessity of a period of syllabic hypothesizing before beginning to attach sound value to writing.

When we shift from writing names to writing sentences, children may conserve syllabic writing, assigning a sound value to each graphic character, or they may try to represent other units (always smaller than the originally proposed unit) but without assigning sound values. We continue with Griselda. The sentence writing takes place in the second session.

Mi mamá sala la sopa (my mom salts the soup) is written as *iamaaaa*, while *la nena está comiendo* (the girl is eating) is written as *dma aolo*. (We proposed the first sentence and she proposed the second in response to a picture.)

Griselda's fluctuation between assigning a sound value to the letters while not using spacing (as in the first sentence) and using spacing to produce separations in the written string while not assigning a sound value to the letters (as in the second sentence) typifies this group. Of the six children, five alternate between these two solutions. When Group II children think they must represent sound value (according to either the syllabic or an approximate alphabetic hypothesis), they are not capable of thinking about segmenting the sentence into smaller units (see chapter 4). While they work on immediate constituents (subject and predicate) they cannot think simultaneously about the sound value of the elements.

Comparing the responses obtained from Group II to the results obtained on the operational test, we confirm that all the children are at the INT level at the end of the year, reached through the following progressions: NC/INT/INT in one case, NC/NC/INT in two cases, and INT/INT/INT in three cases.[1]

The fluctuating behavior reflected by this group in writing coincides with behavior typical of the INT period, when children may give different kinds of responses depending on which aspects of the situation they focus on. The children in this group reflect progress in conceptualizing writing which parallels advances in operational level. Although we are not able to describe in detail the advances in each session and consequently cannot give a thorough explanation of the mechanisms and reasons for this growth, this development takes paths not expected within the school program.

Group III (twelve children). This group starts the year at level 3 (syllabic hypothesis). At the middle of the year six of them continue at level 3 while six others have moved on to level 4 (transition between the syllabic and the alphabetic hypothesis). All twelve of them reach level 4 by the end of the year. (Two of the children who were at level 4 in the second session could not be evaluated in writing a third time).

The progress evidenced by Group III confirms what we conclude from Group II: the internal and constructive nature of the period of syllabic hypothesizing and the necessity of passage through this level. These children are at level 3 at the beginning of the school year and they arrive at level 4 as a group by the end of the year. What does this finding tell us? Achieving the final point of this process—access to alphabetic writing—is closely related to the starting point. Or stated in other terms, children who begin school at level 3 have a good prognosis with respect to the learning that will develop in the school year. This good prognosis is because they initiate learning with a specifically linguistic hypothesis for approaching writing.

In terms of operational stage, all the children except one are at the INT or C levels by the end of the school year, despite great differences at the beginning of the year.

---

[1] Authors' Note: The children who remain at the INT level throughout the year make progress within this level. In our detailed analysis we differentiate the INT level as: INT−, INT, and INT+.

In writing sentences, the fluctuations described in Group II continue in Group III, although they are observed characteristically only at the middle of the year. Later, these children overcome this vacillation, demonstrating a more exhaustive search for the constituent units of the whole. Observe these two examples:

Javier, in the second session, writes *la nena cocina* (the girl cooks) as *nana moisin.* In the third session he writes *un sapo salta en la pileta* (a toad jumps in the pool) as *usapo salta enlapileta.*

Marcelo, during the second session, writes *mi mamá sala la sopa* (my mom salts the soup) as *mimamasabonsa.* During the third session he writes *un sapo nada en la pileta* (a toad swims in the pool) as *1 sapo nada pi le.*

These responses demonstrate clearly a vacillation between the units searched for. In the second session Javier separates the sentence into two, attributing the subject to one part and the predicate to the other. Marcelo is more concerned with sound values than with units smaller than the sentence and writes without leaving blanks. During the third session, both arrive at segmentation into smaller units while they conserve the sound values to an approximate degree. But while Javier joins the written string where it should be separated, Marcelo separates what should be joined together. This is not a random difference; if we analyze their earlier productions, we see that Javier was previously more concerned with finding units, while Marcelo focused more on letter-sound correspondences.

The alternate consideration of one or the other of these aspects and the attempts at reconciling them is what characterizes Group III and also explains a high percentage of the errors they commit. In fact, we encounter among these twelve children the greatest number of responses categorized by the school as errors—omissions, reversals, substitutions, and so on. (Only at this level does the school begin to view things as errors, since it treats earlier writing as scribbling or nonwriting.) Is it legitimate to label as error the product of profound intellectual work? When children apply the syllabic hypothesis they match one graphic character to syllables that may have one (as in the case of vowels in Spanish), two, three, or even four letters in their alphabetic transcriptions. It is evident that they omit in their writing what they do not know: the alphabetic transcription of each syllable. Reversals may also be the result of attempting letter-sound correspondence, a task so difficult that it often involves losing track of the order. One example may serve to clarify this point.

Cesar, while trying to write *pato* (duck), dictates to himself in the following way: "pa-to, *T,* (writes *pa*), pa, *P* again, *P,* pa-to" (adds *p* to get *pap*). While writing *pie* (foot): "pie, pie, *e,* pie, (writes *p*), *e, E,* pie" (adds *e* to the left of *p,* ending up with *ep*).

Substitutions can also be explained. When children do not identify the letter corresponding to each sound value, or the sound value corresponding to each letter, they inevitably produce substitutions. Even though they are unfamiliar with all the rules of graphic transcription, children at this level know that it is a question of attaching sound value to writing. In other words, they have discovered the underlying principle of our system of writing. Reversals, substitutions, and omissions appear as much in the writing of words as they do in the writing of sentences. Why do we encounter these so-called errors with such frequency in this group of children who have the best prognosis of the groups presented? Schools tend to interpret intermediate steps in a constructive process as definitive results. Contrary to what has been generally thought, we believe these errors reflect the mechanisms of constructing knowledge.

Group IV (three children). This group, the smallest, is composed of children who are at level 4 (or between 4 and 5) at the beginning of the year and who have learned the rules of the alphabetic code by the end of the year. They do, however, have some difficulties with spelling and word boundaries. All three of the children in Group IV are at the C operational level by the end of the year. Their progressions are as follows: INT/C/C; INT/INT/C; and C/C/C.

The fact that the members of this group, who know in a strict sense the functioning of the alphabetic code, have spelling or word boundary problems tells us that it is necessary to distinguish these two aspects. Discovering the possibility of graphically representing the sounds of language does not mean understanding the entire writing system. One does not automatically imply the other, because writing is not solely the representation of the sound aspect of oral language. Writing employs "markers" which carry specific meanings.

Let us think, as an example, about the plural. In Spanish many plural nouns are formed by adding the morpheme /s/, represented by the letter *s* in writing, to the base morpheme. There is no apparent reason why the writing of a plural noun should present difficulties.

The task consists of presenting a picture of two girls jumping rope and asking the children to write something to go with the picture. We did this task with six children: the three from Group IV and three of the most advanced from Group III. They all describe the picture orally as "two girls jump" (*dos nenas saltan*) or "the girls are jumping" (*las nenas están saltando*). Of the six, only one—from Group IV—is able to distinguish the plural by using the final *s*, ending up with the written text "girls jumping" (*nenas saltando*). All the others propose rather curious solutions: two children place the numeral 2 in front of the sentence written in the singular; one child writes "girl" (*nena*) twice, ending up with "the girl girl jumps" (*la nena nena salta*); one child simply writes the sentence in the singular; and another writes the whole sentence twice.

The graphic transcription of the phoneme /s/ clearly does not present difficulties to these children. One might argue that their problem with the plurals' is due to dialect charcteristics (the final /s/'s are often not pronounced in the regional dialect). The plural issue for these children is more than a problem of sound transcription; it is the discovery of a marker with a functional value in writing. The diverse solutions to this situation are another demonstration of the cognitive approach the children are taking. The problem of which language elements are represented in writing and how they are represented continues even at this level. Children do not use sound analysis exclusively. They also analyze the content to be represented. This why they offer such original solutions: repeating the noun or repeating the sentence, since there are two people, or using the numeral 2 as a marker which takes on an ideographic value leaving intact the alphabetic writing of the utterance. These data show that writing cannot be reduced to a transcription of speech, because in addition to rules of sound transcription, there are other internal rules which children discover gradually.

The results of this year-long study illuminate some points raised in our original questions:

• While teachers follow a program utilizing the same methodology for all children, not all children advance at the same pace.
• Those who learn to write by the end of the school year are those who start out at rather advanced levels of conceptualization. Those who do not learn in the same period of time start at beginning levels of conceptualization.
• There are no radical leaps in learning. All the children develop, passing through the levels of conceptualization we describe for the preschool children.
• It appears that systematic instruction, as practiced currently, is directed exclusively toward children who have come a long way in conceptualizing writing before entering school.
• There are no great differences between responses from first graders and those from preschoolers.

We gathered the data on children in the course of schooling before we did the research on preschool children. Our research procedures at that time were not sufficiently refined to permit us to observe the details of their development. Subsequent studies will allow us to explore the development of conceptualizing writing in first grade children in a new way, thanks to what we have learned from preschool children.

There remains an important problem that only longitudinal studies can resolve: starting at the same level, Group I children advance very slowly while Group II children advance more rapidly. Progress in writing coincides with progress in operational stage (we are referring explicitly to coincidence here, not to a causal relationship). Problems of developmental pace are related but distinct from problems of the sequence of developmental levels or periods. Our analysis focuses on the sequence of levels. In this sense, our results are surprising because they indicate a regular progression, with or without the intervention of schooling. Moreover, with an intervention that attempts to push children immediately into the alphabetic writing system, we see children advance through a series of levels unforeseen by both method and teacher.

VII READING, DIALECT, AND IDEOLOGY

It is a common belief that students' pronunciation must be corrected to avoid difficulties in learning to read and write. In this chapter we argue a counter thesis: the supposed correct or standard pronunciation ignores dialect variations, imposes the speech norms (real or idealized) of the dominant social class, and, in doing so, introduces ideological content into the learning of written language.

The ideological content of typical basal readers has often been examined. These readers rarely mention workers and refer too often to the middle class family: well groomed with nice clothes, fair skin, and light hair, living in a house that has at least two bedrooms and a living room as well as a bathroom and kitchen, with a mother who sews, knits, and cooks while father reads the newspaper—in short, a family that has nothing to do with the living conditions of the majority of the Latin American[1] population and that projects a model image of the ideal middle class child.

First grade teachers (mostly women) are rarely conscious of the incongruities they transmit when they teach middle class ideological cliches. Two anecdotes will serve as examples. A first grade teacher in a school on the outskirts of the Argentinean capital, in her sixth month of pregnancy, teaching the famous "mother, father, sister, brother" series, does not hesitate to ask her class, "Who is the one who works in the family?" She, of course, expects her pupils to answer, "the father." What, then, is she, teacher and future mother, doing? Is it not work? Why is it that the mother must always busy herself with household chores, going from one never-ending task to another, while at school another woman teaches her children that women do not work?

Another teacher in a similar school gives a lesson on "rooms in the house," apparently for vocabulary enrichment: kitchen, bedroom, living room, bathroom. However, this lesson is directed toward children who live in *villas miserias*,[2] in precariously constructed houses where one room fulfills all functions. In reality this lesson achieves a very different purpose. The children learn that where they live is not really a house. They thought their homes, although different from the places where others lived, were still houses, but in school they learn that this is not so.

The ideology of the dominant social class is not only transmit-

---

[1] Translator's Note: This applies to North America as well.
[2] Translator's Note: These are makeshift slums on the outskirts of the city.

ted through history and geography lessons and through the pages of the basal readers. It also works its way into the transmission of "neutral" notions in apparently ideology-free areas of instruction, such as the introduction of the alphabetic code. In Spanish the letter *ll* is the orthographic representation of different sounds in different regions of the Spanish-speaking community.[1] A phonological phenomenon of great significance and geographical extension is known in Spanish as *yeísmo*. It consists of loss of the distinctive pronunciation represented by *ll* (phonetically, a lateral palatal consonant, similar to the medial sound in "million") which assimilates to the pronunciation represented by *y* (Malmberg, 1977, pp. 53–54).

In Spain and the Americas the dominant articulation of *ll* and *y* is technically a voiced palatal fricative with a sound similar to the initial consonant in the English word "yes" or the medial consonant in the French word *piller*. But "in the Rio de la Plata zone and surrounding areas, particularly in the cities of Buenos Aires, Rosario, and Montevideo, *y* and *ll* are pronounced with a sibilant sound, similar to the initial consonant in the French word *jambe*, characterized by palato-alveolar articulation and by vibration of the articulating organs" (Malmberg, pp. 59–60).[2]

The phonetic description of this phenomenon is not important for our purposes, but the fact that two graphemes (*ll* and *y*) represent one phoneme is important. (We are not concerned here with cases in which *y* represents the vowel *i* in Spanish as in *hoy*, *ley*, and so on.)

Two issues come together here in terms of instructional practice in Argentina. One is the tendency to present the alphabetic system as a system where one sound corresponds to each grapheme. The other is that in Buenos Aires, the distinction between *ll* and *y* is considered a sign of correct speech. The joint force of these two issues leads teachers to introduce the letter *ll* with its traditional sound value (a sound value very seldom used in current speaking norms). This fulfills a double objective. It avoids a new exception to the rule and at the same time it introduces children to proper speech using correct pronunciation. The temptation *ll* inspires is difficult to resist: since we know how it "should" be pronounced, why not teach that sound?

However, that sound does not correspond to any real sound in either the teacher's or the children's speech. Let us suppose that the teacher comes from the Rio de la Plata region and teaches in a school near a *villa miseria*. In Argentina, officially speaking, there

[1] Translator's Note: *Ll* is considered one letter in the Spanish alphabet.

[2] Translator's Note: This sound is similar to the medial consonant in the English word "vision," the phonetic transcription of which is [3].

are no linguistic problems, but this teacher would find great linguistic variation in her classroom since children in a *villa miseria* come from different provinces of Argentina or from bordering countries such as Paraguay and Bolivia. Which pronunciation norm can this teacher adopt?

This situation is not atypical. Of the twenty-eight children we interviewed in a school of this type in our first research study, only six came from families who were native to the region. The remaining families came from ten Argentinean provinces (Salta, Entre Rios, Corrientes, Mendoza, Cordoba, Santiago del Estero, Tucuman, Chaco, Misiones, and Santa Fe) and two bordering countries (Chile and Bolivia). One of the girls in this group, Laura, born in Entre Rios of a father from Tucuman, provides the following dialogue toward the end of the first grade. Laura is seven years old at the time of the dialogue. Her teacher has introduced the letter *ll* with a word such as *pollito* (chick). (In the transcription of the dialogue we use *ll* for the traditional pronunciation of this consonant, *y* for the pronunciation of the Rio de la Plata region and *i* when referring to *y* as representing a vowel sound.)[1]

Do you know this letter? (*y*)[2]	That's *I*. When it's by itself it's *I*. When it's with something else too. . . . And there's also another *I* of another kind.
(Writes POYO [unconventional spelling for *pollo*—chicken].) What does this say?	. . . I don't know what it says . . . u u . . . *po-i-po*. I don't know.
(Writes YO [pronoun I].) Do you know how to read it now?	Not that because we . . . only when it's in the title (of a lesson), you know, it's by itself and also in dictation, it's also by itself in dictation.
(Writes YA [adverb meaning "already" or "now"].) Can you read it like that?	No, not that either.
(Writes POLLO [chicken].) And this?	It says *pollo* (emphatically pronouncing the *ll*). Yes, because we also learned *lluvia*. You don't say *yuvia*, you say *lluvia*.
Oh. You don't say *yuvia*?	No. The teacher taught us that you say *lluvia*.
And when you go to the meat market, what do you ask for, a *poyo* or a *pollo*?	*Poyo*, you say *poyo* for that, but . . . but for *lluvia* you say *lluvia*.

[1] Authors' Note: This data was originally presented in Ferreiro, 1975.

[2] Translator's Note: In Spanish the *y* can represent a consonant or the vowel also represented by *i* in Spanish and similar to the long *e* in English. It can also appear as a single-letter word meaning "and," which is pronounced in the vowel form.

And what did it say here? (*pollo*)

There it says . . . *pollo* (stressing the pronunciation of the *ll* with confidence).

How do you say it, *pollo* or *poyo*?
And how do you write it?
Poyo!

You say *poyo*.
How do you write what?
Poyo, I don't know how you write it . . . (in a low, doubtful tone). We know how to read, but some letters are . . .

What's this? (*pollo*)
And what's *pollo*?

Pollo.
Pollo? *Pollo* is . . . is an animal. You can also say *pollo, pollo,* and *poyo.*

You can say it both ways?

Yes, because the animal is the same word and it's the same animal.

It's the same animal . . . does it have two names?

It doesn't have two names. It has *poyo* and *po*. . . . Well, it has two names. You can only call it any name of those, but it doesn't have two names.

It's *poyo* or *pollo.* And when I write, what do I have to put, *poyo* or *pollo*? Either one. But, *yuvia* and *lluvia,* how is that?
You don't say *yuvia*?

Whatever!

Llu, lluvia. Just *lluvia, lluvia.*

No; it has two names, but you can't call it *yuvia.* If not, the word's upside down.

How's that?

That the word is upside down? If you don't call it *lluvia,* then you can't write it! Because, only if you call it *lluvia.*

If you don't call it *lluvia* you can't write it?
When a lot of water is coming down from the sky, what do you say? Look how it's . . .

Yes, you can also write *yuvia* but you say *lluvia.* The teacher told us so.
Look, how the rain (*lluvia*) is coming down (spoken with a forced tone which Laura perceives as artificial and she immediately excuses herself). Well, but that's how you speak, you don't say it another way. . . . The teacher told us so, that you don't say it another way . . .

But in the meat market you ask for a *poyo* . . .
You say *poyo,* not *pollo* . . .

Yes, *poyo,* not *pollo.* A *poyo.* You don't say *pollo.*
Yes, but you can also say that (meaning you can also say *pollo*).

Some people from other places say *pollo,* right? But here we say *poyo.*

Poyo, yes. For example, over where my godmother lives, it's a villa (pronounced *viya*) and there everybody talks a different way.

Where does your godmother live?

You know where the hospital is? Well, it's over there, you turn in, and . . . there's all dirt streets (*calles*—

And why do they talk different there?

Of course. In every town the people speak a little differently.

pronounced *cayes*) and in the back it's all garbage.

I don't know, the people are from somewhere else, from another town. Because we can't understand Italians. Because there's a girl who's my friend whose parents are Italian and every time they call her, who knows what they say to her!

You were born in Entre Rios, right?

No, I wasn't. I was born here in Argentina.

And how do they talk in Entre Rios?

In Entre Rios? They talk a little the same as us but they don't talk . . . right, like Argentineans.

Who talks right like Argentineans?

Us who are Argentineans. Me, for example; my father. . . . No, not my father. My father is from Tucuman but he talks like an Argentinean. . . . I don't know. . . . He is from Tucuman . . .

And if he talked like a person from Tucuman, would it be wrong?

He does talk like somone from Tucuman, but he talks like an Argentinean. He knows how to talk. But sometimes he calls me and who knows what he says. He calls me Laura but he says it another way. He talks to me in a Tucuman way.

But it's like *pollo* and *poyo* . . .

Yes, and in Tucuman they say *poio* . . . (She becomes perplexed by what she has just discovered.)

And which is better, *poio* or *poyo*?

Poyo . . . (in a low voice. She thinks and then continues with conviction). Yes, but there are other countries where they speak different and they have to say it how they say it. They're not going to start to talk . . . as if it was wrong. We're not going to have to teach them, no. They teach them like they know.

The example is eloquent. Laura's ability to reason and become aware of dialect differences is quite remarkable. No less remarkable is the lack of knowledge the instructional system displays regarding this very issue. For the seemingly harmless objective of teaching "one more letter," the instructional program introduces an ideological discrimination between "good" and "bad" dialects, between "correct" and "incorrect" ways of speaking. Effective communication acts are superimposed by prescribed norms alien to language users. Children learn in school that they must speak with *ll*, for how can *ll* be written if it is not pronounced? This attempt to make each grapheme correspond exclusively to one phoneme is misguided, since it is inconsistent from a linguistic point of view, contradictory from a didactic point of view, and dangerously tainted with prejudicial connotations from an ideological point of view.

Without technical terms to explain her thoughts precisely, Laura manages to express all the pertinent distinctions. She tells us that it is not appropriate to consider *pollo* and *poyo* two different names, but rather two different ways of pronouncing the same name, two acceptable variants for articulating one shared meaning. She points out the difficulty that any speaker has in imitatively adopting the dialect of another ("who knows what he says," referring to an unreproducible mode of pronunciation). She makes us see the conflict between rules learned in school for "correct speech" which permit access to writing ("if you don't call it *lluvia* then you can't write it") and existing forms of speech—such as that of her father—recognized as being different from the teacher's and doubly inferior since they are used neither in school nor in the capital of the country.

(The problem of distinguishing Argentineans from residents of Entre Rios or Tucuman is a different problem, not unique to Laura but shared by children of her age. The problem of recognizing double membership—of the province of origin and of the country—requires being able to handle class-inclusion relationships [in logical terms]: if *A* is a subset of *B*, then all *a*'s are also *b*'s while still being *a*'s. This is not established as a logical consequence until eight or nine years of age.)

Finally, Laura ends by expressing respect for dialect variations. How wonderful it would be if teachers shared this respect. "Yes, but there are other countries (for Laura, 'country' is synonymous with region or place) where they speak different and they have to say it how they say it. They're not going to start to talk . . . as if it was wrong. We're not going to have to teach them, no. They teach them like they know."

Laura's clear perception of the differences connoted by the *y*/*ll* pronunciations is shared by other children. One child explains the different pronunciations for chicken, *pollo* and *poyo*: "*pollo* is the live animal; *poyo* is the dead one." Another explains the different pronunciations for street: "*cayes* are the unpaved ones and *calles* are the paved ones." The ideological transmission effectively reaches the receivers. The children understand that the difference in pronunciation is linked to a difference in value: living as opposed to dead, the pavement of the city as opposed to the unpaved streets of the outskirts and rural areas.

This problem goes far beyond the pronunciation of *ll*. Spanish is taken as an example of a written language system in accordance with alphabetic principles, and yet, when one considers the variation in the Spanish-speaking community, the arbitrary orthographic conventions can be seen clearly. The words *cesto* (basket) and *sexto* (sixth), which look quite different in writing, are pronounced identically by speakers from the Rio de la Plata region. The plural *-s,* written regularly, is almost inaudible in these same speakers, as is the *s* in certain consonant clusters (*fo*[s]*foro*[s], *re*[s]*frio, a*[s]*falto*).

An interesting problem is the inverse effect writing has on the ideas speakers form about their own pronunciation. Because we write *hueso* (bone) so much, we are convinced that this is how we pronounce it even though we actually say *gueso*. We write *agujero* (hole) but we say *aujero*. We write *obscuro* (dark) but we say *oscuro*. And so on.[1]

Is it perhaps necessary to introduce a spelling reform to adapt written Spanish to distinct local pronunciations? If such a task were possible, the consequences would be unacceptable. But this kind of reform could never be accomplished because geographic and social mobility result in many speech variants coexisting in the same geographic zone. Even if one were to find a sufficiently homogeneous linguistic community, spoken language still changes more quickly than written language. (The orthographic correspondence established today would not be valid a few years from now, and it is inconceivable that such a reform could take place every few years.)

However, the consequences of such an idea, if it could be done, would be grim, as it would cause difficulties in written communication between members of the Spanish-speaking community. Uniformity in writing, in spite of marked differences in speech, fulfills a social function which cannot be dismissed. It permits written communication between people who use variations of the same language. The same written text read with different pronunciations in Buenos Aires, Mexico City, or Madrid is comprehended in a similar way. Comprehending the meaning of the written message is what matters, even though different readers may have their own way of translating it into sound signs, of oralizing it.

It seems to be relatively easy to tolerate pronunciation differences between nations, but this is often not the case for differences within one nation. Rural speakers of Spanish say *juimos al pueblo* (the written form is *fuimos al pueblo* [we went to town]) as

---

[1] Translator's Note: The pronunciation of words and strings such as asks, poem, wanted, west side, have to, and got to in many dialects of English do not represent the writing system in ways English speakers believe they do.

well as *hicimos juego* (the written form is *hicimos fuego* [we made a fire]). Must these speakers modify their speech and learn to say *fuego* and *fuimos* in order to learn to read and write? Or is the important thing their comprehending these words when they see them in writing (just as we all comprehend the same meanings in spite of variations in pronunciation) even though they read them— out loud—in a different way?

We are referring here to dialect variations, not to individual speech defects or to immature pronunciation forms. A dialect is an adult oral language variation belonging to a particular social group.

Quite probably, most teachers would not be pleased to hear that they speak a dialect of Spanish (or English, as the case may be). They would feel uncomfortable because the term dialect has a negative connotation in common social usage. A language has more social prestige than a dialect, since "dialect is a term that suggests informal, lower class or rural speech." In common usage, "dialect is thought of as being outside of language, as not being correct language." In terms of social norms "a dialect is a language which is excluded from educated society" (Haugen, 1972).

However, in linguistic terms, a language is defined as "the means of communication between speakers of different dialects, within the same linguistic family" (Haugen). In truth, everyone speaks a dialect variation of some language, but recognizing dialects does not imply denying the existence of norms or standards. For a dialect to exist, there must be a set of linguistic norms shared by a social group. There is, then, no opposition between a standard language (the dialect of prestige, identified as the language itself) and deviant forms of speech (the other dialects). The distinction is not represented by an opposition between the absence and the presence of norms. The issue is knowing who decides, and in whose name, which dialect variation enjoys the most social prestige. In this regard, history has been clear and unequivocal, from antiquity to the present: the speech pattern of the dominant social class of the political center of the nation (generally, the capital) has been identified as the national language. In this way, the form of language spoken in Athens became Greek, that of the Paris area became French, that of Castille became Spanish, and so on.

The history of languages is a political history and the language-dialect distinction is a history of the vicissitudes of internal domination. Max Weinreich's definition is extremely apt, although it may appear sarcastic: "a language is a dialect with an army and a navy" (Kavanagh and Mattingly, 1972, p. 128).

The problem of dialect differences and their role in literacy development is far from exclusive to Latin America. In the United States an emotional debate—still unresolved—has arisen because dialect differences between black Americans and white Americans involve not only marked differences in pronunciation but also important syntactic differences. Black English has also been called nonstandard Negro English (NNE) in opposition to the standard dialect of English, or standard English (SE). Here are some parallel constructions which give an idea of the differences. (Examples are taken from different texts of Baratz and Labov):

SE:	He RUNS home	NNE:	He RUN home
	She HAS a car		She HAVE a car
	He IS GOING		He GOIN'
	I don't HAVE ANY		I don't GOT NONE
	I ASKED IF he DID it		I ASK DID he DO it

The differences are significant. In NNE the third person singular -*s* marker is omitted; the copulative is omitted; the double negative is permitted, and so on. These differences were long considered to be poor forms of speech, deviations from the norm, and not norms in their own right. After a series of extremely serious linguistic studies—among which those of William Labov deserve special mention—it is no longer possible to support that opinion. These studies have demonstrated that black English is not an inferior dialect, but rather a dialect different from standard English. The title of one of Labov's most widely quoted articles is "The Logic of Nonstandard English", a title that is a definition in itself.

In demonstrating the internal linguistic structure of black English, Labov is conscious that he is not carrying out a strictly academic task. The notion that black children's language is so deficient as to be responsible for school failure had been maintained authoritatively by numerous educational psychologists with no background in linguistics. Bereiter's and Englemann's compensatory preschool education programs (mid-1960s) are the best example. They establish the necessity of teaching black children to talk, because what they have learned in their "culturally deprived" homes is not even language. Labov states clearly, "the myth of verbal deprivation is particularly dangerous, because it diverts attention from real defects of our educational system to imaginary defects of the child" (p. 202).

Once the dialect of black Americans is accepted as a valid form of language, the problem becomes how to handle this dialect in teaching reading. Three positions arise offering these solutions (Wolfram, 1970): (*a*) prepare special beginning readers written in black English; (*b*) revise existing books to neutralize dialect differences, avoiding all structures which differ between dialects, but without introducing any black English structures; and (*c*) utilize existing materials, but allow children reading out loud to translate what they read into their own dialect.

The first alternative has given way to decided (and foreseeable) opposition from parents and community leaders who see it as a new form of discrimination. The second alternative presents serious problems. A considerable number of syntactic structures must be avoided (for example, all third person singular structures). Also, this alternative deals only with grammatical differences, while the most pervasive dialect differences in English involve pronunciation.

The third alternative is the most innovative. As Goodman, one of its most explicit supporters, expresses it: "No special materials need to be constructed but children must be permitted, actually encouraged to read the way they speak" (1965, p. 860).

The most immediate objection to this alternative would be: how can someone read in one dialect something written in another? This objection dissolves immediately with another question: written English is the transcription of which English—the English of England or of the United States ("two countries separated by a common language," according to Shaw)? Written Spanish is the transcription of which spoken form? Throughout Latin America we are able to read and understand the same newspapers and books without interpreters or translators. But which spoken language does the written language transcribe?

The contribution of two contemporary linguists, Noam Chomsky and Morris Halle, allows us to clarify this discussion. In "The Sound Pattern of English" (1968) these authors demonstrate that English orthography, usually considered highly irregular (due to numerous divergencies from phoneme-grapheme correspondence), is actually quite regular. This regularity does not appear in the superficial phonetic form (that is, the apparent, observable form) but at a more abstract level of lexical representation. There are words close in meaning but different in pronunciation, as in the case of "nation/nationality," "medicate/medicine," and "resident/residential." Many of these pronunciation shifts are systematic, as are shifts in stress (as in "telegraph/telegraphic/telegraphy"). A phonetic representation would make it difficult to recognize the semantic relationship between these pairs or sets of words, each of which constitutes one lexeme with one meaning. "Nation" and "national" differ at the level of articulation, but at the lexical representational level they are forms of the same lexeme and correspond to one meaning (contrary to minimal pairs at the phonemic level that are very different at the lexical level, such as "nation/notion" or, in Spanish, *contaba* [counted] and *cantaba* [sang]).

Carol Chomsky, commenting on the pedagogical implications of these developments in phonology (1970), argues that English orthography helps the reader, since words which belong to the same lexeme are similar in writing. This helps the reader in that it permits more direct access to meaning and avoids wasting time on superficial details irrelevant to comprehension. Also, the same written text can be interpreted in all dialects. If we remember (something often forgotten) that children already know how to pronounce the words when they learn to read, the problem becomes identifying the word through its meaning in order to pronounce it, and not producing sounds through deciphering to find the meaning later.

This leads to a discussion on the definition of reading itself, included in the conclusions to this book (see "Reading Is Not Deciphering; Writing Is Not Copying" in chapter 8). Here we will simply point out that the answer to the question "which dialect variation does written Spanish transcribe?" is neither obvious nor immediate. Inspired partially by Chomsky and Halle, we tentatively give this answer. Written language should not necessarily be, and usually is not, a phonetic transcription of speech. The written signs may correspond to phonic forms that do not coincide exactly with the actual sounds, but if the semantic similarities linking different forms of the same lexeme are reflected in writing, then the writing system lends itself easily to dialect variations of pronunciation. Consequently, none of these dialect variations enjoys the status of correct pronunciation for learning to read.

(This interpretation of Chomsky and Halle describes certain aspects of the English writing system as being similar to ideographic writing. The ideographic components of French writing have been pointed out by several authors. For example, Blanche-Benveniste and Chervel [1974] analyze many cases where written French establishes a visual difference between words when there is no auditory difference, as in the series *pin, pain, peint*; *vain, vint, vingt, vainc, vin*; *tan, tant, temps, tend*. The difference between alphabetic and ideographic writing systems is not as clear-cut as it would seem, not only because alphabetic systems introduce ideographic principles but also because ideographic systems frequently use characters with phonetic value. For a technical discussion of the notion of optimal orthographic representation, we refer to Klima, "How alphabets might reflect language" [1972].)

Returning to Goodman's proposal, it is not necessary to change materials, but rather to allow children to read the way they speak. It serves no purpose to merely change materials; we must change how the process is conceived. There are reasons why this alternative has been the least explored. It goes against linguistic prejudices (in maintaining that there are no "bad" dialects) and also against traditional conceptions of learning to read through deciphering (or phonics). (It also goes against the industry linked to instruction, always ready to produce new texts, new materials, and new manuals.) It has been the least explored in spite of indications in the literature of its feasibility. Cases of black preschool children who learn to read by themselves, and who read, in black English, texts written not in white English but simply in English, are examples of this (Smith, 1973).

Should schools, then, refrain from correcting the pronunciation of their pupils? Since this is a critical issue, it must be answered with precision.

One must not confuse dialect variation with pronunciation defects. The mode of pronunciation or of construction belonging to a dialect is very different from the persistence of "baby talk" forms or idiosyncratic pronunciations. Linguistic rejection is one of the most serious forms of rejection and has detrimental affective consequences. Individuals cannot change the way they speak at will. When we reject the language children bring from home, we are rejecting them as human beings, along with their family and the social group to which they belong.

Homogenizing speech based on written language is an impractical school objective. Whenever schools attempt to stop language change in their lifesaving missions to preserve cultural values, they play on the losing team. Language is a live instrument of social interchange and its evolution takes place outside of school. Schools can help to conserve a language in contact with other languages (a typical situation in border schools or schools of national minority groups within a larger national community). Schools can perpetuate certain stylistic variations, independent of their communicative function. Schools can assume the distinction between correct and incorrect speech, stigmatizing dialects and appropriating the hierarchy established by the dominant classes within the society. But they cannot stop the development of the linguistic community they serve. For many years schools in Argentina fought against *voseo* (informal second person singular pronoun and verb conjugation form used commonly in Argentina) and in favor of *tuteo* (parallel form used in many other parts of the Spanish-speaking world). Teachers were obligated to use with their pupils—and pupils with their teacher—the *tuteo* form, viewed as the correct linguistic pattern (*tu eres* instead of *vos sos* [parallel expressions of "you are"]). This became one more barrier to the already difficult communication between teachers and students, but it did not change to the slightest degree the linguistic pattern of the Argentinean capital.

Finally, national educational policies may establish the need to provide all children access to a speech form which will facilitate future social integration. (For example, black Americans encounter many barriers to upward social mobility because they are black, but the barriers are greater if they do not know how to speak like white Americans.) This is not the place to discuss whether such a policy is justifiable or not. We know that it is feasible. It involves teaching another form of speaking. Forms of speaking are learned, especially by children, in speaking contexts, in communicative situations. Let us teach people, if judged necessary, how to speak other dialects. But we must not establish this as a prerequisite for learning to read, because it would establish an invalid causal relationship. We would also be setting up a double barrier to learning: to the learning of reading by forcing future readers to change dialects before allowing them access to written language; and to the learning of the new dialect by presenting it outside of any real communicative contexts.

VIII CONCLUSIONS

Guided by the hypothesis that all knowledge involves a psycho-genesis, we have attempted to discover the initial forms of written language knowledge and the accompanying conceptualization processes. Conceptualization is a dynamic process involving the interaction of the ideas of the knowing subject and the reality of the object of knowledge. Our central question is directed toward learning how children come to be readers in the psychogenetic sense before they are readers in the conventional sense. The problems involve both the nature of written language as an object of knowledge and the appropriation of written language by children.

We hope that the data presented here contribute new elements to the psychogenetic theory of knowledge, and that some of the results of our work will lead to a reconsideration of educational practice in the field of literacy.

As a general summary, we will outline the development of reading and writing in four to six year olds, listing the problems they pose along with their ways of solving them.

Problems Children Pose

By the age of four most children have already solved an initial problem: writing is not just lines or marks but a substitute object representing something external to the graphics themselves. (We hope to verify the psychogenesis of written language as a substitute object in our current longitudinal studies beginning with three year olds.) The fact that children view print as a substitute object does not mean that they initially conceive of it as a representation of language or, even less likely, as a representation of the formal aspects of speech (the sound elements or phonemes). The first problem to solve, then, is what does written language substitute, what meaning is attached to it? In other words, what does print represent and what is the structure of this representational mode? At this age, drawing is the preferred form of graphic representation. Picture and print are material substitutes for something which comes to mind, manifestations of the more general semiotic function, and they have a common origin in terms of graphic representation. However, the relationship between the two cannot be reduced to simple confusion. Most four year olds know when the result of graphic marking is a picture and when it can be called writing. Attempting to understand what writing represents, children try to establish a dividing line between drawing and writing and, in a parallel sense, between picture and print. The following summarizes the sequence of solutions children explore.

When interpreting a text accompanied by a picture, the meaning of the picture is attributed to the print. Both are assimilated in terms of the meaning attached to them. Pictures are easily interpretable in themselves, but how is the print interpreted? Children suppose initially that picture and print are close in meaning but different in form. There is a differentiation in terms of signifiers, but children expect to find similar meanings attached to each.

Children at this level do not share with adults the knowledge that print is "language written down." That is, they do not suppose that print represents language even though they interpret it as a visual expression of differentiated meanings. Because of this children move back and forth between picture and text without modifying their interpretation, since both form a unit and together express the meaning of a graphic message.

We find the same thing in the production of texts: children at this level expect writing—as a representation close to but different from drawing—to conserve some of the properties of the object it substitutes for. This figural correspondence between the written string and the object referred to relates to quantifiable aspects of the object. For example, large objects are given graphic representations proportional to their size. This happens because the written representation of objects does not yet correspond to particular sound patterns. Including some of the object's characteristics in its representation is a way of ensuring an appropriate interpretation. In this period children also produce written strings next to their drawings, as if to guarantee the meaning. This leads some children to insert the written strings in their drawings. However, the initial graphic lines children label as writing are distinct from their drawings and retain the most outstanding characteristics of the adult writing they imitate. The differentiation between drawing and writing is not restricted to their form of execution. In spite of certain temporary difficulties, four year olds can also distinguish the activities of drawing and writing, because the way the drawing refers to objects is not the same as the way the writing refers to them although similar meanings are attributed to the products of each. This similarity means that at this level, writing, like drawing, symbolically expresses the content of a message but not its linguistic elements.

The first explicit indication of distinguishing between picture and print (and between drawing and writing) consists of eliminating the articles when predicting the content of a text, while including them in reference to pictures. This resource of erasing the article is systematic in moving from picture to text. While a picture is identified as being "a ball," for example, the text accompanying it is attributed only the name: "ball." This important moment in the evolution of writing constitutes what we have called the *name hypothesis.* The print retains only one of the potentially representable aspects of the object in the picture, its name.

Thinking that print represents names does not imply conceiving of it as the graphic representation of language, but it is an important step in that direction. Print functions as a registry of names which identify represented objects. Children at this level expect to find as many names in the text as there are objects in the picture. Names are the only linguistic forms to appear in writing. Writing does not directly represent language to these children, and so their interpretation of what is actually written does not always correspond to their verbalizations. There is a necessary distinction between what is written and what can be read. This distinction indicates a different conceptualization of what actually appears in print and what can be read from print.

The name hypothesis is a construction of children and it appears even in the absence of pictures. If the content of an unillustrated text is revealed by an adult, children at this level still expect only names to be represented in writing. The texts children respond to in our experimental tasks are complete sentences (transitive verb with simple nominal phrases), and, even so, only names are conceived as being written. This is a frequent response both in reading, with or without pictures, and in children's spontaneous writing. To understand this kind of response, consider these two hypotheses: either children think that only nouns of the sentence are represented, or they think that writing represents the objects themselves. The difference between these alternative hypotheses is not insignificant. The first one assumes that children can segment the oral message and attribute isolated parts of it, the nouns, to the written text. But according to the second interpretation, children attribute the referential content of the message to the text and not parts of the message in linguistic form. We believe that the name hypothesis is related to the second explanation, that print is seen as a particular way of representing objects. It is particular in that what is written are not figural elements of the object, but rather its name. However, complete sentences can be read from the written names (once again, we must differentiate what is written from the subsequent oral interpretation). Analogous to drawing, given certain elements in the representation, others may be added to complete its interpretation. Herein lies the difference between what is drawn and what it means, parallel to what is written and what can be read.

To this point our explanation accounts for children's efforts to interpret print while they attempt to distinguish it from pictures. Once they have established this distinction, children begin attending to certain properties of the written text itself.

Children cannot consider specific text properties before making a distinction between print and picture. To conserve the interpretation attributed to a text, children match certain quantifiable properties of the object to quantitative variations in the substitute which represents it. These quantitative variations (length, number of lines, number of parts or fragments of a line) are the first text properties children notice. Attributing names of large objects to long strings of print is an example of an initial consideration of text properties.

Considering qualitative properties of the text (individual letters in terms of form and kind) comes much later, generally when children can recognize socially transmitted written models, such as the initial letter of their names or the names of people they know. In addition, qualitative properties are taken into account when children achieve a certain stability in the meaning attributed to a particular piece of writing. They must have gone beyond the period in which any written text can represent any given meaning. While children attempt to differentiate print from picture, they overlook differential characteristics in print itself. Letter graphics, number graphics, and graphics accompanying letters (such as punctuation marks) look alike as nonrepresentational characters distinct from the elements of a picture. Once the picture-print distinction is resolved, a new problem appears: taking into account the specific formal characteristics of what is written. The properties established by children are not what adults would expect them to be. The first of these properties is that a minimum quantity of graphic characters must be present for a written text to be readable. According to this criterion, graphics can be classified as "are/are not something to read." The minimum quantity tends to be three graphic characters, because "with a few letters you can't read."

The notion that quantity determines whether a text can be read or not is a hypothesis constructed by children. This hypothesis cannot have an exogenous origin because no adult could have transmitted this idea and also because one- and two-letter words appear in any written text. We have called this construction the *minimum-quantity hypothesis*. Its most curious consequence is the following: applied to any character type (letters, numerals, and so on) and regardless of labels children may be capable of using ("letters," "numbers," "names"), it gives way to two well-defined groups of graphics—readable (many characters) and not readable (few characters). The first group is generally labeled "letter", the second, "number." Determining which group a graphic character belongs to does not depend on specific properties of the character itself, but rather on whether it appears with others or by itself. It might seem that this classification criterion results from perceptual confusion, since children do not focus on the distinctive features of each character. Although lack of distinction may be involved, this is a conceptual problem, a good conceptual problem, not a case of perceptual confusion.

Evaluating the properties of an object in terms of putting it with or separate from others (and in other contexts, making it bigger or smaller, removing it, interchanging it, and so on) is a characteristic of the preoperational period. All the subjects at this level of conceptualizing print are preoperational. Through this construction children seem to have discovered a fundamental property of the graphic universe: a graphic character by itself does not constitute a written text while a number by itself expresses a quantity.

The second property children discover is that the graphemes must be varied for a text to be readable. For children at this level, quantity and variety are the abstract properties that define the objects necessary for reading to take place.

The quantity hypothesis defines properties the object must have. The name hypothesis, however, relates to interpreting the object; it is elaborated through the act of attributing meaning to print. These hypotheses are completely compatible and coexist in children's thinking during long periods of written language development.

Closely linked to distinguishing picture from text (produced by others) is the problem of distinguishing drawing from writing, activities children perform. Identifying texts as being something to read or not corresponds in children's graphic productions to the distinction between picture-graphics and writing-graphics. All the children in our study are able to make this distinction: writing, as opposed to drawing, has specific graphic characteristics which depend on the model being imitated. Initially, all written products look alike, because what counts is the writer's intention rather than the objective results. Later (and seen more clearly in cases where print rather than cursive characters serve as the model), criteria regarding the formal conditions necessary for something to be readable are used to express different meanings. The demand for a constant number of graphemes and for variation of these graphemes appears in children's writing. That is, the need to distinguish meanings is expressed through differences in the signifiers.

At this level writing is clearly distinguished from drawing and there is a beginning consideration of written products as well as a utilization of resources to distinguish meanings: basically, variation of characters. Once the resource of variation is used, it expands and develops gradually toward consideration of qualitative characteristics: use of different letters, cursive-print opposition, and variation of the linear position of characters. At the same time, children begin to differentiate letter-graphics, number-graphics, and other graphics which accompany letters, such as punctuation marks. In other words, the specific characteristics of print become observable when they become necessary variables within the writing system.

Finally, we must include a concurrent problem: the distinction between reading and looking, and more generally, between text-specific actions and those that are not.

From very early ages (two to three years old in the middle class), children are able to identify objects carrying printed texts by their specific function: they are something to read. Children at this age are also able to imitate the actions of holding, looking, and speaking as they occur while reading objects which lend themselves to such activity, usually picture books. This is the first step in appropriating the adult social practice relative to written texts. Initially the imitated actions are quite general, but in the course of development they give way to more specific actions. One of the first specific differentiations consists of distinguishing looking from reading. Although looking is necessarily involved in reading, the inverse is not the case. To read one must look and do something more, which can only be defined as reading itself. This something is cued by the direction in which the eyes are focused and the amount of time they take to move across the print. To make this distinction one must accept the idea that reading can be done silently.

Another specific differentiation is between telling and reading. The picture book, or storybook, tends to be the prototype text (at least for middle class children) with which two actions, initially undifferentiated, can be carried out: one can either tell a story or read a story. Later, these two actions are differentiated: one "tells" from the picture and "reads" from the text.

From an incipient differentiation between the actions of drawing and writing and between the interpretations of picture and text, children move toward actions oriented to specifically definable aspects of the object. There is, thus, a parallel construction of these implicit notions.

Children's knowledge can either be socially transmitted or spontaneously constructed. Knowledge coming from the environment develops through interactions between the individual and the environment, but the individual imposes definite constraints through the assimilation process. The presence of the environment is, no doubt, essential: we are dealing with an object essentially cultural and social in nature. How can one come to know the names of letters, the spatial orientation of reading, the specific actions carried out on texts, and the nature of the content of various kinds of texts if one has not seen written material and witnessed acts of reading? Individuals cannot discover on their own certain conventions of the written language system. This kind of knowledge is transmitted socially by those who value it. In our experimental population, only middle class children demonstrate a great amount of practice with texts and readers. Lower class children do not seem to have had the advantages of this practice. Children also construct hypotheses which are products of internal elaboration. The name hypothesis and the criteria of minimum quantity and variety are not transmitted by adults; they are deduced by children. In our experimental population, we find examples of spontaneous constructions in both middle and lower class children. As we note in chapter 6, the different origins of knowledge have significant consequences for learning in school. Schools demand and provide more encouragement for the kinds of knowledge that are specific products of cultural transmission. In addition, the environment—as it presents opportunities for confrontation between internal hypotheses and external reality— provokes conflicts that can eventually modify and enrich children's hypotheses.

Children face the problems we have been discussing at the level of global, nonanalytical correspondence between oral language and print, a correspondence between two wholes: the utterance and the interpretation of the printed text.

At a more advanced level of development the written word is seen as having distinguishable parts (easily distinguishable, since print, rather than cursive, is the dominant writing model). Here the problem becomes how to divide the utterance in order to match it to parts of the written text. One of the solutions developed by children is to divide the utterance into syllables. We call this solution the *syllabic hypothesis*. From this point print is directly linked to oral language, through sound patterns with specific properties different from those of the object referred to. This capacity for analyzing speech does not immediately assume the ability to recognize individual words in a text. Syllabic division is one possible way of breaking up the utterance, one that may coexist with other kinds of segmentation (into words, constituent units, and so on).

The syllabic hypothesis continually conflicts with the minimum-quantity hypothesis (both of them children's original constructions) and also with written models proposed by the environment (in particular, the child's own name). The opportunity to surpass the syllabic hypothesis arises from this double source of conflict. The conflict can only be resolved by searching for an analysis that goes beyond the syllable (dividing the syllable into smaller units of sound). The number of graphemes in written strings produced according to the syllabic hypothesis is often smaller than the necessary minimum quantity, and obviously smaller than alphabetic writing models proposed by the environment.

The syllabic hypothesis can be used with signs that do not resemble letters of the alphabet, or it can be used with letters conventional in shape but not in sound value. Syllabic writing with stable sound values may be vocalic, consonantal, or a combination of the two. The conflict between the syllabic and the minimum-quantity hypotheses is resolved by adding a greater number of graphemes than those required for a syllabic interpretation. In this way, two-syllable words that must be represented syllabically by two letters are written with three letters to fulfill the minimum-quantity requirement. A new conflict appears: not all of the graphemes can be interpreted. Solutions to this conflict consist of repeating the same syllable twice or grouping two graphemes to represent a single syllable. (The similarities to children's attempts at establishing a correspondence between number names and counted objects is evident. In counting situations preoperational children count the same object twice or repeat the same number twice.) In addition, when analyzing globally learned forms provided by the environment, children at this level encounter leftover elements difficult to interpret. They attempt diverse compromise solutions for each particular case but are unable to overcome the disturbances. Whether due to leftover elements (provided by external models) or to added-on elements (produced by internal criteria), children find themselves obliged to abandon the syllabic hypothesis. However, this does not take place immediately. Children can go through long periods of fluctuation between syllabic and alphabetic writing, producing reading and writing which tend to begin syllabically and end alphabetically.

The problem of the whole-part relationship is posed somewhat differently when the unit analyzed is the sentence rather than the word. Here the problem consists of knowing which segments of an oral sentence correspond to textual divisions and discovering which categories of words are represented in writing.

Recognizing that a sentence is written does not imply supposing that all the words composing it are written (because of the distinction children establish between what is written and what can be read from it). In addition, children may recognize that a word is written without accepting its appearance as an independent segment of the text. This occurs initially with verbs and later with articles. Transitive verbs represent a relationship between an actor and a receiver of the action. Children have difficulty conceiving that verbs can be written in separate fragments since the verb expresses a relationship inseparable from the terms it relates. From this come responses that assume that nouns are represented independently while verbs are linked to the direct object complement or to the whole sentence. Once the problem has been solved for verbs, it appears regarding articles, which have even less autonomy. The case of articles is complicated by their graphic notation: a two-letter fragment of writing cannot be read (according to the minimum-quantity hypothesis). Once again the problem of leftover elements appears. Children attempt various solutions to the problem of leftover parts of a written sentence (as they do with leftover letters in a written word). One of the most frequent solutions is attributing an incomplete part of the oral emission (a syllable) to the written fragment conceived of as incomplete (since it has only two letters).

When the previously listed problems have been overcome, children advance to a new problem area resulting from two specific conventions of the writing system: orthography and word boundaries. (Children have previously dealt with the latter as an objective text property but have generally ignored it in their own writing.)

There are two outstanding characteristics in the developmental sequence of solving these problems: the strict consistency children demand of themselves, and the internal logic of the developmental progression.

We have repeatedly shown in analyzing our data how children, following rules they set themselves, are consistent to an extreme. No one asks them to use a certain number of characters to write; no one tells them not to repeat the same letters. And yet, four year olds perform remarkable feats of reasoning such as those characterizing level 2 of writing development: with an extremely limited stock of graphemes children discover that they can express different meanings by rearranging the linear order to produce different written representations.

The problem-solving sequence children construct progresses through what seems to be an ideal programming. They begin by differentiating iconic graphics from noniconic graphics before attempting to make distinctions within the latter. Once these two kinds of graphics have been fairly well differentiated and their respective functions more or less established, children begin to make distinctions within the universe of noniconic graphics in terms of letter-graphics and nonletter-graphics.

Only when there is a beginning stability in certain graphic configurations (in terms of whole forms or cueing elements) can children consider whole-part relationships. Only when they understand the reasons for abandoning the syllabic hypothesis can they advance to phonetic analysis. Only when they comprehend the production rules of the alphabetic writing system can they begin to deal with problems of orthography.

Reading is Not Deciphering; Writing is Not Copying

Our introduction included three basic precautions that guided the elaboration of our research: reading is not deciphering; writing is not copying a model; and progress in literacy does not come about through advances in deciphering and copying. These precautions have allowed us to demonstrate, through new data, the developmental sequence of children's intelligent construction of written language as a cultural object of knowledge. Here we return to these three basic precautions as theoretical affirmations rather than methodological principles.

Reading Is Not Deciphering

Our conclusions regarding reading and deciphering coincide with theses supported by various authors who apply contemporary psycholinguistics (post-Chomskian) in their attempt to understand the reading process. The common belief of these authors is that reading cannot be analyzed in strictly perceptual terms. Kenneth and Yetta Goodman (1977) express it brilliantly: "If we understand that the brain is the organ of human information processing, that the brain is not a prisoner of the senses but that it controls the sensory organs and selectively uses their input, then we should not be surprised that what the mouth reports in oral reading is not what the eye has seen but what the brain has generated for the mouth to report" (p. 319).

Frank Smith (1975) also asserts that reading "is not primarily a visual process" (p. 353). In reading we utilize visual and nonvisual information. The visual information comes from the arrangement of letters on the printed or handwritten page, but the nonvisual information comes from readers themselves. The essential nonvisual information is the reader's linguistic competence. (If the text is written in a language the reader is not familiar with, reading does not take place in any real sense even though the reader may visually explore the page, look for similarities and regularities, and so on.) Other nonvisual information, such as knowledge of the topic (which is not the same as knowledge of the text), is used as well.

To Smith's list of nonvisual information we wish to add something we believe is essential: identification of the object that carries the text. Before we begin reading we know something about the text from our categorization of the printed material in which it appears. If we identify the material as a technical book, we predict that certain stylistic structures will be excluded (such as "once upon a time . . ." or "it gives me great pleasure to inform you . . ."). If we identify the material as a medical prescription, the absence of verbs does not surprise us ("one spoonful every three hours" is interpreted as "take one spoonful of this medication every three hours"). And so on.

There is clearly an inverse relationship between the nonvisual information utilized and the visual information required. Smith and other authors remind us of classic data from experimental laboratory psychology. The eye operates by "leaps"; each fixation lasts approximately 250 milliseconds after which the eye "leaps over" ten to twelve letters (or equivalent spaces) where it fixes again. The eye also moves backward, leaps farther toward the end of a line, and so on. In each fixation four or five different items are identified. If the visual stimulus consists of random letters, four or five letters can be identified; if the stimulus consists of written words, twice that amount of letters can be identified (two words, approximately ten letters); if the words are organized syntactically (constituting a written sentence) twice again as many letters can be identified (about four words, approximately twenty letters).

What is seen, then, depends on how the stimulus is organized. It is not that the eye sees more things, but rather that the capacity for integrating information increases with the organization of the stimulus. In other words, readers use nonvisual information (knowledge of the lexicon and the grammatical structure of the language) to complete the sparse visual information gathered by the eye.

Data of this nature, along with what we know about the limitations of short-term memory, have led many contemporary authors to consider reading to be an essentially nonvisual activity. Smith maintains that reading is not possible without prediction. There are two basic kinds of predictions: lexical-semantic predictions, which allow us to anticipate meaning and make subsequent self-corrections; and syntactic predictions, which allow us to anticipate the syntactic category of a word and again make self-corrections when an essential syntactic element has not been appropriately identified. The following is an example of the first kind of prediction: skimming over newspaper headlines (a reading activity in which all adult readers, as proficient as they may be, tend to misidentify certain words), an adult has identified the sentence "Meditation successful in labor dispute." The semantic incongruence is evident and the reader regresses to the only place where the identification error could have occurred ("meditation" for "mediation"). An example of the second kind of prediction is the experience common to adult readers on reaching the end of a sentence without having found the verb. In this case the reader's syntactic knowledge forces self-correction and a new search.

A series of new pedagogical proposals have arisen based on the importance of prediction (intelligent, linguistically controlled prediction, not to be confused with wild guessing). Smith asserts that the opportunity for developing and using prediction should be an essential part of learning to read. In France, educators such as Foucambert (1976) and Hebrard (1977) have come out in support of this pedagogical position.

Obviously, intelligent predictions can hardly develop with sentences such as *"mi mama me mima," "Susi asa sus sesos sosos,"* or similar tongue twisters, structures of the ritual language which traditionally has permitted access to the sacred shrine of written language. These kinds of sentences can be found across languages. English-speaking children are faced with "the fat cat sat on the mat." French children begin with *"bebe a bu, bebe bave"* or *"Riri a ri; Lili a lu"* and move on to *"la poule rousse couve sur son petit nid de mousse"* (which has come a long way from what French first graders had to read in the nineteenth century: *"Hugues subjugue ses juges par la fugue qu'il composa a Bruges"*). As Hebrard points out, "today children learn to read French as if it were Latin." This is true for learning to read Spanish (and English) as well.

Actually, such sentences set a double trap. They look like real sentences, and yet they do not correspond to any real language form (neither the dialect spoken by the teacher nor that spoken by the children). They also sound like real utterances in spite of transmitting no information and lacking any communicative intent. Once again, children must forget all they know about their home language in order to learn to read, as if written language and the activity of reading had no relationship to real language functioning.

We are not claiming here that written language is a simple transcription of oral language. To the contrary, there are marked differences between the two (even without considering the various styles of oral and written language). Written language has its own lexical terms, complex expressions, way of using verb tenses, rhythm and continuity. To appreciate this difference, think of how difficult it is to read the transcription of a recorded conversation and how much easier it is to interpret when we listen to it. On the other hand, it is difficult to listen to a lecture read out loud from a written manuscript. The issue here is not to deny the necessary distinction between oral and written language, but rather to allow written language learners to approach learning with their linguistic competence, an element essential to both oral and written language.

Our results reflect the tremendous difference between children who have been introduced to reading in school through the narrow use of deciphering and those who have organized their own learning. The first group exhibits two unique behaviors: a blind confidence in deciphering as the only possible access to a text; and the inability to use internal syntactic knowledge for making judgments while deciphering. The restrictive use of deciphering leads to its own caricature as children proceed to sound out, oralize graphic marks, or, according to an accurate expression, "make a noise with the mouth based on what they see with the eyes" without comprehending a thing. As any teacher or educational psychologist knows, a correctly deciphered text does not indicate comprehension. It is useless to look for memory defects to account for this problem. It is far too easy to explain that these children are good at analysis but fail at synthesis. Isolated from the constant search for meaning, the text is reduced to a long series of meaningless syllables. When such readers reach the end of the line, they have forgotten the beginning, not because they have poor memories but because the short-term memory cannot possibly retain a long series of meaningless syllables. (This short-term memory limitation has been well established by experimental psychology for decades.) Finally, children lacking confidence in their own syntactic knowledge read some of the most flagrant grammatical incongruities (such as *la mono* or *la pato* (feminine article with masculine nouns—English examples: "she was the book" or "the are in the park"), violating grammatical rules they have been controlling orally for years. They act as if any nonsense could come out of a text, as if the text were a hybrid, as beginning texts truly are, halfway between real language and tongue twisters.

According to the traditional view of reading, meaning appears at some magic moment, through oralization. Meaning arises from the oral emission, transforming the series of phonemes into words. According to various contemporary authors, the cycle of visual sign to oral translation to meaning is not an inevitable part of the reading process. It appears to be so only because of the exaggerated importance oral reading is afforded in school practice.

The question is whether we oralize to comprehend a text or because we are required to do so in school. In the traditional view, written language appears as a secondary system of signs, which refers to another system of signs (those of oral language). In the contemporary view, written language appears as an alternative system of signs, which refer directly to meaning, as auditory signs do.

Current arguments in the literature support the second interpretation. Foucambert states it like this: "reading consists of selecting information from written language to construct meaning directly." Smith states the following: "writing is a parallel or alternative form of language to speech, and . . . reading, like listening, involves a direct 'decoding to meaning,' or comprehension" (p. 348). In another text (1971) Smith maintains that written language does not primarily represent speech sounds but provides cues of meaning. For this reason, the translation of the written text into speech is possible only through the intermediary of meaning.

According to this perspective, readers read visual signs in the same way they listen to auditory signs; in both cases they work through the surface structure to reach the deep structure of the text or utterance. The deep structure is common to both. Because of this, Smith (1975) asserts that "speech and writing are variants or alternative forms of the same language" (p. 348), contrary to the general assumption that written language is the transcription of speech.

In summary: (*a*) evidence obtained from analyzing adult reading behavior coincides in indicating that meaning does not derive from letter-by-letter (or word-for-word) recognition, in other words, from exact deciphering; (*b*) the data we have gathered from preschool children shows that at no time do they opt for pure deciphering as the way to approach print; (*c*) Clark (1976), studying English-speaking five-year-old self-taught readers, confirms that for these children as well reading and getting meaning go together; (*d*) in our own data, only a few children, receiving school instruction, resort blindly to deciphering or sounding out and set aside, also blindly, their own linguistic knowledge.

Foucambert views deciphering (the phonics approach) as the key to all failures in learning to read. He asserts that "deciphering is easy . . . when one knows how to read." But "utilizing deciphering as the medium for comprehending written words sets children up for failure." He concludes that deciphering " is a trap, a poisoned apple" (p. 47). From his perspective, dyslexia is not a reading disturbance but a deciphering disturbance, and deciphering itself is not reading activity (p. 76).

In our opinion, these positions are basically correct, but we hesitate to subscribe to them completely for what we believe to be two nonjustifiable limitations: (*a*) They are based on an analysis of adult reading behavior without including a detailed study of the psychogenesis of this behavior. (Here, as in other domains, an accurate description of the final point is unavoidable, but we cannot deduce the developmental process leading to this point from such a description, accurate and detailed as it may be.) (*b*) The analysis is based almost exclusively on reading, ignoring or treating as secondary the information found in writing. (It is clear that reading and writing are different, though complementary, activities; but just as it is dangerous to look at comprehension and ignore production in the study of oral language development, one runs the risk of constructing a one-sided view of written language development by overemphasizing reading [comprehension] and minimizing the importance of the production of written texts.)

Writing Is Not Copying an External Model

Although there are a significant number of authors who insist on the need to reformulate our view of the reading process, there are considerably fewer who do the same regarding writing. Carol Chomsky (1971) suggests that children "be active participants in teaching themselves to read. In fact, they ought to direct the process," since "children's minds at four, five, six are far from linguistic empty space in which reading information is to be poured." We are wholly in agreement with this statement, but less so with her proposal that "the natural order is writing first, then reading what you have written" and her affirmation that "composing words according to their sounds (using letter sets, or writing by hand if the child can form letters) is the first step toward reading." According to our data, the "natural order" varies from one child to another, some formulating more advanced hypotheses about reading and others about writing. Also, what Chomsky indicates as "the first step toward reading" is, from our perspective, one of the last. The child she studied is only three years old, but his hypotheses correspond to an alphabetic writing system (or perhaps an intermediary level between the syllabic and the alphabetic hypotheses, since he writes KT and reads "Kate"; he writes TODO and reads "Toto"). The argument of Chomsky's that we agree with is at the orthographic level: we must let children write "how it sounds," how they believe the words may be composed. But our argument goes even further: we must let children write, even in a writing system different from the alphabetic one; we must let them write, not so they invent their own idiosyncratic system, but so they discover that their system is not the conventional one and in this way find valid reasons to substitute their own hypotheses with our conventional ones.

Read, studying the invented spelling of preschool children (1975), has shown that when children spell on their own the results are not chaotic but reflect regularities. These spelling regularities appear both within children and across children; they "did not choose letters randomly, or invent additional symbols" (p. 331). These particular English-speaking children have tolerant parents who are not dismayed by messages such as this (accompanying a picture of a fish in water): FES SOWEMEG EN WOODR, read as "fish swimming in water." These studies are extremely useful, both for understanding young children's notion of phonetic variation and for understanding certain systematic orthographic difficulties.

Both Carol Chomsky and Charles Read indicate implicitly that writing is not the same as copying external models (except in reference to letters themselves), but both of them study writing in children who are close to arriving at the alphabetic system. Our work shows that before reaching this point, children explore various hypotheses about writing. The distance between copy-writing and children's spontaneous writing is as great as the distance between copy-drawing and children's spontaneous drawing. The study of children's spontaneous drawing has shown that for young children drawing is not reproducing objects as they are seen but as they know them. The multiple difficulties they encounter while drawing an object are not due to graphic obstacles but to real cognitive problems. In the same way, writing development as revealed in our work does not depend on children's graphic skill, on their ability to make letters which look conventional. It depends on what we refer to as their level of conceptualization about writing, that is, the set of hypotheses they have explored for the purpose of comprehending this object. When we keep children from writing (from testing their hypotheses as they produce written texts) and force them to copy (repeating someone's markings without understanding their structure), we keep them from learning; we keep them from discovering on their own. When we correct their copy-writing in terms of spatial relationships (stick to the left, two sticks instead of three, closed curve) or in terms of letters which don't belong or are left out, we ignore what is essential in the text: what it represents and how it represents it. Although calligraphy is no longer studied in school, the attitude toward writing is the same: the goal is to produce a faithful copy of an established model. The only difference now is a greater margin of tolerance for what is considered to be a faithful copy.

Progress in Literacy Does Not Come About through Advances in Deciphering and Copying

One must reject all assumptions basic to behaviorist and empiricist learning theories to accept the affirmation that progress in literacy does not come about through advances in deciphering and copying. This position is not only based on a redefinition of reading and writing but also on a global conception of the learning process. Piaget's theory of cognitive development allows us to understand the processes of appropriating knowledge involved in learning to read and write. We refer to this learning as appropriation of knowledge, and not as the acquisition of a skill. As in any other domain of cognitive activity, appropriation is an active process of reconstruction carried out by knowing subjects. Knowledge is not truly appropriated until its means of production has been understood, until it has been internally reconstructed.

Pedagogical Consequences

If we define writing as "a system of signs expressing single sounds of speech" (Gelb, 1976, p. 166), we are referring to an alphabetic writing system. Only a small number of children in our sample possess alphabetic writing. If we define writing in a broader sense, taking into account its psychogenetic (and historical) origins, as a particular form of graphic representation, all the subjects in our sample are beginning writers. Our data reflect a long developmental process from children's initial conceptions of print to their final ones. This process takes place in the preschool period. Some children are at the final levels of development as they enter school. Others reach first grade at the initial levels of hypothesizing about print. The former group has very little to learn in school, since first grade instruction will not challenge their capabilities. The latter group has a great deal to learn. The problem is whether traditionally conceived instruction offers them what they need.

On reviewing the problems we have listed here, our conclusion is pessimistic. None of them is taken into account by traditional instruction. The school program operates on an ambiguity. It considers the learning process strictly in methodological terms which implicitly presuppose a series of notions learners must have, but no one ever bothers to find out if learners actually have these notions.

To understand print, preschool children have reasoned intelligently, elaborated good hypotheses about writing systems (although they may not be good in terms of our conventional writing system), overcome conflicts, searched for regularities, and continually attached meaning to written texts. But the logical coherence they impose on themselves disappears when faced with what the teacher demands from them. They must worry about perception and motor control instead of the need to understand. They must acquire a series of skills instead of coming to know an object. They must set aside their own linguistic knowledge and capacity for thought until they discover, at a later point, that it is impossible to comprehend a written text without them.

The traditional school program ignores the natural progression. It proposes an immediate introduction to the mysteries of the alphabetic code, believing the task to be easier if they are unveiled all at once. But doing so only contributes to the mystery. Children do not understand that noises made for letters have something to do with language. They do not understand that the tongue twisters which pass as sentences have something to do with the language they know. Everything is reduced to irrational convention, letters joined together in incomprehensible ways.

The distance between methodological proposals and children's conceptions can be measured by what the school teaches and what children learn. What the school intends to teach does not always coincide with what children manage to learn. Attempting to unveil the mysteries of the alphabetic code, teachers proceed step by step from simple to complex. However, simple and complex are defined in terms of adult notions. This definition attributes simplicity to the alphabetic code itself. The underlying assumption is that all children are prepared to learn the code, if a teacher helps them. The help consists, fundamentally, of transmitting sound equivalents of letters and providing graphic models to be copied. What children learn, according to our data, is relative to how they go about appropriating the object through a slow construction of criteria. Children's criteria only coincide with teachers' criteria at the final point of the process.

Because of this, school is directed toward those who already know. Success in learning depends on the child's condition when he or she begins receiving instruction. Only those at quite advanced levels of conceptualization can benefit from traditional instruction; they are the ones who learn what the teacher intends them to. The others fail, accused by the school of having "incapacity to learn" or "learning disabilities." (Perhaps these labels should be qualified difficulty in learning what teachers attempt to teach, in the conditions in which it is taught.) If we attribute the method's deficiencies to incapacities in children, we are denying that all learning implies a process. What is only a difference in the timing of the child's conceptual development is viewed as a deficit.

No child starts from zero when he or she comes to school, including lower class children who are always at a disadvantage. Six year olds know many things about the writing system and have solved numerous problems to understand the rules of written representation. They may not have solved all problems, as the school expects them to have done, but they have started down the path. Of course, their path differs from the one assumed by instruction because their problems and the means of solving them are the result of great cognitive effort.

The school assumes, on the other hand, that the critical initiation to the learning of written language comes through the acquisition of skills and through specific exercises. The classic reading sequence of mechanical, comprehensive, expressive and copying exercises in writing assume that the secret to written language is producing sounds and reproducing graphic forms. The writing system is reduced to exchanging auditory and visual signals for graphic ones. Year-long daily school practice fills the class schedule with a repeating sequence of dictation (the children write what the teacher dictates), copying, deciphering, and drawing.

The routine nature of this practice responds to methodological principles derived from empiricist conceptions of learning. School is directed toward passive children who know nothing, who must be taught. It is not directed toward active children who not only pose their own problems but spontaneously construct mechanisms for solving them, who reconstruct the object to appropriate it through the development of knowledge and not through the exercise of skills. In short, school is not directed toward children as we know them from Piagetian psychology.

When we follow closely the ways children construct knowledge, we are exploring conceptualization processes that differ from processes implicit in traditional methodology. This is clearly exemplified by our data from children in first grade. Their processes of coming to know the object are different from those proposed by the teacher.

The school's ignorance of these underlying processes implies the following presuppositions imposed on children: (*a*) they know nothing, and so are underestimated; or (*b*) the writing system reflects language in an obvious and natural way, and so they are overestimated because they do not naturally share this assumption. It is based on an adult definition of the object to be known and poses problems from the perspective of the final point of the process. Also, its implicit definitions of reading and writing are wrong. We believe that schools must revise their definitions of these concepts in light of current knowledge.

They must also revise the concept of error. Piaget has demonstrated the necessary passage through *constructive errors* in other domains of knowledge acquisition. Literacy cannot be an exception. When teachers do not allow errors to occur, they do not allow children to think. At the other extreme, errors are produced by the instructional method, resulting from blind application of a mechanistic technique. We must differentiate these two kinds of error and attempt to understand the process. In doing so, we are forced to reconsider the problem of learning disorders: on what basis can a learning disorder be defined, according to what concept of error? In turn we must revise the concept of maturity or "readiness" for learning as well as the foundations of psychological tests which attempt to measure it.

Finally, we must revalue criteria for evaluating progress along with the conception of preschool preparation for learning to read and write. Both of these have traditionally derived from associationist theory; both have been thought of in terms of performing the mechanistic skills of deciphering and graphic copying.

In summary, reading and writing are taught in a mechanistic way as something foreign to children, rather than being viewed as an object of interest children come to know in an intelligent way. As Vygotsky (1978) says, "Children are taught to trace out letters and make words out of them, but they are not taught written language. The mechanics of reading what is written are so emphasized that they overshadow written language as such" (p. 105). He adds, "It is necessary to bring the child to an inner understanding of writing, and to arrange that writing will be organized development rather than learning" (p. 118).

The conception of writing as copying inhibits real writing, but the conception of reading as deciphering not only inhibits reading, but creates other problems as well. Attempts at establishing phoneme-grapheme correspondences lead to "proper" (or "correct") pronunciation, the pronunciation form of the dominant social classes within the society and the only one supposed to permit access to written language. Schools perform an initial selection between those who will learn to read more quickly—because they already speak "the way they should"—and those who must change dialects to learn to read. Aside from the obvious pedagogical consequences, the results of this linguistic discrimination have not yet been evaluated in depth. Operating in this way, schools do not increase the number of literate members of society. Rather, they contribute to illiteracy.

Historical Solutions to the Writing Problem

It is extremely surprising to see how the progression of children's hypotheses about the writing system reproduces some of the key periods of the evolution of written language. This occurs even when children are exposed to only one system of writing. The historical developmental line goes from the stylized pictogram to the writing of words (logography). Later the principle of phonetization is introduced, gradually evolving toward syllabic writing systems. Then, a complicated transitional period culminates in the purely alphabetic system of the Greeks. (Gelb [1963] and Jensen [1969] discuss the importance of syllabic writing systems as necessary predecessors of alphabetic ones, and the interpretation of consonantal writing systems as syllabic [Gelb] or syllabic-alphabetic [Jensen].)

The line of psychogenetic development we have traced also begins with the separation of iconic and noniconic representational systems. It then proceeds to a kind of logographics with unquestionably ideographic elements (similar representations for words related semantically, although very different in sound). It painstakingly develops the principle of phonetization, goes through a syllabic period, and finally reaches the alphabetic system.

This parallelism between cultural history and psychogenesis should not be interpreted as an attempt to reduce the former to the latter. It is true alphabetic writing is the final point (historically speaking) in the development of writing and during the last twenty-five hundred years "no reforms have taken place in the principles of writing. Hundreds of alphabets throughout the world, different as they may be in outer form, all use the principles first and last established in the Greek writing" (Gelb, p. 198). "Further evolution is conceivable still in only two directions: (*a*) in the direction of greater accuracy in the reproduction of the various sounds of a language . . . and (*b*) in the direction of a greater simplification of the letter-signs themselves" (Jensen, p. 53). Although other written systems for representing specific technical languages (such as mathematical and logical) have been developed, no new system for representing natural languages has been created. It is also true that other writing systems are still in use and fulfill with similar efficiency the same functions as the alphabetic system. (Chinese writing, basically ideographic, has fulfilled a historical function which alphabetic writing could not easily have satisfied. It has conserved over centuries a uniform written language in spite of great diversity in dialects. Japanese writing, known as Kana, is strictly syllabic and very well adapted to the syllabic structure of Japanese.)

If the children we have studied arrive, finally, at an alphabetic hypothesis, they do so, undoubtedly, because any other hypothesis enters into unsolvable conflict with information provided by the writing system they experience. This experiential information could eliminate all previous hypotheses children explore, and yet it does not. A strictly empiricist theory cannot account for our data. The coincidence with historical development is not limited to essential periods; certain details arrived at late in individual development are also arrived at late historically (such as adopting a conventional spatial orientation which does not change from one line to the next, using spacing to separate words, and graphic distinction between letters and numbers).

What, then, can explain this parallelism? Although detailed comparative studies are required to discover the precise meaning of the comparison and its epistemological implications, we propose a hypothesis which cannot be immediately refuted: similarities between both processes reflect the mechanisms for becoming aware of the properties of language. To have access to a writing system, historically and individually, it is not enough to have a language; it is also necessary to reflect on the language and thus become aware of some of its fundamental properties.

Phonemes have existed from the beginning of human language. Individuals speaking their native language have an implicit knowledge (underlying or unconscious) of the phonetic structure of the language (which permits them, among other things, to identify a sound pattern as being or not being a possible word, regardless of whether they can attach a meaning to it). However, the discovery of the phoneme as a linguistic unit is a recent fact. Bloomfield points out:

> The existence of phonemes and the identity of each individual phoneme are by no means obvious: it took several generations of study before linguists became fully aware of this important feature of speech. It is remarkable that long before scientific students of language had made this discovery, there had arisen a system of alphabetic writing, a system in which each character represented a phoneme. . . . It is important for us to know that alphabetic writing was not invented at one stroke, as a finished system, but that it grew gradually and, one could almost say, by a series of accidents, out of a system of word writing (p. 228).

Our hypothesis supports a necessary process of reflecting on language in order to approach a writing system, but, at the same time, the writing system itself permits new processes of reflection which cannot easily take place without it. (There are no known examples of grammatical reflection in peoples who do not have written language.) We would have to look for similarities in historical and psychogenetic progression in analyzing the obstacles that must be overcome—cognitively speaking—to become aware of certain fundamental properties of language. (The sociohistorical reasons for the appearance of different writing systems play a similar role to the motivation of the individual, but they do not explain the specific mechanisms leading to the creation of this cultural object.)

This is only speculation, but it permits the elaboration of a series of new hypotheses to be tested, hypotheses leading in a quite different direction from traditional ones. It has traditionally been thought that to learn to read children must possess good language (or a sufficient level of oral language development) evaluated in terms of vocabulary, diction, and grammatical complexity. If we believe that we must consider language awareness, the perspective changes. Rather than being concerned with whether children know how to speak, we should help them become conscious of what they already know how to do, help them move from "knowing how" to "knowing about," a conceptual knowing.

Theoretical Implications

In addition to pedagogical implications, there is a series of theoretical implications.

We used the conceptual framework from genetic psychology to elaborate our hypotheses. This book is reiterated proof of the pertinence and fruitfulness of Piaget's theory for understanding the processes of acquiring knowledge in a domain not directly explored by Piaget himself.

With Piaget's theory we have been able to take a different approach to a topic that has accumulated an overly abundant literature. Through his theory we have been able to discover knowing subjects who reinvent written language to make it their own; we have discovered a process of actual construction and an originality in conceptions previously ignored by adults.

Using Piaget's theory to explore a new area is an exciting intellectual adventure. It does not simply mean employing Piagetian tests to establish new correlations, but utilizing the assimilation schemes based on the theory to discover new observable data. From this point, a new possibility occurs: the possibility of constructing a psychogenetic theory of the acquisition of written language.

In a field where it has been thought, in spite of a variety of viewpoints, that learning cannot take place without specific instruction, and where the learner's contribution has been thought to depend on and derive from the instructional methods, we have discovered a developmental line in which cognitive conflicts play an essential role. These conflicts are similar to the cognitive conflicts involved in constructing other fundamental notions. They are similar in the smallest details.

The kind of object knowledge we have studied allows us to pose a series of problems not yet approached by genetic epistemology. Written language is, in fact, a particular object sharing the social properties of language but possessing a consistency and a permanence oral language does not have. It is precisely this characteristic of objectivity, this existence prolonged far beyond the act of emission, that allows children in their exploration of written language to carry out a series of specific actions similar to those they carry out on physical objects. Written language has a series of properties observable through the child's interaction with print (the only intermediaries being the child's cognitive and linguistic capacities). It also has other properties which cannot be "read" directly from it. These properties can be observed only through actions that others carry out with the object. Social mediation is indispensable for understanding such properties. Through the exploration of written language as an object of knowledge we may perhaps approach a tremendously vast and complex issue: the psychogenesis of the knowledge of sociocultural objects.

As we were finishing this research, we discovered that without knowing it we were doing what Vygotsky (1978) clearly pointed out decades ago: "The first task of scientific investigation is to reveal this prehistory of children's written language, to show what leads children to writing, through what important points this prehistorical development passes, and in what relationship it stands to school learning" (p. 107).

BIBLIOGRAPHY

Ajuriaguerra, Bresson, Inizan, Stambak, et al. 1977. *La dislexia en cuestión.* Madrid: Pablo del Rio Editor.

Berthoud-Papandropulou, I. 1976. "La réflexion métalinguistique chez l'enfant." Doctoral dissertation, University of Geneva.

Blanche-Benveniste, C., and A. Chervel. 1974. *L'orthographe.* Paris: Maspero.

Bloomfield, L. 1942. "Linguistics and reading." *Elementary English Review* 19. Rpt. in *Linguistics for Teachers: Selected Readings,* ed. J. Savage. Chicago: Science Research Associates, 1973.

Braslavsky, B. P. 1973. *La querella de los métodos en la enseñanza de la lectura.* Buenos Aires: Kapeluz.

Bronckart, J. P. 1976. *L'acquisition des formes verbales chez l'enfant.* Brussels: Dessart et Margade.

Chomsky, C. 1970. "Reading, writing and phonology." *Harvard Educational Review* 40, no. 2.

Chomsky, C. 1971. "Write now, read later." *Childhood Education* 47, no. 6. Rpt. in *Language in Early Childhood Education,* ed. C. Cazden. Washington: NAEYC, 1972.

Chomsky, N. 1957. *Syntactic Structures.* The Hague: Mouton.

Chomsky, N. 1965. *Aspects of the Theory of Syntax.* Cambridge: MIT Press.

Chomsky, N., and M. Halle. 1968. *The Sound Pattern of English.* New York: Harper & Row.

Clark, M. 1976. *Young Fluent Readers: What Can They Teach Us?* London: Heinemann.

Cohen, M. 1958. *La grande invention de l'écriture et son évolution.* Paris: Imprimerie Nationale—Klincksiek.

Cohen, M. *La escritura y la psicologia de los pueblos.* 3rd ed. Mexico City: Siglo XXI.

Ferreiro, E. 1971. *Les relations temporelles dans le langage de l'enfant.* Geneva: Droz.

Ferreiro, E. 1975. *Problemas de la psicologia educacional.* Buenos Aires: Producciones Editoriales IPSE.

Filho, L. 1960. *Test ABC.* Buenos Aires: Kapeluz.

Foucambert, J. 1976. *La maniere d'etre lecteur.* Paris: SERMAP.

Gelb, I. J. 1952. *A Study of Writing.* Chicago: University of Chicago Press.

Gibson, E. 1970. "The ontogeny of reading." *American Psychologist* 25, no. 2.

Goodman, K. 1965. "Dialect barriers to reading comprehension." *Elementary English,* **42**, no. 8, December 1965.

Goodman, K., and Y. Goodman. 1977. "Learning about psycholinguistic processes by analyzing oral reading." *Harvard Educational Review* 47, no. 3.

Gray, W. 1975. *La enseñanza de la lectura y de la escritura.* Paris: UNESCO.

Haugen, E. 1972. "Dialect, language, nation." In *Sociolinguistics,* ed. J. Pride and J. Holmes. Harmondsworth, England: Penguin Books.

Inhelder, B., H. Sinclair, and M. Bovet. 1974. *Learning and the Develop-*

ment of Cognition, trans. Susan Wedgewood. Cambridge: Harvard University Press.

Jensen, H. 1969. *Sign, Symbol and Script.* New York: Putnam.

Kavanagh, J., and I. Mattingly, eds. 1972. *Language by Ear and by Eye.* Cambridge: MIT Press.

Klima, E. 1972. "How alphabets might reflect language." In *Language by Ear and by Eye,* ed. J. Kavanagh and I. Mattingly. Cambridge: MIT Press.

Labov, W. 1969. "The logic of nonstandard English." Georgetown Monographs in Language and Linguistics, no. 22. Rpt. in W. Labov, *Language in the Inner City.* Philadelphia: University of Pennsylvania Press, 1972.

Lavine, L. 1977. "Differentiation of letterlike forms in pre-reading children." *Developmental Psychology* 13, no. 2.

Lentin, L., C. Clesse, J. Hebrard, and I. Jan. 1977. *Du parler au lire.* Paris: Editions ESF.

Lurçat, L. 1974. *Etudes de l'acte graphique.* Paris: Mouton.

Malmberg, B. 1977. *La fonetica.* Adapted by G. Bes. Buenos Aires: EU-DEBA.

Mialaret, G. 1975. "The experimental psychology of reading, writing and drawing." In *Experimental Psychology: Its Scope and Method,* ed. P. Fraisse and J. Piaget. Language, Communication and Decision Making, vol. 8. New York: Basic Books.

Piaget, J. 1951. *Play, Dreams and Imitation in Childhood,* trans. C. Gattegno and F. M. Hodgeson. London: Heinemann.

Piaget, J. 1970. *The Child's Conception of Movement and Speed,* trans. G. E. T. Holloway and M. J. Mackenzie. London: Routledge and Kegan Paul.

Piaget, J. 1977. *The Development of Thought: Equilibration of Cognitive Structures,* trans. Arnold Rosin. New York: Viking.

Piaget, J., and B. Inhelder. 1969. *The Psychology of the Child,* trans. H. Weaver. New York: Basic Books.

Piaget, J., and A. Szeminska. 1952. *The Child's Conception of Number,* trans. C. Gattegno and F. M. Hodgeson. London: Routledge and Kegan Paul.

Piaget, J., E. Ferreiro, and A. Szeminska. 1972. "La transmission médiate du mouvement." In J. Piaget et al., *La transmission des mouvements.* Paris: PUF.

Read, C. 1975. "Lessons to be learned from the preschool orthographer." In *Foundations of Language Development,* ed. E. Lenneberg and E. Lenneberg. New York: Academic Press.

Reid, J. 1966. "Learning to think about reading." *Educational Research* 9.

Saussure, F. 1966. *Course in General Linguistics,* ed. C. Bally and A. Sechehaye, trans. W. Baskin. New York: McGraw-Hill.

Smith, F., ed. 1973. *Psycholinguistics and Reading.* New York: Holt, Rinehart and Winston.

Smith, F. 1975. "The relation between spoken and written language." In *Foundations of Language Development,* vol. 2, ed. E. Lenneberg and E. Lenneberg. New York: Academic Press.

Smith, F. 1978. *Understanding Reading: A Psycholinguistic Analysis of Reading and Learning to Read.* 2nd ed. New York: Holt, Rinehart and Winston.

UNESCO, Office for Latin America and the Caribbean. 1974. *Evolución reciente de la educación en America Latina.* Santiago.

Vygotsky, L. 1962. *Thought and Language.* Cambridge: MIT Press.

Vygotsky, L. 1978. *Mind in Society,* ed. M. Cole, V. John-Steiner, S. Scribner, and E. Souberman. Cambridge: Harvard University Press.

Wolfram, W. 1970. "Sociolinguistic alternatives in teaching reading to nonstandard speakers." *Reading Research Quarterly* 6.